QUINTERO DIRECTS O'NEILL

QUINTERO DIRECTS O'NEILL

Edwin J. McDonough

a cappella books

a cappella books
an imprint of
Chicago Review Press

Editorial offices:
PO Box 380
Pennington, NJ 08534

Business/Sales offices:
814 N. Franklin St.
Chicago, IL 60610

Cover art © Al Hirschfeld. Drawing reproduced by special arrangement with Hirschfeld's exclusive representative, The Margo Feiden Galleries, New York.

Cover design by Fran Lee
Editorial direction: Richard Carlin

Library of Congress Cataloging-in-Publication Data

McDonough, Edwin J.
    Quintero directs O'Neill/Edwin J. McDonough.
       p.   cm.
    Includes bibliographical references and index.
    ISBN 1-55652-105-7 : $29.95
    1. O'Neill, Eugene, 1888-1953—Stage history—United States. 2. O'Neill, Eugene, 1888-1953—Dramatic production. 3. Theater-United States—History—20th century. 4. Quintero, José.
I. Quintero, José. II. Title.
PS3529.N5Z693   1991
792.9'5—dc20
                                            90-28314
                                             CIP

For my beloved parents,
who took me to the theatre

CONTENTS

ACKNOWLEDGMENTS

If this project has grown beyond its modest beginnings, it is due to the conscientious work of Professor Theodore Hoffman, the eleventh-hour encouragement of Professor Albert Bermel, N.Y.U. Professors Brooks McNamara and Michael Kirby, and the generosity of those interviewed: Paul Andor, Richard Blofson, Jacqueline Brookes, Jerome Collamore, Colleen Dewhurst, Jack Dodson, Ben Edwards, Mitch Erickson, Crystal Field, Geraldine Fitzgerald, Laura Gardner, Don Garner, Frank Hamilton, Andrew Harris, David Hays, Geoffrey Horne, Leonora Landau, Jane Macfie, Armina Marshall, Elliot Martin, Paul McCrane, John McCurry, Dermot McNamara, Betty Miller, Jane E. Neufeld, Kristine Nielsen, Geraldine Page, Addison Powell, William Prince, Jason Robards, Larry Robinson, Campbell Scott, Ned Schmidtke, Jamey Sheridan, Barry Snider, Quentin Thomas, Jennifer Tipton, Ellen Tobie, William Weaver, and Jim Wooley.

INTRODUCTION

By 1988, Eugene O'Neill's Centennial year, an O'Neill cottage industry had emerged. It included three biographies, full-length studies and articles too numerous to chronicle, and an *O'Neill Newsletter*. O'Neill criticism is overwhelmingly biographical or literary and most theatrical reviews are judgmental, rather than descriptive. Until such Centennial publications as Ronald Wainscott's *Staging O'Neill: The Experimental Years, 1920–1934* (New Haven, CT: Yale University Press, 1988) and Gary Vena's *The Iceman Cometh: Reconstructing the Premiere* (Ann Arbor, MI: UMI Research Press, 1988), nuts-and-bolts information about how O'Neill's plays were staged had been scarce.

Since 1956, José Quintero has directed 13 productions of O'Neill in New York City. Quintero ought to be a significant source of information about the plays in production, but his 1974 memoir, *If You Don't Dance They Beat You*, from a production point of view, is a disappointment. The only rehearsal period he discusses in detail is *Long Day's Journey Into Night*. The book has glaring factual errors and appears not to have been proofread. More than unfactual, however, the book is fanciful. Quintero's friends call it "José's first novel."

Quintero Directs O'Neill reconstructs Quintero's 13 productions of O'Neill, based on published criticism and reviews (there are lacunae because of the New York newspapers' strike in 1963)*; memoirs; and personal interviews of producers, actors, designers, and stage managers.** Quintero's O'Neill career falls into divi-

---

* In a few cases, it was impossible to track down the exact page number for newspaper reviews drawn from clipping files. In these instances, the author's name and the date are cited, followed by "?," indicating that the page reference is unknown.

** All unattributed quotes in the book are drawn from personal interviews conducted by the author.

sions, which are represented in the book by Parts, each of which opens with a section that describes the development of Quintero's career. The plays follow in chronological order according to the date of Quintero's productions. Data about the scripts and premieres precede discussion of each play.

The original production is examined for the production demands O'Neill wrote into the play and how it was initially staged (by "original" is meant the premiere that O'Neill himself oversaw). Of the four plays that were not staged in his lifetime the genesis of the text is discussed instead. The Quintero production is then analyzed to show how he directed the same play a generation later.

The progress from script to realization moves step by step, from formation of the production unit through acquisition of a designer, director, and cast, preproduction work and rehearsals, to the critical assessments that followed opening night. Quoted material is cited by date and page after the author's name; full bibliographical information is given in the reference list at the end of the book.

My access to these rehearsals and productions varied widely. The first Quintero production of an O'Neill play I saw was the 1967 *More Stately Mansions*. I have seen every subsequent O'Neill production he has staged in New York City. Quintero cast me as Mike Hogan in the 1973–74 *A Moon for the Misbegotten* just prior to its pre-Broadway tryout. All the rehearsals for that summer's Lake Forest production took place before I joined the production. Quintero also cast me in the 1977 *Anna Christie* as a longshoreman and understudy to Mat Burke. I attended almost all of those rehearsals. I even took some notes, although it was not until a month later, seated stage-right in the Royal Alexandra Theater in Toronto, that it occurred to me that I might document Quintero's O'Neill career. For consistency's sake, and because my access did vary, all rehearsals and productions are described in the third person, even when this requires referring to myself in the third person.

José Quintero encouraged me to undertake this project, but, for various reasons—scheduling, geography, health—did not make himself available for interviews.

Edwin J. McDonough

There are a few people in the theatre, in the arts, who inspire within an artist that belief that what you are doing is important, that you're in a noble profession: people like Balanchine, Lee Strasberg, and Sandy Meisner, those very rare, few people like José who come along and make an actor feel like saying "I was right to join this profession." There are so many things in this profession to make you feel otherwise.

Barry Snider

Part One

O'NEILL AND QUINTERO

"**B**orn in a hotel room—and damn it—died in a hotel room."
With this final, Beckett-like summation of his life, Eugene Glad-
stone O'Neill died in a Boston hotel on November 27, 1953. If
production were all, O'Neill had been effectively dead for 20 years:
Ah, Wilderness! had been a great commercial success in 1933,
while *Days Without End,* produced three months later, barely
eked out its Theatre Guild subscription performances. There was
no new O'Neill play produced for 12½ years. His two postwar
productions consisted of the misconceived Broadway production
of *The Iceman Cometh* in 1946 and the abortive pre-Broadway
tour of *A Moon for the Misbegotten,* which closed in St. Louis
in 1947.

O'Neill's position as America's foremost dramatist was being
attacked by critics as influential as Mary McCarthy (1956:81–88)
and Eric Bentley (1952:331–45). In 1956, however, José Quintero
directed a revival of *The Iceman Cometh* and the American premiere of *Long Day's Journey Into Night,* the two productions that
ignited the O'Neill revival. To date, Quintero has remained the
most influential director of O'Neill's plays.

O'Neill and Quintero, who never met, would seem to have
little in common, biographically or personally. O'Neill was a first-
generation Irish-American, who married three times and fathered
three children. Quintero, who was born and raised in Panama,
is homosexual. (Barbara Gelb [1977:128] wrote of Quintero in the
New York Times that "it was not without difficulty that Quintero confronted and accepted the fact of his sexual preference. He
does not discuss it, but he has never made any attempt to conceal
it.")

Quintero has attempted many times to explain his affinity
for O'Neill. He is given to mysticism, to discussing the ghost of
O'Neill, which haunts him, and his many long talks with O'Neill's
widow Carlotta, very little of which is applicable to how he actually stages the plays. Quintero writes (1974:223):

> Although they are always labelling O'Neill as a
> realistic playwright, every time I have done any
> of his plays I have had a sense of existing in two
> entirely different kinds of realities: the common-
> place, photographic reality and the interior real-
> ity of a fantasy. I think the struggle of these two

realities—where the impossible can happen among the commonplace; where the figures become regal, monumental and totally equipped for tragedy— gives that unbelievable tension to his works. O'Neill just happens to have had double vision, that's all.

Quintero is more persuasive when he discusses the resemblances between his own family and that of O'Neill:

The fact is that O'Neill's life so paralleled my own life and feelings that it was as if he had a hand in my upbringing. When I read him, there is nothing strange about him. It is all so painfully familiar. His mother was raised in a convent, so was mine; his father was an actor, mine a politician who behaved exactly as his father did. Outside the house, my father was absolutely charming and everyone said, "Viva Mr. Quintero." But at home, if you wanted twenty-five cents to go to the movies, you had to give all the reasons why you were good enough to deserve it (Funke, 1974:20).

With this biographical insight, the common ground the two men shared begins to emerge.

O'Neill was raised as an Irish-Catholic, Quintero as a Latin-Catholic. Their youthful experiences of Catholicism influenced the antithetical approaches they followed into professional theater. The overwhelming majority of Catholics experience the gamut of religious services (mass, benediction, novena, procession, and stations of the cross) long before they attend a theatrical production. Eugene O'Neill was a conspicuous exception; he encountered the theater long before he partook in Catholic religious services. He began touring as an infant with his famous actor-father James O'Neill Sr. "My mother nursed me in the wings and dressing rooms," O'Neill claimed (Gelb, 1960:59). Louis Sheaffer (1968:69) examined O'Neill's Catholic upbringing by interviewing Joseph McCarthy, a schoolmate of O'Neill's at one of the two Catholic schools that O'Neill attended: "He didn't seem particularly religious to me. He went to church every Sunday because we all had to go. Whatever his inner feelings may have been, he showed little interest in the things they taught us, no great feelings about them." Catholic dogma impressed itself upon O'Neill eventually, as it would upon Quintero, but because he had experienced so much bad theater so early, the ritual signification of Catholicism, which was to so fascinate Quintero, was lost on O'Neill.

O'Neill was a playwright for whom the process of production became unendurable. In 1937, he wrote that "the play, as written, is the thing, and not the way actors garble it with their almost-always-alien personalities" (Sheaffer, 1973:469). He had developed, early in his career, a deep and abiding antipathy toward actors. In 1921, he wrote, "I can't help seeing with the relentless eye of heredity, upbringing and personal experience every little trick they pull as actors. Thus in the most tense moment of a play, I am struck by the sly, insidious intent—plain to me—of a gesture, a fillip, a change of tempo, a body wriggle. The actor stands revealed in his egoistic childishness" (Sheaffer, 1973:50–51). The Gelbs (1961:39) quote O'Neill as having said, "The theatre of the present must be destroyed. Let us then first—oh sweet and lovely thought—poison all the actors."

O'Neill never learned to translate the play in his head into a language he could share with actors. In *The Fervent Years*, Harold Clurman (1957:7–8) describes a rehearsal he attended of Stark Young's *The Saint*. The play was produced in 1924 by the Kenneth Macgowan–Robert Edmond Jones–Eugene O'Neill triumvirate, which had taken over the Greenwich Village Theater and the Provincetown Playhouse. The attitude expressed by Robert Edmond Jones reflected O'Neill's views on actors:

> What I remember best was a talk given by Robert Edmond Jones . . . to the actors engaged for the whole season. It was all rather solemn . . . Jones rose diffidently and spoke in a voice that suggested a slight spiritual grief and a noble yet humble exaltation. This is approximately what he said: "Recently I heard the story of a blind child on whom a successful operation had been performed. When the bandages were finally removed from its eyes, the child looked around in ecstasy and murmured: 'What is this thing called light?' To me, the theatre is like a light that blind people are made to see for the first time. The theatre is a dream that the audience comes to behold. The theatre is revelation. I look about me here, and I do not see light,

> I do not perceive dream, I do not feel revelation.
> That is what I want to tell you." He walked up the
> aisle and disappeared . . . I realized immediately
> that he had made no connection with the actors.
> They could not be blamed for being embarrassed
> by his talk. They did not speak his language, and
> he had been at no pains either to teach it to them
> or to translate himself into a language that might
> affect them . . . Here was no unity of point of view
> or any attempt to make one. Where was the con-
> necting link? Since, obviously, Jones felt he couldn't
> function—his dream couldn't be realized without
> the assistance of those to whom he addressed
> himself—it seemed to me to be Jones' fault that he
> was not understood. It was the leader's task to fash-
> ion a common language and a common point of
> reference with those whom he hoped to lead.

These were the circumstances in which O'Neill functioned. He
seldom addressed himself to the actors, preferring to leave that
task to the director. When O'Neill intervened, tempers flew.

Quintero's background, on the other hand, was steeped in
Catholic rituals and he did not see his first play until he was 18
years old:

> I was brought up in Panama City, Panama, and
> during most of my early life spent nine months a
> year in a Catholic convent, where I was taught by
> Spanish monks. Ritual has been a meaningful and
> eloquent kind of communication for me, since my
> environment not only included Christian
> ceremonials, but also those of pagan origin . . .
> From the richness of church ceremonials, I learned
> the restrained pantomime which springs so com-
> pletely from the chest, where the heart and the soul
> lie (Quintero, 1957:17).
>
> "Maybe not consciously, but I learned quickly
> that the imagination was more real than the fac-
> tual world . . . because one could, for example,
> give life to wooden statues. Just by the fact of
> believing, one endowed them with life. That is why

it is so easy for me to believe a tree in the theater is a real tree, although it is made of cardboard." Quintero is a lapsed Catholic who, as a child in his native Panama, was intensely religious and served as an acolyte, and whose play included the building and adornment of miniature altars. Historically the church is, of course, a foundation of the theatre and Quintero thus experienced its double nature in the most fundamental way. As its religious significance receded, the rigidly stylized, unvarying drama of the liturgy remained (Millstein, 1960:10).

Quintero brings to production the very gifts that O'Neill conspicuously lacked: a love of the process, trust and respect for the human element, and a means of communication with actors. Phyllis Funke (1974:20) wrote of him:

It isn't Mr. Quintero's affinity with O'Neill alone which makes him the sensitive director he is. Colleen Dewhurst has noted that she would rather be directed by José Quintero dead drunk than by any other director in the world. "He is one of the few men I have ever met in the theatre who has no desire to destroy anyone working with him," she says. "As a director, he makes you go where in your gut you could go but you're a little nervous to go there for fear you'll make an ass of yourself. José says, 'Trust me and come on, come on, come on,' and he makes you break through and release something for you."

When Mr. Quintero begins to translate a play into stage terms, he moves, he says, on instinct. But as the production progresses and the layers of the work begin to peel away, more and more meaning is revealed, providing intellectual grounds for proceeding. Mr. Quintero is quick to explain, however, that many of these revelations come from the actors themselves and consequently he feels that one of his principal jobs is to make certain that his actors are at ease. Knowing that actors, in portraying their

roles, must often bear their own souls, he needs an
empathy with them by expressing their own emotions as well.

In an interview with Gilbert Millstein (1960:12), Quintero
gave his fullest expression of his working relationship with actors:

> Persuasion of the actor is paramount to Quintero
> and a kind of authoritative tenderness is his means.
> "You have to understand," he says, "that they are
> not just actors. You must peer into what you think
> are the ways to make them act, what works for one
> does not work for another. We are all people in the
> dark trying to touch each other. So the director
> must become vulnerable first to the play and then
> to each one in it. The moment a barrier is set up,
> the vulnerability is lost. It is my obligation to seek
> out the actor, rather than demand that he disrobe
> himself at once to produce the emotions the play
> requires. The director has to be a lover and, for
> those weeks of rehearsal, be worried and concerned
> about the actor as though he or she were the loved
> one. Because what, after all, you are after—the
> genius in actors—is, as in all of us, a frightened
> child afraid to expose itself."
>
> He was reminded of an analogy. "Do you
> recall the scene in the picture *Symphonie
> Pastorale*?" he asked. "An old man seeks to coax
> a frightened child out of a woods. He says softly,
> over and over, 'Petit, petit, petit,' and the child
> finally emerges. What with readings, agents,
> producers, one thing and another, actors are para-
> lyzed by the time they come to the play. That real
> and vulnerable part of them has gone back into the
> woods. I have had to be strong as a director, but
> I have been fortunate that I've always operated on
> the idea that the dignity of man is more important
> to preserve than just to get a moment the director
> has secured as if the actor were an animal. If I can-
> not reach an actor in the manner prescribed for me,
> that matches my idea of man, then I find someone
> I can reach in that way."

Quintero came to America to study medicine, but became involved in theater. He spent four years at the University of Southern California, one year at Los Angeles City College (from which he graduated), and one year at the Goodman Theater in Chicago. In 1945, he crossed the country by bus to join a fledgling theater company in Woodstock, NY. The company, composed of local amateurs, soon closed. He then alternated between New York City and Woodstock until 1949 when, with several partners, he formed a company of actors and took them to Woodstock as the Loft Players. He directed seven of the nine productions that summer. The surviving members then determined to move the company to New York City if the funds could be raised and the correct theater found.

As Quintero recalls the event in his memoir, he and Ted Mann were taking a postdinner walk in Greenwich Village and passed 5 Sheridan Square, an abandoned nightclub (the old Greenwich Village Inn) with a "For Rent" sign tacked on the door. The following evening, the two men gained entrance to the building. Quintero was undismayed by three cement pillars in the dance floor. With the two men standing at opposite ends of the space, Quintero announced to Mann that the stage would not be on the raised bandstand, but on the ballroom floor: "We may have to raise it and elongate it, but that wouldn't cost very much. Come on up. It will give you a real perspective." Mann was conditioned to the conventional actor-audience relationship, whereas Quintero was experiencing an aesthetic epiphany:

> I didn't move. Instead I touched the pillar again. I hated everything about the place—carpets, bar, ceiling—yet my hand would not move from the pole. As a matter of fact, I tightened my hand around it, the way a drowning man holds onto a broken mast . . . Looking at one of the walls, I saw a painted leopard. I permitted him to become real for a few seconds. He jumped onto the bandstand and began to walk, knocking down the music stands as he went. Then making a semicircle, and rubbing his back against the last pole, he gracefully jumped down into the dance floor. He began to circle the center pole where I was standing, then proceeded in a series of curves until he had reached the farthest poles of the arena. Finally he returned

to the center pole, paused for an instant, and leaped
back onto the wall to reappear as a badly painted
leopard in a shabby mural . . . The leopard never
walked a straight line. He curved himself around
as he walked, almost in the shape of an S. At that
moment I began to understand the kind of movement that the three-quarter arena demanded
(Quintero, 1974:78–79).

The following afternoon the board of the Loft Players
gathered to examine the site. Quintero (1974:84) writes that "the
three poles which divided the arena downstairs seemed to have
grown into four hundred redwood trees, obscuring the minds and
eyes of the board members into a panicky blindness. I assured them
that the poles, as if by magic, could become trees, lampposts,
statues, masts of galleons, in short anything and everything that
the scenery of our future plays would demand." They suggested
and junked a series of names for their projected theater, until Quintero himself linked the Sheridan Square location with a theater
"which has to do with a circle" (Quintero, 1974:85) to form Circle-
in-the-Square. Quintero had found the style that would dominate
the next dozen years of his career. The company literature billed
the Circle-in-the-Square as "the only theater-in-the-round in New
York City, an unusual combination of an arena performing area
and a proscenium backdrop."

Quintero sought to supplement the few actors who had come
in from Woodstock. He interviewed actors, rather than auditioning them, because "I despise readings, and unless truly pressured
by the producer I won't conduct them" (Quintero, 1974:89). The
actors selected were offered living quarters upstairs and $10.00
a week.

Quintero (1974:93–94) writes of his directing qualifications,
"I have never taken a lesson in directing. I am glad I never have.
What I know I learned by introspection and observation." In
preparing to direct the Circle's premiere production in 1951, *Dark
of the Moon*, Quintero absorbed as much as he could of the
Appalachian world of the Martha Graham/Aaron Copland ballet *Appalachian Spring* and concentrated "on the intricacies of a
curved gesture on the real and known plateau of a stage" (Quintero, 1974:88).

Staging *Summer and Smoke* a year later, Quintero placed the Buchanan household at one end of the stage, the Winemiller household at the other end, and, between them, the park with the center pole standing for the stone statue of the angel. Geraldine Page immediately grasped the implications of the set: " 'To get to his house I will have to make a long curve, won't I, José? Otherwise, it will seem that we are living next door.' I said, 'Yes, darling. I'm glad that you have already begun to understand that everything on the stage has to be done on a curve' " (Quintero, 1974:113).

The Brooks Atkinson review of *Summer and Smoke* in the *New York Times* read: "Nothing has happened for quite a long time as admirable as the new production at the Circle-in-the-Square—in Sheridan Square to be precise. Tennessee Williams' *Summer and Smoke* opened there last evening in a sensitive, highly personal performance." Atkinson's review marked the legitimization of the off-Broadway movement and Quintero's introduction to the dangers of success.

Part Two

CIRCLE-IN-THE-SQUARE

The initial productions at Circle-in-the-Square ran for several weeks only. Quintero had no sooner directed one production than he began casting another. With the long run of *Summer and Smoke* in 1952, the face of Circle-in-the-Square changed. Quintero had time to direct *Legend of Lovers* (1953), *In the Summer House* (1953), *Portrait of a Lady* (1954), and *The Innkeepers* (1956) on Broadway. Only *In the Summer House* had a successful run. Repertory at the Circle continued to be catholic, in the off-Broadway fashion: revivals of American classics and more recent European plays. At the Circle, Quintero directed two short-run productions, *American Gothic* (1953) with Jason Robards and *The King and the Duke* (1954), and three long-run successes, *The Grass Harp* (1953), *The Girl on the Via Flaminia* (1954), which moved to Broadway, and *La Ronde* (1954).

The success of *The Iceman Cometh* in 1956 need not have altered the repertory of the Circle any more than the success of *Summer and Smoke* had influenced Quintero to direct a series of Tennessee Williams revivals. Mrs. O'Neill's bestowal of the American rights to *Long Day's Journey*, however, proved to be the point of no return for Quintero. The production reestablished O'Neill as America's greatest playwright and Quintero as the preeminent director of O'Neill.

In his remaining years at the Circle, Quintero successfully directed Brendan Behan's *The Quare Fellow* (1958), Thornton Wilder's *Our Town* (1959), Jean Genet's *The Balcony* (1960), and Wilder's *Plays for Bleecker Street* (1962). For his final production at the Circle, Quintero chose *Desire Under the Elms* (1963), which ran for 11 months. By the time he left the Circle, Quintero had every reason to see himself as a merchandisable virtuoso director of a wide repertory of plays.

1

The Iceman Cometh

Writing

Begun June 8, 1939; first draft completed October 12, 1939; second draft completed November 26, 1939; final version completed January 3, 1940.

Premieres

Original: October 9, 1946; New York, Martin Beck Theater.

Quintero: May 8, 1956; New York, Circle-in-the-Square.

1946 Production

Cast List

Harry Hope	Dudley Digges
Ed Mosher	Morton L. Stevens
Pat McGloin	Al McGranery
Willie Oban	E. G. Marshall
Joe Mott	John Marriott
Piet Wetjoen	Frank Tweddell
Cecil Lewis	Nicholas Joy
James Cameron	Russell Collins
(Jimmy Tomorrow)	

Hugo Kalmar	Leo Chalzel
Larry Slade	Carl Benton Reid
Rocky Pioggi	Tom Pedi
Don Parritt	Paul Crabtree
Pearl	Ruth Gilbert
Margie	Jeanne Cagney
Cora	Marcella Markham
Chuck Morello	Joe Marr
Theodore Hickman	James E. Barton
Moran	Michael Wyler
Lieb	Charles Hart

O'Neill's final creative writing period lasted from 1939 to 1943. By June 1939, he had been working on his American Cycle of plays for five years. He had just revised *A Touch of the Poet* and was scheduled to forge ahead with the never-to-be-completed *The Calms of Capricorn*, but chose, instead, to write a play outside the Cycle:

> For years, intermittently, O'Neill had been turning over in his mind bits and pieces of a "lower depths" play, a drama set in a scruffy saloon and peopled with the sort of drifters he had known in the days when he was drowning himself in booze in an effort to escape himself. Unable to conceive a unifying theme and narrative, he made no attempt to force the play but, as usual, relied on the "back of my mind" to develop it. As he was revising *A Touch of the Poet* in 1939 . . . he became aware that the barroom play had suddenly begun to crystallize in his thoughts, the bits and pieces to fall into place (Sheaffer, 1973:485).

On June 6, 1939, O'Neill read over his workbooks and wrote, "Read over notes on various ideas for single plays—decide outlines of two that appeal most, and see—the Jimmy the Priest, Hell Hole, Garden idea—and New London family one" (Floyd, 1981:281). Jimmy the Priest was the person on whom O'Neill was to model Harry Hope; the Hell Hole and the taproom of the Garden Hotel served as models of Harry Hope's saloon. On the same day, O'Neill chose to write what would eventually become *The Iceman Cometh* and *Long Day's Journey Into Night*.

O'Neill stipulated that no new plays of his were to be staged during the war. By summer 1944, however, he agreed to discuss plans for renewed productions of his plays when the war ended. Theatre Guild producer Lawrence Langner and his wife Armina Marshall travelled to California to discuss *Iceman* with O'Neill. Langner (1951:402) writes that O'Neill "felt that the timing for the play's opening was very important, and that if it were to be produced immediately after the war was over, the pessimism of the play would run counter to public optimism, and would result in a bad reception by the audience. He thought a year or so after the peace there would be considerable disillusionment, and that then the public would be more inclined to listen to what he had to say in this play." Two years did elapse before the play was staged.

In 1944, however, the Theatre Guild was no longer the highly professional organization it had been. As Louis Sheaffer (1973:551) describes it, "A few years earlier, after behind-the-scenes feuding with other board members, director Phillip Moeller and designer Lee Simonson, the most talented of the founders, had resigned (or been pushed out)." For O'Neill's purposes, Simonson was replaceable, but Moeller, O'Neill's most sympathetic director, was not. Sheaffer (1973:489) compares Moeller's sensibilities to the specific needs of directing *Iceman:*

> Phillip Moeller, a gifted amateur musician, used to say that O'Neill's plays had a musical structure—an observation that appears particularly true of *The Iceman,* a complex resonant work with contrapuntal effects, recurrent motifs and a symphonic amplitude. The play has also a sort of oceanic quality, born of the slow-moving passages that recall the lazy swells of the sea, then a gradual mounting of tension which finally boils over that is like the hunching up of the waves and their crashing on the shore.

On the advice of George Jean Nathan, O'Neill went to San Francisco to see Eddie Dowling play in *The Time of Your Life.* O'Neill met Dowling and decided that he was right to play Hickey. The Theatre Guild engaged Dowling not only to play Hickey, but also to direct the production. O'Neill finally came to New York in fall 1945 , and the Theatre Guild spent that winter casting *Iceman*. A full-cast reading was held in May 1946. Langner (1951:405) describes the reading and its ramifications:

> We were all impressed with the very sensitive reading given by James Barton in the part of Harry Hope, the owner of the saloon. At the same time we all felt that the task of directing the play would be enormously difficult, and that Dowling would have about as much as he could handle in that department without attempting to play the role of Hickey as well. This was a disappointment for Dowling, but he deferred to our collective judgment. Later on, Gene felt that James Barton would be excellent for Hickey and thought that we should engage someone else for the role of Harry Hope.

As a result of the reading, O'Neill attempted to cut *Iceman*. Six years earlier, in a 1940 letter to Kenneth Macgowan, he had defended the play's length at the expense of the fact that it would eventually have to be performed on a stage:

> It's hard to explain exactly my intuitions about this play. Perhaps I can put it best by saying *The Iceman Cometh* is something I want to make life reveal about itself, fully and deeply and roundly— that it takes place for me in life, not in a theater— that the fact that it is a play which can be produced with actors is secondary and incidental to me— and even quite unimportant—and so it would be a loss to me to sacrifice anything of the complete life for the sake of stage and audience (Sheaffer, 1973:572).

When production neared, however, O'Neill tried to cut 45 minutes from the script, but succeeded in cutting only 15.

Robert Edmond Jones, the chosen designer, took O'Neill's wish for slice-of-life as his guide: "After steeping himself in the script, he had sought out Manhattan's ancient saloons, starting with McSorley's, and worked his way from South Ferry to Harlem" (Sheaffer, 1973:569). In a postproduction interview, Jones described O'Neill's contribution to the set:

There are so many things bound up in designing
a play by O'Neill. There's knowledge of the man,
of course, and friendship and memories. It's hard
to say, otherwise, why you spend twelve hours of
every day trying trimmings for dresses, looking for
1912 underthings, hanging around disreputable
saloons, getting the exact type of keg to look right
on the bar, selecting mosquito netting to keep the
flies off the mirrors, raiding a waterfront hash
house for dirty, checked table-cloths, exploring junk
shops for straight-backed chairs, traveling upstate
for a nickle-in-the-slot Edison talking machine,
searching photograph collections for pictures of
John L. Sullivan and Dick Crocker.

Gene knows exactly what he wants. His
descriptions are definite. All a designer has to do
is follow them. I've been complimented on the
colors for the sets and costumes, but it was really
all Gene's idea. He knew so well that dirty white
would be the best background . . . Without ever
having painted, he's a true artist. His creativeness
embraces the visual aspect (Rhodes, 1946:V,3).

The Iceman Cometh went into rehearsal in September 1946.
Langner (1951:405) writes that "every move of every actor had
been clearly thought out in 'Gene's mind, and he was of enormous
help in the staging of the play." Any author who attends rehearsals with every movement of the actors already preconceived can
only be a Jonah. O'Neill was at his most unyielding. Langner also
records that "on one occasion I told 'Gene that at my request my
assistant, Paul Crabtree, who played the part of Don Parritt, had
counted the number of times a certain point was repeated, and
this, in actual fact, was eighteen times. 'Gene looked at me and
replied in a particularly quiet voice, 'I intended it to be repeated
eighteen times.' "

O'Neill was deeply disappointed with Dowling's direction:

At first Eddie Dowling tried to enliven the leisurely
drama with some movement and pieces of "business," but every afternoon the playwright eliminated what the director had introduced in the

morning. The playwright wanted no unessential action that might distract, even momentarily, from his words. After being told by the Guild brass to follow the text scrupulously—no stage business unless specified in the text—Dowling, according to cast members, was "cowed," "like a whipped child," "afraid to suggest anything." Dowling himself confided to stage manager Karl Nielsen: "I dread their coming in the afternoon."

On his side, O'Neill who had become thoroughly dissatisfied with the director, felt that he had been unduly influenced by George Jean Nathan's enthusiastic recommendation. "Nathan," he complained privately, "may know plays, but he doesn't know actors and directors" (Sheaffer, 1973:574–75).

O'Neill refused an out-of-town tryout, but Actors' Equity allowed the production a fifth week of rehearsal, rehearsal pay being less than performance pay.

New York's drama critics had been sent advance copies of the play so that they would be familiar with the text before they saw the production. The curtain went up at 5:30 P.M. and came down at 11:30 P.M. There was a 90-minute dinner intermission during which, Langner (1951:406) writes:

James Barton . . . was forced to entertain a crowd of friends in his dressing room instead of resting, so that by the time he came to make the famous speech, which lasted twenty minutes in the fifth act, he had little or no voice left with which to deliver it. As a result the last act, which should have been the strongest of all, fell apart at the center.

O'Neill had imposed his will on the production, but achieved only the letter of the law, not its spirit. "There is little movement," wrote Rosamond Gilder (1950:665), "there is only an antiphonal development of theme . . . As the play progresses, the way the tables are grouped in the barroom and bar and the manner in which actors are grouped around them—slumped over asleep or sitting in a deathly daydream—provide a constant visual comment on the developing theme."

Stark Young (1946:518) reported:

> Eddie Dowling has directed in his by now well
> known style. His is a method sure to be admired;
> it consists largely in a certain smooth security, an
> effect of competence, of keeping things professional
> and steady, and often of doing nothing at all. To
> this he adds in *The Iceman Cometh* a considera-
> ble degree of stylized performance, actors sitting
> motionless while another character or other groups
> take the stage. Since there is a good deal of styli-
> zation in the structure of *The Iceman Cometh*, this
> may well be justified. But in my opinion the usual
> Dowling method brought to the direction of this
> O'Neill play would gain greatly by more pressure,
> more intensity and a far darker and richer texture.

George Freedley (1946:2) wrote of the first act:

> The first act certainly reads better than it plays.
> There I would be inclined to blame Eddie Dowl-
> ing, the stage director, for the static quality.
> Though the author has called for it, Mr. Dowling
> is too astute a stage manager not to realize that
> some movement is necessary for an act which is
> entirely given over to exposition and in which there
> is no real dramatic action until almost the close of
> its ninety-minute length. In the subsequent acts,
> Mr. Dowling has enlivened the action and is par-
> ticularly effective in his handling of the comedy
> which is bawdy, lusty stuff.

When it was pointed out to O'Neill, after several months of
performances, that 10 percent of the audience did not return after
the dinner break (on which he had insisted), he agreed to elimi-
nate it. "Under the new schedule, the performance ran from 7:30
to 11:20, with 15 minutes cut from the original time by quicken-
ing the pace" (Sheaffer, 1973:585).

O'Neill deviated from his normal practice and attended
several subsequent performances of *Iceman*, but such excursions
brought him scant pleasure. According to Sheaffer (1973:590–91)
"he was so unhappy about the performance, and kept muttering
imprecations against Dowling's direction."

Like O'Neill, Stark Young thought James Barton's performance as Hickey of a piece with Dowling's direction:

> Mr. James Barton as Hickey, a most central character in the entire motivation and movement of the play, plays the part very much, I should imagine, as Mr. Eddie Dowling would have played it, judging from his performance in *The Glass Menagerie* and elsewhere, and from his direction, which means a sort of playing that is competent, wholly at ease with a something which appears to settle the matter, to close the subject as it were, so that for the moment at least you are prevented from thinking of anything else that could be done about it. Only afterwards do you keep realizing what might have been there and was not (Young, 1946:518).

On one occasion O'Neill saw E. G. Marshall substitute for an indisposed James Barton. O'Neill admired Marshall's performance and insisted that he play Hickey in the road company.

The Iceman Cometh did well enough in New York to warrant sending out a road company, but with the wrong director and leading man it was perceived as a botched production. Stark Young (1946:518) wrote, "I am not even sure as to the extent to which I can judge *The Iceman Cometh* after seeing such a production of it."

1956 Production

Cast List

Harry Hope	Farrell Pelly
Ed Mosher	Phil Pfeiffer
Pat McGloin	Al Lewis
Willie Oban	Addison Powell
Joe Mott	William Edmundson
Piet Wetjoen	Richard Abbott
Cecil Lewis	Richard Bowler
James Cameron (Jimmy Tomorrow)	James Greene

Hugo Kalmar	Paul Andor
Larry Slade	Conrad Bain
Rocky Pioggi	Peter Falk
Don Parritt	Larry Robinson
Pearl	Patricia Brooks
Margie	Gloria Scott Backe
Cora	Dolly Jonah
Chuck Morello	Joe Marr
Theodore Hickman (Hickey)	Jason Robards
Moran	Mal Thorne
Lieb	Charles Hamilton

As of 1956, José Quintero had never read or seen any of Eugene O'Neill's work. His Circle-in-the-Square partner, Leigh Connell, suggested that he direct an O'Neill play. When Quintero asked which O'Neill play, Connell replied, " 'Of course, the one we could never do is *The Iceman Cometh.* That is the one for you. Not that you couldn't do any of the others, but right now that is the one for you. Unfortunately, I think it is out of the question . . . It requires an extraordinary ensemble performance from a group of people and it also requires a truly remarkable performer to play the leading role. I don't think he exists' " (Quintero, 1974: 150).

Quintero read the play that evening and decided that he wanted to direct it. Ted Mann phoned O'Neill's agent, Jane Rubin, and "after answering a few questions such as when, where, who and how, she told him that no O'Neill play was being released at that time" (Quintero, 1974:153). In an interview with Lewis Funke (1968:19), Ted Mann said, "We kept getting turned down. Thinking we'd better play it safe, we named some of the more obscure ones. But Jane said 'How about *Iceman?*' " Jane Rubin subsequently arranged a meeting between Quintero and Mrs. O'Neill on March 15, 1956, at Mrs. O'Neill's apartment in the Lowell Hotel.

By 1956, Carlotta Monterey O'Neill (born Hazel Neilson Tharsing; she and Quintero did not share a Spanish heritage) was a formidable 68-year-old keeper of the O'Neill flame. Unlike Richard Wagner's widow Cosima, a vigorous woman who ran Bayreuth until her death, Carlotta was a recluse, there was no Bayreuth to run, and her late husband's popularity was decidedly on the wane. Carlotta's position more closely resembled that of Alban Berg's widow, who possessed only the power to prohibit tampering with her dead husband's oeuvre. Such widows are the terror of the earth to those who presume to interpret the work of the dead husband.

Having devoted her life to O'Neill, Carlotta threw herself into mourning as devotedly as Queen Victoria. The apartment Quintero visited was an O'Neill museum. In one brief visit Quintero gained Carlotta's complete and undying confidence. He took her at her own evaluation and she committed herself to him, not on a business level, not even on a professional level, but on some personal level whereby Quintero accepted her conviction that she had participated in the creation of *Iceman*. He quotes Carlotta as saying:

> "*Iceman* broke his heart and mine too which was not any new thing. We broke each other's hearts time and time again. He thought that I broke his more times than he did mine. But he was wrong. Sometime I would like to tell you, but not now. I'm sounding morbid and you didn't come here to hear a sad tale. You came here to get the rights for the play . . . You can have them. I trust you. I like you . . .Will you come and see me every once in a while and tell me how it's going? I get so lonesome here . . . I'll tell you more about him. Maybe it will help you understand the *Iceman* better" (Quintero, 1974:156–57).

With the rights secured, Quintero contacted David Hays, who had designed the previous Circle production, *The Cradle Song*. Quintero (1974:157) writes, "To this day, I consider him the greatest and most resourceful designer I have worked with. His work has the deceiving simplicity of the Orient and, when called for, the frenzy of a Caribbean carnival."

When asked how Quintero discusses a set, what suggestions he makes, Hays answered:

> He doesn't. I read the play and come up with a thought and then we discuss it. We can talk about the script a little, as we did in those days, and maybe there's an impression or something vague,

vague but stimulating, and then we go at it and take it apart.

We could express ideas as theoretical as warmth or cold, but then we'd back it up with things that we might have seen or been in our common knowledge, anything like paintings or settings that we might have seen; not to copy, mind you, but to illustrate the direction in which our thoughts are traveling. He might mention some staging considerations, but, by and large, you have a lot of leeway with José.

Hays had seen pictures of Robert Edmond Jones' set for the original *Iceman*, but, he said, "It was on such a different kind of stage that there wasn't any relevance to it. I mean it was a hell of a design, but it had no relevance to this space."

When asked what was the basic difference designing for a three-quarter stage rather than a proscenium, Hays answered:

On a three-quarter you have a scenic wall, that fourth quarter is a scenic wall. You're dealing with that scenic bit that you have, but it can't be your whole scenic bit. It has to be something that you can then pull out and make flow into all the rest of your stage; it can't stop there. Instead of being like a ball of wool up there, it's got to be a ball of wool that's shredded out all over the rest of your stage. Whatever design elements are there flow out to the rest of it through the floor patterns that might be established up there (the floor is very important on a three-quarter), the way the furniture continues or the way something hangs overhead. In this case, it was a ratty old chandelier with strings and cobwebs that went to that wall and then connected it to all the rest because it went out all the way to the audience.

So you try to tie the whole stage into that back wall instead of its being there just willy-nilly behind the rest of your stuff and you have to watch the furniture very carefully to see that it doesn't block sight-lines.

Quintero said of Hays' *Iceman* set, "it only cost us a hundred and some-odd dollars. Tables, chairs and a stained-glass window, a light fixture like a wheel . . . and that was it. We had our bar" (Lawson, 1978:38). Brooks Atkinson (1956:39) described the set as "a few tables and chairs, a squalid bar, a flimsy door leading into the street, a handful of fly-blown chandeliers and a few ranks of benches for the audience, they are all part of the same setting and closely related on that account."

After his first reading of the play, Quintero had examined the wide range of characters he was to cast: " 'My God,' I thought . . . 'What O'Neill's got here are representatives, ambassadors from every major and revered institution. All the characters at Hope's bar are not Americans and they're not of the same race, or religion, or of the same political convictions' " (1974:152).

When asked by Frederick Morton (1956:II,3), in a preopening interview, if the four-hour length of *Iceman* had created difficulties, Quintero shook his head and replied that "the toughest problem was casting seventeen important parts, mostly older men. There are few good older actors who want to subject themselves to the conditions of an experimental theater. But I found them, after interviewing over four hundred."

Quintero's casting methods are unabashedly visceral: "Casting a play is like love. You fall in love or you don't" (Morehouse, 1960:?). His memoir reads as if the casting were completed in two days. In his 1957 "Postscript to a Journey" article, however, Quintero wrote, "We sent out a casting call and began listening to actors, 100 to 125 a day. After four weeks we had cast all of the characters—with the exception of Hickey"(1957a:28).

According to the memoir, Farrell Pelly was cast as Harry Hope without an audition, although he warned Quintero that his memory was not to be trusted. Three-hundred-pound Phil Pfeiffer was cast as Ed Mosher without an audition, although he had never acted on a stage. Peter Falk was cast as Rocky the bartender without an audition, although he had only one previous credit. Quintero said of Al Lewis that "as soon as I saw his face, the face of a police sergeant, he had the part" (Tallmer, 1974:15).

The actors who had not worked with Quintero before expressed astonishment at being cast without being asked to audition. Paul Andor could not remember if he auditioned or not, but said, "I remember that he gave me a choice. Because I have a German accent, which could also be Dutch, he asked me whether I wanted to play Hugo Kalmar or the Dutchman, Piet Wetjoen." Larry Robinson was submitted by an agent for the pivotal role of Don Parritt: "I only had to read a few lines and Quintero cast me as Parritt."

Addison Powell had to audition for the role of Willie Oban. Quintero had seen Powell several years earlier in a Broadway production. A mutual friend, Jason Wingreen, told Powell that Quintero had liked his work very much. He sought out Quintero at the *Iceman* interviews:

> I think I met José for the first time when I read for Willie. My having to audition may possibly have had to do with the demands of Willie. There are certainly acting demands to the other parts, but they are broader caricatures in a sense; the con-man, the circus barker, and Al Lewis' part, and so on, but Willie is the most drunk. The others are sodden with drink. Willie is like a trout that has just been hooked, still flashing and jumping out of the water in agony. That is possibly part of the reason why I had to read for Willie. You can't just cast Willie to type, you can't have a guy who looks right and let it go at that. The role I played on Broadway that José saw was nothing like Willie, a nice guy that I played out of myself, but José liked it well enough to consider me for Willie.

Casting the three whores proved to be a problem. Quintero (1974:165) dismissed one actress who was grotesquely decked out as a whore: "She was no whore. Specially an O'Neill whore." He telephoned Dolly Jonah, an actress who had worked at the check-room of the Circle-in-the-Square: "Dolly had short hair tinted red, a gravelly voice, and a figure that would slow down any car, day or night." Yes, she did know the role of Cora:

> "Dolly, do you play the piano?"
> "No."
> "Not even a little?"
> "Yes, a little."
> "How much is a little?"

"Very little."
"Well, the part is yours. We start Monday at ten."

Quintero had already sensed that music would play a significant part in his production.

The remaining two whores also went to "family": Patricia Brooks, who was married to Ted Mann, and Gloria Scott Backe, who had been married to actor Jimmy Greene. Both actresses had worked for Quintero previously. Patricia Brooks commented on the casting:

> He picked me. He picked Scottie, who had a won-
> derful bosom and was rather waspy, proper, almost
> a Westchester matron sort of type. When you saw
> Dolly you'd say, "Oh yeah, that's a hooker." She
> had a gravel voice, this incredible raspy voice that
> sounded like a man in drag. She was an extreme,
> like a Bette Midler or Sylvia Miles, but underneath
> it there was a little lost girl, a Jewish princess being
> needed and spoiled. I think José was very drawn
> to qualities in actors more than to their professional
> experience. He felt that he had the ability (and he
> had a lot of the time) to mold somebody into the
> way they would go.

The casting of Jason Robards as Hickey is an epic unto itself. According to the memoir, Quintero's first casting choice was to call up Robards, with whom he had worked at the Circle-in-the-Square in the 1953 *American Gothic*, and offer him the role of Jimmy Tomorrow. When Robards came to the Circle unexpectedly, Quintero assumed he had come to refuse the role, but Robards had come to read for Hickey. Quintero agreed and Robards began, from memory, to deliver Hickey's final-act monologue, beginning "I picked up a nail from some tart in Altoona." Quintero (1974:168–69) describes the audition: "He kept on with the speech, and I sat there watching him gouge his eyes out and tear the very flesh from his bones. His arms stretched out, begging for the crucifixion. Rivers of sweat distorting all his features. But driving his points cleanly, with the precision and clarity of the mad, of the holy, of the devil." Quintero then imposed himself on the audition and insisted that Robards' Hickey justify himself for having killed his wife, spurring Robards on to greater depths of characterization. Robards left the office before Quintero could collect himself. He told his secretary to call Robards and offer him the role and not to leave the office until she reached him.

According to Jason Robards, "José never sought me out for *Iceman*. He'd cast the play and hadn't even called me."

Unlike Quintero, Robards had already had some exposure to O'Neill. During World War II, Robards happened upon *Strange Interlude* in the ship's library: "What fascinated me was that it had unspoken things, both dialogue and their thoughts." Robards was very specific that he had no interest in the material from an acting or technical point of view: "I didn't care about how you did it as an actor. I didn't know anything about acting and didn't care about it either. My father was an actor and I had no desire to be an actor." Robards was fascinated by the psychology, "the fact that you could say the unsaid things that you don't say to people, that the actors *said* them. I thought, 'Isn't this wonderful, that you can read inside the people while they're saying something else?' "

After the war, Robards entered the American Academy of Dramatic Arts where he had his second O'Neill experience. In 1946, he went with his class to a performance of *The Iceman Cometh*, in which James Barton was playing the role of Hickey "as a middle-aged man with little luster" (Gelb, 1974:64). Ten years later, in 1956, Robards told John Bryson (1973:36), "I was going to do a Studio One, and I went by the newsstand and Jimmy Greene, an actor who was selling newspapers, says José is doing *Iceman*. I never made it to the studio. I dropped everything. I went down to see José, hadn't seen him for a year, went into the office and he said, 'Where the hell did you come from?' "

Robards told Quintero that he wanted to be in *The Iceman Cometh*. According to Robards, Quintero paused and said, " 'Well, if I were going to use you in *Iceman*, I'd see you as Willie Oban.' I was the right age for Willie. I think José already had Howard da Silva or Franchot Tone in mind for Hickey because he pictured a guy in his 50s, the age O'Neill specifies. That age works well with Hickey's marriage because it's a real jolt when a guy kills his wife after a quarter of a century, not just some young Turk doing it."

So Robards was offered Willie Oban, a terrific part, but he wanted to read for Hickey: "I told José I wanted to read for Hickey because something had stuck in my head about Barton, about the play as well, but about Barton. It wasn't his acting, it was the way he looked. It was something that would stick with anybody, something that stuck out like a death's head or a skull."

Robards auditioned and nailed down his great role, much to the disgust of his agent Archer King. Addison Powell, who was also represented by Archer King at that time, stated, "Archer told Jason that he was out of his mind to go into a five-hour bomb by O'Neill, the thing that had bombed out on Broadway, and that nobody in his right mind was going to sit through all that shit. Archer just viewed this whole *Iceman* thing as an annoyance at a time when he was beginning to get good money and parts for Jason in live television."

In his "Postscript" article, Quintero (1957a:28) described his *Iceman* cast: "It was an oddly assorted and most unorthodox cast, ranging from highly trained and experienced actors to ones who were beginning their careers at the age of fifty. Some of them had never been in a play before."

Michael Murray (1973:II,3), who was the stage manager of Quintero's *Iceman*, recalled that unorthodox cast in a commemorative article:

> Most of them worked for 30 dollars a week to start with, the off-Broadway minimum at the time. They were mainly older men who were too far along to be starry-eyed or even very ambitious. They didn't noticeably like each other, which is to be expected. Among them were an Irishman who had worked with Lady Gregory, a German who had trained with Reinhardt, and a middle-aged fat man from Brooklyn who had never been on a professional stage before. There were intense Method addicts who required long and agonized preparation before making an entrance playing scenes with British types whose main goal was "to get on with it." The company did share a wary respect for one another as being at least well cast. They also shared a feeling of awe about the play,

a capacity to be hypnotized by the remarkable work
of José Quintero, the director, and a basic belief
that this lumbering vessel would probably float no
matter what happened.

Quintero seldom makes major prerehearsal judgments, but
Iceman was an exception. He said to John E. Fitzgerald (1959:8)
that "I worked on that one and I had elaborate staging and movements planned. Something was wrong. I didn't know just what.
It didn't 'play' right. Later on I decided to scrap all the trappings.
I let it run under its own steam. I could see the genius of O'Neill
and I adapted to him rather than forcing his work to fit my conception."

Quintero (1957a:28) wrote:

My approach in directing The *Iceman Cometh* was
different from that used in any play I had ever
done. It had to be, for this was not built as an ortho-
dox play, it resembles a complex musical form, with
themes repeating themselves with slight variations,
as melodies do in a symphony. It is a valid device
though O'Neill has often been criticized for it by
those who do not see the strength and depth of
meaning the repetition achieves.

My work was something like that of an orchestra
conductor, emphasizing rhythms, being constantly
aware of changing tempos, every character
advanced a different theme. The paradox was that
for the first time as a director I began to understand the meaning of precision in drama—and it
took a play four and a half hours long to teach me,
a play often criticized as rambling and overwritten.

O'Neill did think in such musical terms. In a 1931 notebook
entry he writes:

A play form—return of my old idea of using structure of symphony or sonata—justification of my
unconscious use of musical structure in nearly all
my plays—impulsion and chief interest an attempt
to do what music does (to express an essentially

poetic viewpoint of life) using rhythms of recurrent themes—is my, at times, blunderingly vague groping and missing caused by just the very fact that my use of musical structure *is* unconscious and ignorant of its own laws?

Jason Robards said, "José has mentioned the musical structure of O'Neill's plays to me, many times. He would say that *Iceman* is a full symphony and *Long Day's Journey* is a string quartet." Quintero made no such mention to his *Iceman* cast. Patricia Brooks, a professional opera singer, remembered no mention of musical structure in Quintero's direction. Paul Andor spoke of the play "with its oratorio style, with repetitions which are intended, written by a professional writer of great quality," but stipulated that Quintero "never mentioned the musical structure. You became conscious of the oratorio style which is inherent in the piece, but he did not force it, he did not mention it. He made no effort to control the repetitions. I think it would have made the actor too conscious of it, it was better to be left alone."

Addison Powell said of the repetition:

> I think it just happened. I think that's part of the organic way that it grew. I think it became a great virtue that it was hatched very quickly. No one came in with any premeditated salivation about what it might mean. Although we got a telegram from Vladimir Horowitz, a yard long, praising the production and going into a musical analysis, symphonic structure of *The Iceman Cometh* in which he wrote, "Theme one, stated." Then he would put "line" and so forth, "theme one restated, theme two stated." A complete musical analysis.

Larry Robinson who played Don Parritt said that "Parritt is the alter ego of Hickey, the role Jason played. He is the minor key in O'Neill's theme of guilt, punishment, and redemption," but Robinson said that this terminology was his own: "Quintero never mentioned music to me."

Quintero also made no reference to the 1946 production of *Iceman*, although he had cast Joe Marr as the daytime bartender, a role he had played in 1946. Paul Andor said:

We had no information about the original production other than Joe Marr. We interviewed him, we
were all around him. He was not especially elo-
quent, but he had seen O'Neill who, to all of us,
was a great man and writer, so it was fascinating
to talk to someone who had worked with him, especially about his deep blue eyes. He did not talk so
much about the original production, but about Barton's getting stuck on opening night.

When first addressing his company, Quintero spoke very little about the play's drinking or alcoholism. Addison Powell recalled
that "José spoke more about the world of pipe dreams than alcoholism." For Quintero, O'Neill's genius in *Iceman* is that "he knew
what man has to put up with, what he has to invent, in order
to endure his own fate" (Richards, 1985:K10).

Addison Powell recounted vivid memories of the first reading:

The first reading was upstairs at the Circle and
there was a matinee performance of *The Cradle
Song* downstairs so we could not speak too loud.
I'll never forget Jason, particularly that long speech
at the end. He just quietly put his book aside and
he knew the whole thing, practically by heart. It
was the most moving reading of that scene I ever
heard because he had to keep his voice down and
he was literally thinking it through. Jason is such
a bravura actor; for him to have that technical
imposition put on him and work with it, that's
when we realized that something big was going to
happen.

Larry Robinson recalled that after a reading of the play,
"Quintero turned to each of us and asked 'Why are you in this
bar?' The actor playing Larry Slade was fired that day because
whatever he said to Quintero seemed unsatisfactory. Jason then
brought in his friend Conrad Bain to play Larry Slade." There
was another replacement during the first week, Addison Powell
recalled, "a nonactor, a little guy who was cast completely to type,
not an actor at all, a painfully shy little guy who, it became quickly
evident within the first four or five days, that he just couldn't do

it. He was terrified to begin with. José very reluctantly let him go and that's when Jimmy Greene came in."

With so many actors new to the Circle, it would have seemed natural that Quintero lead an orientation into the mysteries of playing three-quarter style, but he never did so. Paul Andor said, "I was not exactly used to a three-quarter stage, but I had worked on such a stage before. You were in that room and you instinctively adapted to it." Patricia Brooks said, "You never thought about that, never. It became an environment, it became Harry Hope's and that was how Harry Hope's looked, that space."

Addison Powell said:

> I'd never worked at the Circle before. I never considered working on that stage a problem, that anything had to be dealt with. I'd never done arena style or even three-quarter, almost all my work had been straight proscenium. I think the main thing I noticed in rehearsal was that José kept moving all the time. He kept popping up which was a constant reminder that you had to be aware that the audience was on all sides because wherever you looked you might see José. He was constantly moving in that space, but as far as articulating in his direction "Now you must be here because we must think of this side of the house, you play this scene to this side of the house," that never came up.

Quintero knew the space well enough to take it for granted, but he also knew that he'd stumbled onto a more specific use for it. May 1956 was well in advance of environmental staging, but Quintero announced in the Frederic Morton (1956:II,3) interview, two days before the production opened, that "it is time we tried O'Neill. Important, too, is the atmospheric quality of *Iceman*. In a proscenium theater the most you can do is look at its setting, Harry Hope's bar. But in an arena theater, you are in Harry Hope's bar."

Addison Powell recalled Quintero's commitment to that space:

> I can remember at midpoint in the rehearsals when José was looking haggard and probably hadn't slept well in two or three nights. It was the time just

before rehearsal when he was summoning up his
energy; he just sat there at one of those tables,
looked at that space and said, "Thank God it's happening in the womb." He used to refer to that space
as the womb. I think that gave him enormous
strength, that he was on his home space, that old
territorial imperative.

Jimmy Greene said of Quintero's rehearsal habits, "I think
José rehearsed longer hours then than he would today and I'm
certain it must have been a case of breaking down scenes so that
we weren't all called at the same time."
Addison Powell remembered:

José had a wonderful way of working at that time,
taking it section by section. He knew the precise
point at which to begin a piece of work and the
precise point where to stop. He would take each
beat and start it very intimately. We would sort
of murmur it to each other, put our heads together
with loads of contact, no acting, just talk it through
so that we were never intimidated by the sweep
of it. Because he kept our attention so strongly on
each section as we went along, we always knew
where we were. The beats varied; it might be just
a page and a half or it might be six, seven, or eight
pages. There was no set length of time. It was just
what he conceived of as the beginning of an idea,
a new idea or a marked change of mood and the
duration of that, but whatever it was, it seemed
organic and infallible. As hard as we all worked,
we never seemed off-balance. There's always that
awkward stage in a production and we never
seemed to have an awkward stage. It isn't that
things came full blown, they didn't. It grew gradually. Everything seemed to be centered. We found
a center.

Quintero spent the first week on the first act, putting into
practice the "elaborate staging and movements" he had planned.
Like Eddie Dowling, he tried to make the first act move. Robards
said that, after a week, "José decided 'I have done this wrong and

I'm throwing out the week. We'll start from scratch,' which was a very brave and daring think to do; to rehearse a company for a week in a lot of hard work and look at it and say, 'I'm commenting on the play. I'm putting my stamp on the play, trying to jazz it up and not letting the play do its work.' When I came in was when he threw out the first act. He said, 'No, I haven't got it ready for you.' "

In handling the individual actors, Quintero trusted his casting because, as Jimmy Greene pointed out, "so many of the actors were so much like the characters they were playing. The kind of fights that broke out on stage were often happening offstage as well, people would be bickering all the time and picking at each other. The life just seemed to flow from the dressing room to the stage and back again."

Quintero did not cast a large authoritarian shadow. Patricia Brooks said that "he wouldn't really direct you so much, he would let you go and do it and you would bring a certain way of how you wanted to walk or get up and he would say, 'No, don't do that. All right, yes, do that.' So, in a way, it was creative in that you could do your own stuff and he would edit that."

Paul Andor remembered:

> He let the actors go quite a bit. If he liked what you did, he just said, "a little more here, a little less there." He didn't change anybody. He told me almost nothing. He didn't get up on the stage at any time, fortunately, no. He walked around quite a bit and listened to us. He did not interfere, that's as much as I can say. I liked his directing, but he didn't stop anyone from doing what they shouldn't do either. Dolly Jonah did too much and he wouldn't stop her.

Jimmy Greene said:

> José talked a lot about the play, talked a lot about himself and parallel experiences and so on. He did a lot of observing of you and leaving you pretty much alone. When you got into trouble, then he would help you physically or he'd actually suggest things. He stood apart unless he felt that you were getting tied into knots and then he would try to find

ways to relax you and give you something physical to do.

Addison Powell insisted that Quintero's direction was always achieved through suggestion:

> José had very little to say in a concrete way on how to work on Willie. I remember a beautiful statement . . . "Just think, I was once a prince in velvet, and now I'm a piece of shit and isn't that the funniest thing you ever heard in your life?" He said that's the attitude in which you tell that whole story of your past. That triggered it and gave me the whole character. I mean, my instincts were starting to go in that direction, but José's statement . . . Well, he had a genius at that time, heightened by the fact that he didn't have time to ramble on and get verbose anyway, but, by the necessities of it, he was forced to be as economical as possible.

Quintero's control of the various actors depended on the specifics. Larry Robinson recalled that "José had to clamp down on the natural hamminess of Al Lewis and Phil Pfeiffer who sat at the same table." Peter Falk had a day job to make ends meet and was invariably 30 to 40 minutes late for each rehearsal. Addison Powell said that "José would shrug and say, 'Well, that's Peter.' One of José's great strengths was his tolerance for eccentricity, a marvelous prismatic personality. He could accept wildly variant, aberrant behavior and incorporate it and make it work."

Quintero spent most of his direction on Larry Robinson:

> I found the role of Don Parritt very difficult to play and found that Quintero gave me no help. José was fascinated by the part and he began to overdirect me; he tried to accentuate the hatred of this character for his mother. I was playing such hatred when I came on stage that I looked guilty. I was a guy who'd done something wrong. Bud Powell, who's a very smart guy, took me aside and said, "I think you're tipping your hand. You should be more of a mystery." I was playing that because Quintero told me to play it. He kept saying, "You hate your

mother, you hate your mother. It should be your primary action."

Like Robards, Robinson had seen the 1946 production:

I saw Paul Crabtree in 1946 and I saw José's revival in 1985 and felt that the actor there had been misdirected as well. Quintero had not learned anything in all those years about this particular part. The actor came on looking as if there was a cop on the sidewalk chasing him. They hated him from that moment. I don't think the audience should hate this guy. They ought to wonder who he is, even be disturbed by him, but not say, "Oh, he's a bad guy, he's up to no good." And that's what Quintero has directed this part to be; a furtive, sneaky character.

The only actor who has had an unqualified success with Parritt was Robert Redford, who played it for Sidney Lumet's 1960 televised version. Robinson said that "Redford was exactly what the part should have been. He's a mysterious guy and you don't catch on to what he's up to until the last act. Just as you shouldn't catch on to what Hickey is up to until the last act. And Jason, who was on the level of genius, never tipped his hand until the end."

Robinson concluded by saying, "I remember walking on in the opening performance as a puppet. I was doing what I was told, but I was not in control of my performance. I don't consider José Quintero a great director or the genius he's cracked up to be. He's a nice man, interesting, and intelligent, but I consider him a very lucky guy to have had Jason Robards thrust himself into the production."

Jason Robards used Quintero's direction of Larry Robinson to make the point that Quintero came into the acting space only if it got difficult:

Larry Robinson did not have an image of how his mother had behaved with men while he was growing up. José told Larry it was like having a whore around with all those men coming in. It made home seem rotten. Larry was having trouble with the imagery, with the memory, because he hadn't had that experience of a woman who was a tramp. José would tell Larry stories. He would come into the acting space, sit at the table with Larry and say, "Larry, the bedsprings were creaking, you hear this, they're fucking your mother." He'd say these things to try to get Larry to feel something about it. That's what José does when he *has* to make a point.

Quintero's impact on Robards' magnificent performance was muted. Paul Andor recalled that "with Robards he didn't have to change much, he was so intense and strong." Addison Powell specifically remembered: "I know that José and Jason said that the day that Hickey happened was very early on in that second week when Jason came in, made his entrance and did something like that [arms forming a Y] and José was down at the other end of the space and José mirrored that back to him, like 'That's it, revival, preacher, savior,' and they said that they hardly had words beyond that, that words were not needed."

Robards maintained that he was simply responding to the religious imagery in the text: "I got none of that revival material from Barton." Robards emphasized his dependence on the text and added, "In 1956, I crossed out all the stage directions and as soon as we started rehearsing, took my eraser out and put them all back in. I don't think they are stage directions, they are the play. For the actor, they are as much a part of the play as the dialogue."

Robards could recall only one major discussion with Quintero:

It's not until Hugo and Harry break in the third act that Hickey begins to doubt. We had him doubting sooner, but José and I had a talk one night and agreed, "Let's string it out like a piano wire, as tight as we can get it before it breaks: and see how long Hickey can remain confident without any doubts, not even a beat." So we took it up until Hugo broke. Harry came back and broke. Still, Hickey wasn't thrown, but when *Hugo* broke, right at the end of that act, *that's* when it turned. And that worked for us.

Because Quintero had decided to restage the first act, the fourth act rehearsal time was minimal for Robards:

The Iceman Cometh, 1956. L to r: Larry Robinson, Patricia Brooks, James Greene, Al Lewis, Richard Bowler, Paul Andor, Farrell Pelly, Phil Pfeiffer, Conrad Bain, Jason Robards, Gloria Scott Backe, Dolly Jonah. Photo by Jerry Dantzic.

That cost me a week. José couldn't stage the final act until about three days before we opened. José said, "Say that speech for me—yeah—that part we'll start there and feel free when you want to move. When you leave home and go to town, then come down here." I said, "Yes, and I think I'll end up behind the whore when I talk about picking up a dose," and then José said "and end up there in the middle part and then, at the very end, go back up to the bar." That was how we did it. We had no time. We did that in about five minutes just to get it staged. We ran it three times and that was it.

When Robards was asked the all-too-familiar literary question, "What about the relationship of Gregers Werle in *The Wild Duck* to Hickey in *Iceman*? Is that relationship, that similarity, of any use to him as an actor?" Robards raised his arms in comic desperation:

I've heard that about a thousand times, right from the beginning. That doesn't mean anything to me. I don't use that. I can't even get through *The Wild Duck*. I can't read it. It's dull to me. I've never acted it. It's hard for me to read plays in a literary way. I have to *act* them. I don't care where O'Neill got it from. He got it from his old man, from melodrama; all that stuff was born and bred in him. Those things are in people. It's like actors. You either have it or you don't have it. It comes down to that, nothing else. There's no way to put your finger on what O'Neill had. It's a gift.

After four weeks of rehearsal the production opened to overwhelming critical response directed to the environmental atmosphere provided by the Circle-in-the-Square.

Brooks Atkinson (1956:38) wrote, "If *The Iceman Cometh* seems to belong in Mr. Quintero's theater, there is a good reason for Circle-in-the-Square was a nightclub originally and all four of the acts of the O'Neill drama are set in a saloon. The audience has the sense of participating. The rows of seats are only an extension of David Hays' setting of the battered, blowsy waterfront saloon and flophouse that is under the fabulous proprietorship of Harry Hope."

Thomas R. Dash (1956:?) said, "the intimate theater-in-the-round technique seems more congenial to this O'Neill play than the conventional proscenium or picture-frame setting staging."

George Oppenheimer (1956:?) described the setting in this way: "The audience sits on three sides of a tawdry, sawdust saloon, so close to its sodden inhabitants that their souls would seem to be in your lap—and on your conscience. It's a terrifying experience . . . Quintero has used the arena stage to greater effect than I have ever seen it used before."

Robert Hatch (1956:458–59) wrote that the "theater-in-the-round (actually this stage has one standing wall) is well suited to the sprawling structure of the play and it puts us all in the saloon which is the point."

Walcott Gibbs (1956:74) wrote, "I would like to say that the platform staging employed at the Circle-in-the-Square is admirably suited to *The Iceman Cometh*. You are apt to feel as if you were sitting right there in Harry Hope's bar along with all the other bums. It is a disturbing experience, but a memorable one. José Quintero's direction accomplishes the complicated task of maintaining equal visibility from all points in the auditorium with commendable ingenuity."

Only Euphemia Van Rensselaer Wyatt (1956:310) intimated that the more realistic proscenium set of the Broadway original was more suggestive: "Next day they go out one by one through the saloon's swinging doors. At least that is what they did on the stage in the first production. Now they are seen through a window ascending some steps and a certain finality suggested by the doors swinging back is lost."

In addition to the participatory aspects of the production, critics found rhythms in the play that they had previously thought to have only a single, protracted theme. Brooks Atkinson (1956:38) wrote: "Mr. Quintero is a versatile conductor who knows how to vary his attack with changes in volume and rhythm; he knows how to orchestrate a performance."

Walter Kerr (or Walter F. Kerr as he then signed himself) explained (1956:18): "O'Neill is determined that every key strain in a despairing symphony be sounded again and again until its possible variations are exhausted. He refuses to surrender his fierce

grip on the material until it—and we—are drained dry." In a Sunday column, written a week-and-a-half later, Kerr (1956:IV,1&2)
examined Quintero's impact on the musical structure of the
production:

> There's a battered old piano standing near the bar
> in the cobwebbed, gas-lit saloon of Eugene O'Neill's
> *The Iceman Cometh.* It isn't played much. Dur-
> ing the disturbed and half-hearted merriment of
> the third act, when there's some chance that out-
> of-towner Hickey is going to throw his pals a party,
> one of the neighborhood tarts does finger it
> forlornly, plucking out a few slightly sour notes in
> an effort to get the doomed revel going. Yet I had
> the eerie feeling . . . that the box in the corner was
> a player piano and that it was rolling out an
> unsteady but perpetually rhythmic tune from the
> play's first fade-in to its last long sigh. Something
> about José Quintero's restrained and endlessly
> orchestrated stage direction suggests an odd kind
> of music, music that has a bright, drunken clatter
> to it, that jerks backward and forward as though
> the feet on the pedals were speeding up and slow-
> ing down on a lunatic whim, and that—under all
> the inspired vagaries of tempo and volume—
> maintain an insistent, unbroken, out-of-key rattle.
>
> And Quintero has been wise, I think, not to
> hurry his author. By simply taking time for every-
> thing, by refusing to blur the passing moments in
> a conventional anxiety to make them pass, he has
> brought the characters harrowingly close to his
> ringside audience. These lurching, sweating, gasp-
> ing figures breathe down your neck not because the
> production is an "in-the-round" operation, but
> because they insist—in the regularity of their
> rhythms, in the painstaking fullness of their
> portraiture—on occupying your whole attention.

Patricia Brooks was surprised to learn that Quintero had first
asked Dolly Jonah if she played the piano, only to see it show up
in Kerr's review. She concluded, "José was a man of some kind

of inspirational visions and I'm sure that he suddenly woke up and saw Cora playing the piano."

In praising Quintero's refusal to "blur the passing moments in a conventional anxiety to make them pass," Kerr had pinpointed what Quintero was later to call his own directing style. A week before *Long Day's Journey* opened, Quintero said:

> I know myself. I cannot do fast-paced shows. I like silences; they are as eloquent as words. A character without silences tends to be too secure, too mechanical. I could never do high comedy, the witty comedy of manners. I don't understand that kind of world. In Latin America, society is not light and superficial. I remember once seeing a great lady whip her husband's mistress in a restaurant. I would probably turn Wilde's *The Importance of Being Earnest* into a tragedy (Lewis, 1956:13).

The chronology of Quintero's production of *Iceman* is particularly revealing. From his securing the rights to opening night was a little over two months. Addison Powell said, "I think his reactions to it were instinctive because he didn't have time to plan; it was the most instinctive piece of direction I have ever seen in my life." The Theatre Guild production took over two years, conceived by seasoned Broadway veterans in the waning years of the Guild's effectiveness. Quintero's production, by contrast, was conceived in a white heat by a director, designer, and leading man who were half the age of their predecessors.

2

Long Day's Journey Into Night

Writing
Begun June 1939; first draft completed September 20, 1940; second draft completed October 16, 1940; final version completed March 30, 1941.

Premieres
Original: Not produced in O'Neill's lifetime.

Quintero: November 8, 1956; New York, Helen Hayes Theater.

On June 6, 1939, O'Neill determined that his next two projects would be *The Iceman Cometh* and *Long Day's Journey Into Night* (Floyd, 1981:281). Carlotta wrote in her diary for June 21, 1939, that "Gene talks to me for hours—about a play (in his mind) of his mother, his brother and himself" (Gelb, 1960:6).

Virginia Floyd (1981:196), who edited O'Neill's work diaries, writes that "the dramatist draws two set designs for the play. The intricate first floor plan of the Tyrone home is an exact replica of the O'Neill family's New London home before it was renovated . . . The other sketch is an accurate visual representation of the living room as it is described in the published text."

The secrecy of the play's subject matter was such that "he left scarcely any recorded comments on it, referring to it only obliquely on the few public occasions that he mentioned it at all" (Gelb, 1960:838). The single exception to this rule was an unpublished June 15, 1940 letter to George Jean Nathan. Louis Sheaffer (1973:509) writes:

> Without disclosing that it was autobiographical, he had told Nathan, after finishing the first act, that the play would cover one day in a family's life, "a day in which things occur which evoke the whole past of the family and reveal every aspect of its interrelationships. A deeply tragic play, but without any violent dramatic action. At the final curtain, there they still are, trapped within each other by the past, each guilty and at the same time innocent, scorning, loving, pitying each other, understanding and yet not understanding at all, forgiving but still doomed never to be able to forget."

The majority of O'Neill's plays are, to one extent or another, autobiographical: *Long Day's Journey* is the most nakedly autobiographical. In 1926, when O'Neill was still married to Agnes Bolton, he took part in a study directed by Dr. Gilbert V. Hamilton, "a psychiatrist with a commission from a scientific organization to research the sex life and problems of married people . . . The Macgowans were part of the survey, and Kenneth thought that Dr. Hamilton might be able to help the O'Neills with their drinking problem and the conflict between them" (Sheaffer, 1973:188). O'Neill saw Hamilton for six weeks, who told him that he had an Oedipus complex. Hamilton "apparently believed that O'Neill was able to reform once he accepted that oedipal impulses, with consequent guilt feelings, were at the root of his self-destructive drinking." O'Neill took this diagnosis lightly enough: " 'Why, all he had to do,' Gene said, 'was read my plays' " (Sheaffer, 1973:190). He did, however, stop drinking. More importantly:

> His participation in the research project and his consultations afterward with Hamilton (which he incorrectly liked to call his "analysis") launched O'Neill on a journey into the past that led him to drawing up two papers in which he summarized

his early years and the family forces that had shaped him. The two documents are in a script so minuscule that they almost defy reading even with a magnifier; he evidently tried to make them illegible, except to himself, in case they ever fell into another's hands.

One paper, a diagram, outlines his relations from birth into adolescence with his parents and his nursemaid . . . The other document, also on one side of a single page, summarizes a great deal of the background history that would be divulged in his family portrait. Taken as a unit, the two papers can be considered his first step toward writing, some fifteen years later, *Long Day's Journey Into Night* (Sheaffer, 1973:190–91).

In writing *Long Day's Journey*, O'Neill purged himself of more than just his personal demons. He finally disciplined his compulsion to control the means of production. Travis Bogard (1972:423) writes:

Ironically, O'Neill's ultimate "experiment" was a return to four boards and a passion—to, in other words, a confident reliance on his actors. He, who had gone to such elaborate lengths to ensure that his actors would fulfill his purposes, loading them with masks, asides, choral support and an infinity of pauses, now removed all exterior pressures . . . Everything, now is in the role. An actor in these plays cannot hide behind personal mannerisms, clever business or habitual stage trickery. O'Neill has stripped all but the most minimal requirements from the stage. They must play or perish.

Long Day's Journey is eminently actable, but O'Neill never intended it to be staged. On November 29, 1945, O'Neill delivered a sealed copy of the play to Bennett Cerf at Random House. Cerf was not allowed to open the seal until 25 years after O'Neill's death, at which time it could be published but not produced (Sheaffer, 1973:560). In a 1951 letter to Cerf, O'Neill reiterated his instructions about the play: "That, as you know, is to be published twenty-five years after my death—but never produced as a play" (Sheaffer: 1973:635). Based on O'Neill's work notes, however, Virginia Floyd (1981:294) concluded that "one page of computations is certain to lead to new speculations about O'Neill's plans for *Long Day's Journey Into Night* . . . He makes a concerted effort here to determine the running time for both a five-act and four-act production."

By the terms of O'Neill's will, Carlotta had the legal right to dispose as she saw fit of O'Neill's literary estate. In 1955, two years after O'Neill's death, Carlotta directed Cerf to publish *Long Day's Journey*. Cerf felt himself bound by O'Neill's wishes and refused to publish the manuscript. Carlotta "thereupon withdrew the manuscript from Random House. She presented it to the Yale University Press, which published the play in February, 1956" (Gelb, 1960:862). Simultaneously, Carlotta awarded the Royal Dramatic Theatre in Stockholm the rights to stage *Long Day's Journey*, where it had its world premiere on February 2, 1956.

1956 Production

Cast List

James Tyrone	Fredric March
Mary Tyrone	Florence Eldridge
James Tyrone, Jr.	Jason Robards
Edmund Tyrone	Bradford Dillman
Cathleen	Katherine Ross

Shortly after the May 1956 opening of *The Iceman Cometh*, Carlotta offered Quintero the rights to the American premiere of *Long Day's Journey Into Night*. Quintero (1974:206) describes her gesture: " 'I let it be done in Sweden first. Sweden proved to be more faithful to O'Neill than his own country. Now I am ready to have it produced here and I want you to do it. But you must promise to do it exactly as he wrote it, without cutting a line. Will you?' I managed to say, 'I promise.' "

David Hays was especially faithful to O'Neill's directions. When asked if verisimilitude had been a concern in designing the set, he answered:

> None to the original house, none whatsoever. I
> never saw the house. People were invited up there

Long Day's Journey Into Night, 1956. L to r: Florence Eldridge, Bradford
Dillman, Jason Robards, Fredric March. Photo by Sy Friedman.

and a photograph was published in the *Times* of Leigh, Ted, and José. I wasn't invited that day. It seemed curious, because I was the one person dealing with the physical structure, but I wasn't invited. I went up to New London to see the types of houses up there and someone showed me photographs of the actual house, but when I drove up there, no one from the management pointed out to me which house it was. I didn't particularly care. The only thing from the house that came out in the set was a little bit of porch detail, a very small bit of it, quatrefoil, which was outside the windows anyway and was seen by no one but a few people and me.

Hays had never seen the set rendering O'Neill himself had made for the play (the notebooks were not published until 1981), but commented that "I recreated that exactly from the stage directions. I drew my own sketch from his description. That's a replica of the house itself in which I later lived for two years when I was with the O'Neill Foundation. One of the funny ironies, after designing a play that took place in a specific room, is that I subsequently moved into it and lived there for two years."

Elliot Martin, who stage-managed the production, stated that "the set bore no resemblance to the house at all. The house is a pretty solid piece. O'Neill in his directions runs the house down and in the text the characters run down the house. The actual house was wonderful, a marvelous place."

In his memoir, Quintero (1974:219–22) re-created the discussions he had with David Hays in arriving at a set:

It's a long play but it all takes place in one set. Besides, it's very important that, although it is the characters who make their inward journey, we have to match their progression in physical terms. We visually have to travel from morning to afternoon and into night . . . but the journey must be accompanied and intensified by the various speeds and moves that the sun experiences as it makes its long voyage across the sky . . . So, in some way, you have to bring nature into the set. You have to

give me windows where I can see clearly its joyful
rising, its angry noon and its majestical downfall
. . . It has to be a room that does not face the street
. . . Let's use as little furniture as we can. I'd like
to have enough space to be able to isolate each one
of them whenever the script calls for it. And,
David, there must be a rocker . . . How deeply
Florence will have to suffer in that rocking chair.
They will turn it into a witness box and lock her
in it every once in a while . . . The center table
has to be oval. Don't you think of oval as a complete embrace? And the last thing, David, see if you
can place the doorway leading to the upstairs way
upstage right and the door leading to the garden
almost to the very edge of the wall, stage left.

When asked what Quintero had wanted from the set, Hays
answered:

José had the proper reverence for O'Neill's stage
directions without being particularly slavish to
them. For example, O'Neill called for a central
table and José felt, with justice, that that would
give you a funny kind of ping-pong match. If the
table's right in the middle, you're either looking to
the right or to the left. We worked very hard on
the kind of room in which the table would have
the feeling of being centered in the room, but that
the room was seen at a very slight angle, so the table
was actually off to the left. We could compose the
stage much better that way. We even considered
that the play might take place in an entirely different place, like a screened-in summer porch. I didn't
think that we needed two doors upstage so we cut
it to one upstage door which served both the front
parlor and the windowless back parlor.

I don't remember who had the idea of featur-
ing the big windows which can bring into a room
the change of day. In the [Laurence] Olivier
production, he went more to the stage directions
and, while it gave a chance for more sudden

entrances upstage center, it lacked the feeling of a passage of time which was our big thing. That was how the set got off the ground, a phrase designers use, by really having such an expanse of window which could show the four different times of day. I used little bits of colored glass because they dressed up the windows enough so that I didn't need curtains and yet they were perfectly bare. They were built for the house, but it didn't look as if anyone had taken care of them one way or another. The light shooting through these squares of glass made the first act very cheerful, the over-head light of noon didn't come through the glass but you saw the light outside through the glass which was a different look. In the fog, there was a bluish feeling throughout and you weren't aware of the details of the window. In the last act, there was the ugliness that stained glass has from the inside when there is no light outside. That's the act when you want it to seem most inhospitable.

Quintero cast the play very quickly. He had admired Fredric March ever since he saw *Anthony Adverse* as a child. Recently he had seen March and Florence Eldridge three times in *The Autumn Garden*. The Marches were available and eager to play the Tyrones.

Quintero asked Jason Robards, who was still playing Hickey, to play Jamie. "I had been given a copy of *Long Day's Journey* by Leigh Connell on opening night of *Iceman*. I read it and said 'I'd love to do the play some time' and that was that. I did *Iceman* for about six months. I never got to study *Long Day's Journey* until we went into rehearsal because José had not yet replaced me in *Iceman*. He got a little remiss about that. I rehearsed *Long Day's Journey* by day and played *Iceman* by night. I only got a couple of weeks free, at night, before we went to open in Boston."

The role of Edmund proved to be the only casting hurdle, and Quintero saw over five hundred young actors. "Finally a young man named Bradford Dillman came into my office and after two readings I got into a cab with him and took him to see Mrs. O'Neill. She talked to him for five minutes—and the part was his" (Quintero, 1957a:29).

Normally, Quintero does not make contact with his actors before rehearsals, but the Marches proved to be an exception. In his memoir, Quintero describes visits he made with Jason Robards and Bradford Dillman to the March home in Connecticut. Robards recalled: "I did go up to Connecticut in the late morning and read the play for the first time. I got into a car about five o'clock and drove back to do *Iceman*. Brad and José stayed overnight." Elliot Martin confirmed that José did go to the March house for a month of weekends: "I didn't go with him, but I was very close to José and heard all about them. They talked about the roles; Freddie talked about his Academy Awards. That's what those sessions were. José didn't sit down with them to analyze deeply prior to rehearsal. He does not work that way."

When rehearsals began, actors arrived in varying stages of preparedness. According to Elliot Martin, "Freddie and Florence arrived letter-perfect, knowing their parts completely. A four-hour play, both of them. Freddie had two scripts, one for his lines and the other for his business; a book full of notations like 'James O'Neill would cut his cigar a quarter of an inch down before smoking it,' every single detail. He studied every record of James O'Neill and every picture. Jason didn't know word one and neither did Brad."

Elliot Martin recalled the first rehearsal:

> It was a very short preamble. What José really laid out, I remember it very clearly, was that the play dealt with guilt and that he wanted to see this through their eyes. He said, "This is a play about eyes. If there's a sound upstairs, everyone's eyes must register it." That was an element that ran throughout the play. Whenever they heard a creak upstairs from Mama who was walking around, the men were to register that, perhaps look at each other. The three men were to carry that sense of guilt and of fear of what was going to happen.
>
> With almost all of José's earlier productions, his direction was all related to his own family. In his preamble for *Long Day's Journey*, he did identify the guilt of the father with his own father's guilt and the treatment of his own mother. There's so much niggling between the father and mother, they did everything with a barb and a sense of guilt. He

said, "this is so much out of my background, the way they dealt, they would shoot knives at one another in their speech."

Quintero told David Richards (1985:K10) that "when we presented *Long Day's Journey* on Broadway, I invited my sister Carmen to come to the opening. After the curtain had come down, she ran backstage and said in Spanish, 'Oh, José, how could you! How could you do this to Papa and Mama?' I said, 'Carmen, I did not write this play.' "

Frank Hamilton, who stood by for the national company, recalled Quintero's opening remarks for that production:

> José's psychiatrist told him that he had "anxious-ness." José told him, "Don't get rid of my anxious-ness until the play opens." He had to have his anxieties because he understood them to be the same anxieties as the Tyrone family. I remember references to the Catholicism with its whole "don't" system. It's a part of the Tyrone family and of José's. José's family was very straight-laced, he experienced no freedom until he went to USC. They covered over their secrets like the Tyrone family. Edmund wants to create, but the family says no, even though the old man was an actor. He is told that he cannot create, that he is not well. There is a crushing of Edmund in the play. Jamie is oppressed as well. The moral scale is the same in Panama and New London. Oppression is oppres-sion. If there is a leitmotif in the play, however, the word is love, a kind of yearning to be close to people. There's a lot of hatred in *Long Day's Jour-ney*, but if they really hated each other that much they would not stay in New London. It is love that holds them together. The boys have a terrible need to love. José understands that.

Quintero recalled the conversations he had while directing Fredric March:

> You asked me whether I wanted James Tyrone to have a slight brogue all through the play. As I hadn't thought about it, I answered, "I don't

know." "Neither do I," you said, "but we mustn't forget that he was pure potato-famine Irish and regardless of how he tried to hide it, he wouldn't really forget anything, not even his brogue. There is something there that needs to be explored. It may seem strange to you, but I have a feeling that hidden in the brogue business is one of the keys to my character. Leave it to O'Neill to do something like that. He really intended for me to take a long day's journey into night backwards, to go back to the beginning." And, by God, you were right. I had never seen anybody work so intensely and relentlessly on a part. You wore a facsimile of the boots of the period from the first day of rehearsal. It was your idea to wear the gold fob and big-faced gold watch, hidden in the vest pocket (the same gold watch you were going to use later to hide in, pretending to look at the time, but really pitifully trying not to see what you didn't want to see).

It was only in that last act, when all facade had been peeled off, that you used the sad, remembered song of an Irish brogue. As you climbed onto the chair to turn off the extra light bulbs to save on electricity, you lifted the character to a tragic level by having him, as he performed the almost comedic act, accept the responsibility of his situation. Oh, the way you handled that chandelier as if it were the wheel of your life. And the way you loosened the bulbs into black, with the unerring timing of death, was pure artistry (1975: 23–25).

Elliot Martin described March's performance by comparing it with that of Laurence Olivier: "I spent a month with Olivier in 1970 when I was running a theater in Los Angeles. He wanted to do James Tyrone, but he wanted to do it very differently from Freddie. He said, 'Freddie took the actor home. I'm going to be a common man.' And so he was. He played a little fussbudget in the home. I think that was wrong because everything you ever read about James O'Neill, the pictures you see, they were all declamatory. He just wanted to be different from Freddie."

Florence Eldridge wrote, "José Quintero was particularly anxious for me to met Carlotta O'Neill as he felt that O'Neill had woven a bit of her into the character of his mother. The director arranged for us to have lunch and I could find echoes of Mary Tyrone's speeches in Carlotta's love-hate anecdotes. She would start to reminisce so sweetly and suddenly repressed resentment would burst through into bitter complaints or self-pity just as Mary Tyrone does repeatedly when she is reviewing the past with James Tyrone" (1979:287). Eldridge also made reference to the musical structure of O'Neill's writing: "When we opened in Boston, they insisted that it must be cut as it was too repetitious. Fortunately, Carlotta stood firm. Not one word could be touched. The more one worked on the play, the more one realized that it was a symphony. Each character had a theme and the 'repetitions' were variations on the themes. That was the power of the play—the ceaseless pounding of the themes and, had it been cut, it would have unravelled."

Elliot Martin said that there definitely had been cuts made in the script, but of Quintero's direction he said, "The only sense of rhythm that José used was in the foghorn. He said that he wanted to use that rhythm as the heartbeat of the play. He said that to me, he didn't say that to the actors. I didn't get a sense of music. You know the way David Mamet writes, he writes musically. I didn't have a sense that José was directing with pauses, with a sense of loud/slow/fast, in there at all. José doesn't do that."

Martin recalled that, in directing *Long Day's Journey*, Quintero did get up on the stage and act out the roles, "more for Florence than for the men. He acted out everything for Florence: gestures, sitting, everything."

Martin described the relationship between Robards and Quintero: "I think that Jason works very organically, just lets it hang out and happen to him. He doesn't need, at least in his work with José, long speeches. He just needs a little thing. They use a short-cut language between the two of them."

In this instance, Robards had already found a little thing to get him started. While he was still playing in *Iceman*, he made an early discovery about Jamie Tyrone. Addison Powell, who played Willie Oban in *Iceman*, recalled:

> Jason said at one point, after he learned that he
> was going to be doing *Long Day's Journey*, that

Florence Eldridge (foreground); L to r: Bradford Dillman, Jason Robards, Fredric March (rear). Photo by Friedman Abeles.

he began to see in Willie Oban a sketch for Jamie. Willie has the emotional demands in it that Jamie has, the depth of his despair and self-destruction. You've got the father, that's cut from the same plot, and you've got the bitter humor. The self-destructive humor of Willie is very much like Jamie. Jason told me (and I took it as a very high compliment because he had a very long time before his first entrance) that he used to watch my first scene every night after he found that he'd be playing Jamie. He said, "I'm going to be using Willie—not using literally. It's just coming in on me strongly that that scene has so many drum beats foreshadowing Jamie's big scene in *Long Day's Journey*."

Robards corroborated: "That's right. Addison and I talked about that. That's Jamie in the end, when he finally goes, when he's yelling to the winds, 'I want company,' screaming into the night. Willie does that. That's where I saw the connection, not in the stuff that happens earlier; but, when you unpeel him, he's in an area that Willie's in."

In the third week of rehearsal, Carlotta came to watch a run-through. Quintero (1974:213) writes that "almost as soon as the first act started, she started to cry, pressing her handkerchief tight against her mouth, so nobody could hear her. I put my arms around her and she pulled very close to me. She felt like a wounded bird, she was trembling so. She waited until the end of the first act, then unable to control herself anymore, she sobbed loudly and openly. Her sobs echoed from wall to wall until they filled the whole theater." Elliot Martin said of the same experience, "Carlotta only came once to a run-through of one scene. At the end of that one scene she feigned collapse or something and they took her out." When asked why Quintero was so successful in dealing with Carlotta, Martin replied, "José just used his charm, as he's done with all the ladies, and he treated her like a star. I think she was mad for him."

Martin said of Quintero's rehearsal schedule, "I almost never remember José doing eight hours. We had an enormous volume of work so he had to go more than his usual five hours. If he went beyond five hours it wasn't productive, ever. Oftentimes, we would go noon to six without a lunch break."

Following the four-week rehearsal in the Helen Hayes Theater, the production opened in Boston and played in New Haven before moving to Broadway. Martin recalled opening night in Boston. Fredric March had memorized his lines for the opening day of rehearsal, but had not absorbed them for opening night:

> Freddie didn't know a line, not a line. It was terrible. I had two assistants on the show and I put them both behind the porch. They lay there for the whole show with flashlights and a script because Freddie didn't know line one. Our arrangement was that Freddie was to cough if he was going to go up. Everyone thought that this was going to be a disaster. Florence knew her part, she was perfect, so smooth. The notices came out the next morning. "Fredric March is brilliant in this play. Unfortunately he was suffering from a severe head cold and was coughing all the way through the show." Florence was letter-perfect, but didn't get good notices at all. She was also very good on the night after we opened in New York. She was just not a good opener.

The New York reviews dealt almost exclusively with the play. The production and cast were lavishly praised but minimally described.

In February 1977, when the *Anna Christie* cast was exploring Toronto's Royal Alexandra Theater, actor Edwin J. McDonough discovered a wall photograph of Fredric March among the theater's memorabilia. He said to Quintero, "Friend of yours here." Quintero saw the photograph and burst into rapture. He placed his hands on the wall to isolate this one photograph. "That beautiful man," he sighed. Quintero is totally dependent on the confidence of the people with whom he works. March's generosity and professionalism (his opening night in Boston notwithstanding) created the atmosphere in which Quintero was able to utilize his own familial experiences most openly.

3

Desire Under the Elms

Writing
    Begun mid-January 1924; completed July 1924.
Premieres
    Original: November 11, 1924; New York, Greenwich Village Theater.
    Quintero: January 9, 1963; New York, Circle-in-the-Square.

1924 Production

Cast List

Eben Cabot	Charles Ellis
Simeon Cabot	Allen Nagle
Peter Cabot	Perry Ivins
Ephraim Cabot	Walter Huston
Abbie Putnam	Mary Morris
Young Girl	Eloise Pendleton
Sheriff	Walter Abel

In the 1920 play *Beyond the Horizon,* O'Neill had experimented with spatial relationships. The three-act play could have been written in a single, interior set. O'Neill wanted to contrast the interior

61

and exterior, however, and wrote each act in two scenes, alternating the confinement of domestic life with the freedom of the outdoors. The production's scene changes were interminable and destroyed the rhythm O'Neill had hoped to achieve. To his immense frustration, none of the critics even perceived the attempt, but assumed that he was unable to concentrate his drama into the expected single set, "à la Pinero."

With *Desire Under the Elms*, O'Neill grew more ambitious. He wished not only to contrast interior and exterior, but also to show them simultaneously. He always drew ground plans for his plays. Because *Desire Under the Elms* was to be a more complex project than any of his previous works, he went still further:

> He envisioned a set that encompassed kitchen and parlor downstairs and two bedrooms upstairs of the Cabot farmhouse and a strip of farm outside. He drew four sketches, each of them showing the pitched-roof farmhouse nestled between two giant elms; in the first sketch, the wall of the house is closed; in the second, a panel has been removed, showing the interior of the kitchen; in the third, the parlor is revealed; in the fourth, the two bedrooms, separated by the thin walls through which Eben and Abbie were to stare lustfully at each other (Gelb, 1960:568).

O'Neill then gave his sketches to New Hampshire–reared Robert Edmond Jones to be realized. Jones was to serve as both designer and director. He cast Walter Huston as Ephraim, Mary Morris as Abbie, and Charles Ellis from the Provincetown Players as Eben.

The production opened to reviewers who, for the most part, could not see beyond the ferocity of the plot. Jones' set came in for its share of criticism:

> Working from the four sketches by O'Neill, Jones devised a set faithful to the author's conception: stark, whitewashed interior, mean little windows, pinched rooms, sinister over-hanging elms. For some episodes the structure worked fine; in the scene where old Cabot tells his life story to his wife, as she stares hungrily towards Eben's bedroom, the multiple setting shows Eben in his room, restless

Scenic sketches by Eugene O'Neill for *Desire Under the Elms*. Upper left: the farmhouse; upper right: kitchen exposed; lower left: bedrooms exposed; lower right: parlor exposed.

and uneasy . . . On the whole, though, the set was a mixed blessing. If the rooms and other playing areas, all of them small, suggested the constricted life of the Cabots, they also cramped the action; perhaps it would have been better had Jones, disregarding the O'Neill sketches, provided a freer, more impressionistic set (Sheaffer, 1973:157).

Many of the reviewers dismissed the set as nothing more than a mechanical doll house. Like Percy Hammond of the *Herald Tribune* and Stark Young of the *New York Times*, Alexander Woollcott praised the theatricality of the two key simultaneous scenes, but maintained that the set was a heavy price to pay. The negative reviews notwithstanding, the production ran for two months at the Greenwich Village Theater. It transferred to the Earl Carroll Theater and later to the George M. Cohan Theater. Attendance was augmented by charges of obscenity and the production ran until mid-October 1925.

For O'Neill, *Desire Under the Elms* remained unrealized. " 'Has *Desire* ever been produced as I wrote it?' O'Neill asked Kenneth Macgowan, some time after its original showing. " 'Never! There have never been the elms of my play, characters almost, and . . . through lack of time to get the changes perfected . . . the flow of life from room to room of the house, the house as character, the acts as smooth developing wholes have never existed' " (Gelb, 1960:568).

1963 Production

Cast List

Ephraim Cabot	George C. Scott
Simeon Cabot	Clifford A. Pellow
Peter Cabot	Lou Frizzell
Eben Cabot	Rip Torn
Abbie Putnam	Colleen Dewhurst
Young Girl	Leonora Landau
Old Farmer	Jerome Collamore
Sheriff	Charles Mundy

In 1959, the building in which the Circle-in-the-Square Theater had been housed was demolished to make way for a 17-story apartment building. The company moved its quarters to the Amato Opera Theater at 159 Bleecker Street. Quintero eliminated the theater's proscenium arch and imposed a three-quarter stage. David Hays said of the new stage:

> The new Circle-in-the-Square could handle higher spaces, but it wasn't as good. The first space had a wonderful look of used and reused and then used-again rooms. It really got into this old space, it was just a patchwork quilt of everybody's old dreams. It was a fabulously theatrical, emotional space without anything happening in it. The new space was a space that tried to re-create what was there, but on new terms, I mean with modern terms built into it. I helped design it. I wish I'd helped design the one uptown.

Desire Under the Elms was the final production Quintero directed for the Circle-in-the-Square and the only O'Neill play he directed at the Bleecker Street Theater. Once again, he hired David Hays to design the set and lights. (Hays specified, in discussing this production, that he had never been on staff at the Circle; he was always hired one show at a time.)

There are five geographical locations in *Desire Under the Elms*, four interior and one exterior; the master bedroom, the sons' bedroom (used in the first and third acts), the parlor (used only in the second act), and the yard. Hays devised a set with a wooden post at the entrance, a long plank walk, and several benches and beds placed beneath hanging gas lamps, all in gray and black. When asked if he created the specific demarcations of space strictly by lighting, Hays responded, "It helped; to the extent that it can, it did. I think every place was fixed. We had a way of starting in the living room and ending up playing in the yard just as if it were the living room. There were levels to distinguish the bedroom. The house was against the back wall and I suppose the bottom opened up a bit to show the bedrooms."

George Oppenheimer (1963:3C) wrote of Hays' set that "where the original set of Robert Edmond Jones was on two levels and depicted interior and exterior in realistic terms, the Circle set must, of necessity, be on one level and leave a great deal to the imagination." In fact, such is not the case. The fact of the three-quarter stage does not, of necessity, demand staging on only one level. In 1980, the Tyrone Guthrie Theater produced *Desire Under the Elms* on a thrust stage, using both levels of the Cabot house. The distinction is not between a thrust or three-quarter stage, but that the Guthrie Theater is high enough to stage on two levels while the Bleecker Street Circle was not.

For the five geographic locations in the play, the Guthrie production employed four acting areas. Both bedrooms were against the back wall; the master bedroom sat 10 feet above the floor and the sons' bedroom seven feet above the floor. Stairs led down to the floor that served as the kitchen in the first and third acts and the parlor in the second act. The forestage was always the yard. The production was designed for area staging and three of the four acting areas remained the same geographical location throughout and were identified realistically by beds, chairs, lawn, and well. Although one acting area served for both kitchen and parlor, realistic set pieces (changed during the intermissions) provided immediate recognition of location.

In Hays' set, the two bedrooms were fixed, but the remaining three locations bled into one another with a minimum of realistic set pieces. It did indeed "leave a great deal to the imagination." Henry Hewes (1963a:32) specified the complexity of the task Hays and Quintero had set for themselves:

> The mere fact of placing the action on an open playing area changes things immediately. Instead of watching the play's three main characters in conflict with their dominating physical surroundings, the audience views actors as they create the farm around them by their acknowledgement of its presence. And instead of watching a series of dramatic deeds and confrontations, the audience experiences the actors' human reactions to what has been done, and to the events in their own past that have set them on their present courses. David Hays has designed a simple setting using beams and hanging oil lamps to capture the farmhouse flavor. Yet this work is most difficult for open area playing since certain sectors must stand for different locations at different times. And the long walks from the bedroom area at one end to the exits at the other tend to diminish the tension of the action.

On the strength of the cast, Colleen Dewhurst and George C. Scott (both of whom worked for Equity minimum), it seemed to be an all-star revival, but it was not conceived as such. When asked if the production was contingent upon her availability, Dewhurst answered: "No, most of the things with José were just like everybody getting together and saying 'What about doing. . . ?' "

Rip Torn was cast as Eben. Franchot Tone had originally been cast as Ephraim, but was very unsteady on his feet and in no condition to execute the dance in the final act. Rehearsals were put off for two or three weeks until George C. Scott became available for Ephraim. Jerome Collamore (a sprightly 93-year-old when interviewed, he had seen both Duse and Bernhardt act and much preferred the French actress over her Italian rival) was cast in typically off-hand Quintero fashion. The two men had never met. Quintero was working on the stage and took a single glance at Collamore from a distance and cast him.

Quintero asked dancer Leonora Landau (Mrs. David Hays) to choreograph the square dance. Landau specified that she was not a choreographer and didn't know much about square dancing: "But I became an expert in two weeks by reading every book and going to every square dance I could find."

When asked what specifics Quintero had asked for in terms of movement or space, she answered:

> José did not give me specific instructions about the space, but then I *knew* the space. I put the dance together in one four-hour rehearsal and showed it to José. All José told me was that at such and such a moment the dancers must be up here because the actors are down there. We used all the space that was available. The other areas were not lit. We used mostly the center of the stage, but we moved around a lot. When we stopped dancing and went into a freeze the lights would go out on us and onto where the dramatic action was taking place. We danced outside and there was dramatic action inside. The lights would come up on one and down on the other. We danced on the flat stage only, not on the runway.

Desire Under the Elms, 1963. L to r: George C. Scott, Rip Torn, Douglas Roberts, Melba de Beyle, Lee Delmer, Sandra Fisher, Leonora Landau, Colleen Dewhurst. Photo by Ed Rooney.

Landau was also responsible for the last-act jig that George C. Scott had to dance. Rather than impose an entire routine on him, Landau chose to give him a few steps and then give him his head. The jig was therefore extempore, unlike the square dance which was very closely choreographed.

The entire production was rehearsed on stage at the Circle-in-the-Square. Jerome Collamore recalled the first rehearsal: "There was a wooden walk. I remember José walking down that and saying 'Oh, doesn't it impress you?' I didn't know what he was talking about. There wasn't any set. It was just an open space all the time, there was no bedroom or kitchen or anything. There were just benches around for the dance."

Colleen Dewhurst said that there was no discussion of O'Neill's having placed Medea or Phaedra in New England or any discussion of O'Neill's biography: "*Desire* really doesn't lend itself to that." When asked if Quintero attempted to characterize Abbie in conventional terms, for instance, a woman who sets out to acquire property and ends up by committing herself to a love relationship, Dewhurst answered, "José and I don't communicate that way. We communicate with unfinished sentences and end up usually saying 'you know what I mean.' And I say 'I think that maybe what I . . .' We have both confessed that we really have never understood what the other person is saying, but we obviously just communicate in another manner. With George, he didn't have to do anything."

Quintero (1974:185–86) writes of George C. Scott:

> He is thoroughly methodical. Colleen told me once when we were doing *Desire Under the Elms*, George had said to her, "Colleen, do you know that you and José work pretty much in the same way? You both go to rehearsal totally open and make your artistic choices spontaneously, right there on the spot. It's marvelous to watch but it's so unlike me; I don't work that way." And he was absolutely right . . . Directing George is a wonderful experience. He follows direction so easily, knowing that wherever he sits it will be the head of the table. But most important is that you, as a director, learn more from George than George does from you.

In an article about Quintero, Barbara Gelb (1977:126) wrote that "no director has much impact on a performance by George C. Scott. Quintero . . . has found that Scott is completely cerebral. He is so meticulously versed in all the nuances of a role by the time he begins rehearsals and so gifted at finding precisely the attitude, gesture and inflection that will convey character, that only the most minor suggestions are ever necessary for him."

Production stage manager Don Garner described the way Quintero directed Colleen Dewhurst and George C. Scott: "You know how private José is. He talked of dreams a great deal. He always resorted to his stories, his family, pulling out images like that. So much of Cabot and Abbie grew out of that close relationship José has with Colleen and George. And the two of them would work on their own and then bring in things."

Quintero and Rip Torn had great personality clashes, both in *Desire Under the Elms* and the subsequent *Strange Interlude.* Quintero finally fired Torn from the *Desire* production. Jerome Collamore recalled the immediate conditions which brought about Torn's replacement: "My dressing room was next to Rip Torn's with a curtain between us. I heard that Rip had started choking Colleen on stage for some reason. George C. came in and said 'Blankety blank, you ever do that again and I'll wring your neck.' So it went along and then Colleen complained that he'd done it again. George C. told José, 'You have a new man in the part by Saturday matinee or I don't play.' That's when Alan Mixon came in and gave a good performance."

Don Garner said of the Quintero-Torn relationship:

> Rip Torn worked extremely hard and well with José during rehearsal, but after the opening, the terrible flights of fancy began and the disregard for being in a certain place at a certain moment. Abbie would turn around and not have an Eben there. "Acting" began and grew and grew until it grew out of what José had set. Once the play was set it was very definitely set and put into a form. Much to Scott's and Dewhurst's chagrin that form began to break apart. They were both very professional and came to me to ask Mr. Torn to resist or to revert to the original blocking. It got out of hand and,

L to r: George C. Scott, Rip Torn, Colleen Dewhurst. Photo by Ed Rooney.

when the terrible strangling incident took place,
Mr. Scott insisted and Rip Torn left.

In light of the fact that Quintero was about to direct *Strange Interlude,* the first production of the Actors' Studio Theater, Don Garner made an interesting point about the initial cast of *Desire Under the Elms:*

> José had a very mixed cast at first. The two brothers worked, frankly, the way José does *not* work. They were very strict Method actors. José was not able to speak with them of dreams or symbolism, nor, at the same time, was he able to say you must be seated by this time, you have to walk on this line. He wasn't able to block them. (I shouldn't say "block." I should say "move" people because he doesn't seem to preblock.) He can work with Page and a lot of other very Method people, but there was a very definite problem at the beginning of rehearsals because these people could not be stage right at a certain time. They didn't feel it.

Quintero replaced these two actors with Clifford A. Pellow and Lou Frizzell.

When asked how Quintero operated in the Bleecker Street space, Garner answered, "I don't remember any spatial difficulty putting *Desire* into the Circle simply because that was the space which José had used for so many years. The areas broke. José said very specifically, 'Sometimes people don't understand me.' He broke areas; it wasn't sacrosanct that this door be here all the time."

Although the reviewers praised the three principals' individual performances, most of their analyses were devoted to the staging or, in some cases, how the staging influenced the acting.

Many reviewers demanded the proscenium arch. Edith Oliver (1963:64) wrote that "No work was ever less suited to an arena stage." Jack Gaver (1963:?) wanted it "staged in the conventional fashion with scenery." Richard Watts (1963a:27) missed "the spur to the imagination provided by a proscenium setting of the white farmhouse with two elms brooding above it." He lamented that "the important party scene is weakened by the enforced styliza- tion that causes the dancers to huddle in the center of the stage while the drama swirls about them. A concentrated tragedy tends to become diffuse." *Time* ("Suffocated Souls") commented that "*Desire's* sense of puritanically suffocated beings sweeps away on a wall-less stage." Alan Pryce-Jones (1963:8) echoed O'Neill's original complaint: "It is a pity that in the nature of things the elms themselves, whose mingling of protection and threat as their branches join over the roof—the trees were an important symbol to O'Neill—cannot be shown."

The location of specific areas did not prove to be that large a problem. Only Oppenheimer (1963a:3C) complained that "there is also the matter of geography . . . There were times when I was not at all sure which of the several rooms the actors were inhabiting and at other times Eben and Abbie stood only a few feet apart, yet were unable to see each other because of an invisible wall." Michael Smith (1963a:16), however, found just the opposite to be true: "Locations of action are indicated almost casually as the lights change (credit David Hays) and the characters move from bedroom to kitchen to porch to yard. There is none of the self-conscious miming of doorways and unseen walls, yet we are always told as much as we need to know about where the scene is happening."

David Hays addressed himself to the possibilities and necessities of designing for the Bleecker Street stage:

> The set I made was not such a big deal, on a *theoretical* level, as critics would suggest. We were used to the space and knew instinctively how to use it. Upstage indoors, downstage outdoors (and for the dance) is reasonably obvious. You can't *leave* a bed downstage, so put it upstage. Same with the kitchen table. In the old Circle, you were close enough to all areas not to be shut away from upstage action.
>
> The point is that your achievement is bound up in what you reveal, what you wanted to (or had to) achieve. On a proscenium, your needs are defined as Oppenheimer senses them. In a smaller room, surrounding the players, the intimacy dictates that suggested scenic indications are not necessary—are often intrusive—because, in the particular juxtaposition of *that* room they never had the reality of the actors. Oppenheimer should have

>trusted O'Neill more—José and I did. Also—that
>close to the actors, their own sense of the elms
>would be the best chance to take, rather than some
>shabby indication of the trees. Trust actors, trust
>O'Neill. You want to see elms, go to the park. On
>a proscenium—fine. At Circle—better imagined.
>We had good leaf patterns—more suggestive
>anyway.

"More suggestive" was the operative phrase. Howard Taubman (1963:5) found it so: "The extensive open playing space, sparingly set by David Hays, conveys the impression of greater reality than do decors with an abundance of furniture and details." *Show Magazine* (West, 1963a:34) agreed: "Letting suggestion take the place of exposition, he flings his production loose onto the center stage, up the aisles right to the exits and achieves that flow of life through the rooms of the farmhouse that O'Neill complained directors so rarely drew out of his work."

Harold Stern and Harold Clurman stressed the negative impact of the staging on the acting. Stern (1963a:12) wrote:

>*Desire Under the Elms* is so powerful and explosive a drama, involving as it does many of man's basest and most violent emotions, that it literally demands some form of aesthetic distance from its audience. In the arena production the audience is under the gun every step of the way. Drama, intensified by proximity, becomes melodrama at the Circle-in-the-Square. Acting becomes over-acting. The play demands so much intensity from its actors that to adjust performance to stage would dilute the play. It would have been far wiser to adjust the stage to the play and performance.

Clurman (1963a:107) wrote, "It is not only the production's intimacy (perhaps inevitable in the oblong of the tiny playhouse) which makes for melodrama, old-fashioned rural comedy, and pathos of a personal nature that aspires to simplicity but comes close to hamminess."

Only Walter Kerr (1963a:38) fully examined the implications of seeing the play in three dimensions:

What makes the difference is Mr. Quintero's intelligent and super resourceful use of the long vacant space of his floor. Colleen Dewhurst (Abbie, and Abbie absolute) stands prophetically behind a bedstead in the dim recesses of our tunnel; George C. Scott (her aged tyrannical new husband) curses his two departing sons in the opening void at the tunnel's opposite end; between these two poles, head bowed on a lamplit table, waits the remaining son who will destroy them both by catering to their separate passions. The staggered planes are suggestive without being oppressively symbolic.

Better still is Miss Dewhurst's slow silent march from the cradle in which she has murdered her first-born down an undefined corridor which contains only her tension until she has reached the child's waiting father (Rip Torn). The deed moves with her, dictates her pace and charging the air she breathes (and that we breathe) with apprehension.

I find the open floor helpful to O'Neill's play partly because Mr. Quintero has used it evocatively and partly because O'Neill's hard carved figures profit from being *seen* dimensionally. They are altogether dimensional in the writing; they are fashioned with great thickness, but at the core of the thickness there is no real marrow. In fact, with this production we so nearly approach knowing them as flesh and blood that we come to share something of O'Neill's own frustration at their failure to take the last little leap into supple and free poetic life. However, once it is granted that the characters live under this limitation, it also becomes apparent that seeing them in the round suits them.

The production continued to run after the original cast departed and ultimately played 384 performances. Its impact was very clearly delineated by the adjectives used to describe it. Those critics who found it "suggestive" or "evocative" welcomed the three-dimensionality of the production. Those critics who demanded "aesthetic distance" or "illusion" wanted a verisimilitude that is provided only by three solid painted walls to contain the highly wrought emotions built into the play. For the latter critics, without such specific, *visible* boundaries, the actors' overcompensation exploded beyond the boundaries created by suggestion or convention; emotion uncontained became diffuse and lost its focus.

Part Three

THE MARKETPLACE

With the back-to-back successes of *The Iceman Cometh* and *Long Day's Journey Into Night*, Quintero encountered levels of success for which he was unprepared and which he constantly reexamines. He told Phyllis Funke (1974:20):

> The telephones began ringing and the telegrams started coming in and suddenly everyone was telling me how wonderful I was. It was good, only the trouble was that, like so many people, I was educated for failure, reared to think that every other child was brighter. So I really couldn't handle this. Because, you know, a fear comes over you, a fear that you aren't as good as they think, that you have simply fooled everyone, that really you may be a fraud and then a life of terror begins, terror that you will be found out.

Quintero told David Richards (1985:K10):

> A certain amount of success is a frightening thing, particularly when you don't know what it is people are praising. I was doing all the things I was punished for as a child—dreaming, escaping, inventing—and I found myself wanted because of them. How could I believe that? I have a highly developed system and I was consumed by fear and anger. A great deal of fear.

Quintero left the Circle-in-the-Square in 1963, not to better himself, but because of a power struggle with Ted Mann. In "Not for Profit: A History of the Circle-in-the-Square," Sheila Hickey Garvey (1984:258) is unable to specify exactly what legal form the separation took. She interviewed Ted Mann, who maintained that Quintero chose to leave, that "it was Quintero who decided to terminate their partnership. The two men discussed the best way to handle legally their strained situation. Their lawyers suggested that Mann give Quintero a cash settlement to 'buy out' their partnership. Quintero agreed. In effect, Quintero sold Mann the title: The Circle-in-the-Square."

Quintero had put off-Broadway behind him and wanted to work on Broadway, which in the past had been a means for him to direct a play he liked, pay his rent and utilities, and then go back to the Circle. Now, he aligned himself with two institutional theaters operating on Broadway: the Actors' Studio Theater in 1963 and the Repertory Company at Lincoln Center in 1964. Both proved to be one-time experiences.

With institutional theater behind him, Quintero looked to the commercial Broadway theater and soon perceived that he was merchandisable only as a director of O'Neill's plays. After the commercial failure of *Hughie*, however, Quintero did not direct on Broadway for two years. His next project, *Pousse Cafe* in 1966, was a total failure. Financial difficulties and escalating emotional and drinking problems pressured him into adapting and directing O'Neill's incomplete *More Stately Mansions* in 1967. Barbara Gelb (1977:136) wrote that "the production was a flop. And, whereas, in the case of *Long Day's Journey Into Night*, Quintero could not handle success, he found, now, that he could not handle failure any better. The drinking became more destructive."

4

Strange Interlude

Writing
> Begun February 1926; completed spring 1927.

Premieres
> *Original:* January 30, 1928; New York, the original John Golden Theater (202 West 58th Street).
>
> *Quintero:* March 11, 1963; New York, Hudson Theater.

1928 Production

Cast List

Charles Marsden	Tom Powers
Professor Leeds	Phillip Leigh
Nina Leeds	Lynn Fontanne
Sam Evans	Earle Larimore
Edmund Darrell	Glenn Anders
Mrs. Amos Evans	Helen Westley
Gordon Evans (age 11)	Charles Walters
Madeline Arnold	Ethel Westley
Gordon Evans (age 21)	John J. Burns

In Provincetown, in 1922, O'Neill heard " 'from an aviator, formerly of the Lafeyette Escadrille, the story of a girl whose avia-

tor fiance had been shot down just before the armistice. The girl
went to pieces from the shock. She later married, not because she
loved the man but because she wanted a child. She hoped through
motherhood to win back a measure of contentment from life' "
(Sheaffer, 1973:239–40). A year later O'Neill began taking notes
on what he called "my woman play," meant to dramatize "the
life of a woman without the padding of a novel" (Gelb,
1960:589,659). From its conception, the project was large, not
just a woman, but "Woman, weak and strong, benevolent and
destructive, in her various roles as daughter, wife, platonic friend,
mistress, mother" (Sheaffer, 1973:444–45). The working title was
"The Haunted."

Sheaffer (1973:242–43) maintains that the personality of Nina
Leeds was based on Louise Bryant and that "Darrell's long relationship with Nina, the wife of his best friend, was probably
inspired by a page from O'Neill's own history; his comparatively
short affair in the World War I period with Louise Bryant before
and after her marriage to John Reed, a man O'Neill genuinely
liked."

O'Neill's 1925 scenario contains no indications that he
intended to use stream-of-consciousness techniques. *Ulysses* had
been published in 1922, but was banned in the United States. It
was legally available in Bermuda, however, where O'Neill
devoured it in 1926, "a strategic time, for not long afterward, he
would borrow Joyce's stream-of-consciousness technique"
(Sheaffer, 1973:199).

In his workbook O'Neill writes, under the heading "Method—
1926":

> Method—Start with soliloquy—perhaps have the
> whole play nothing but a thinking aloud—anyway
> the thinking aloud being more important than the
> actual talking—speech breaking through thought
> as a random process of concealment, speech incon-
> sequential or imperfectly expressing the thought
> behind—all done with the most drastic logic and
> economy and simplicity of words. (Thought per-
> haps always naturally expressing itself to us—
> thinking itself—or being thought by us—always in
> terms of an adolescent level of vocabulary, as if we
> thereby externally tried to educate to mature self-

understanding, the child in us.) Carrying the method to an extreme—one sees their lips move as they
talk to one another but there is no sound—only
their thinking is aloud (Floyd, 1981:74).

O'Neill had attempted a modified version of asides in the 1924
Welded, in which a husband and wife "speak, ostensibly to the
other, but showing by their tone it is a thinking aloud to oneself,
and neither appears to hear what the other has said" (O'Neill,
1951:266). From this stage direction, it is clear that O'Neill wanted
the asides to be achieved, not with lights or movement, but "by
their tone."

O'Neill was open enough in discussing the subject matter of
the play, but very secretive about its form. Sheaffer (1973:252)
writes that "one thing particularly worrying him, though he had
sworn to secrecy everyone who had read the new play, was that
word of his stream-of-consciousness method might leak out and
be copied by another playwright before *Interlude* was staged."
One of the people to whom O'Neill showed the manuscript in 1926
was Barrett Clark (1947:111):

> [Clark] ventured to question whether an audience
> would sit through nine acts listening to characters
> speaking their thoughts aloud "with no regard for
> the ordinary conventions of the theatre or of nor-
> mal social intercourse." "And why not?" asked
> O'Neill. "Everything is a matter of convention. If
> we accept one, why not another, as long as it does
> what it's intended to do? My people speak aloud
> what they think and what the others aren't sup-
> posed to hear."

In March 1927, Lawrence Langner went to Bermuda to cure
a severe cold and to mend fences between himself and O'Neill;
the Theatre Guild had already turned down five O'Neill scripts.
Langner wished to discuss *Marco Millions*, on which the Guild
was uncommitted, and was told of the existence of another script.
O'Neill said that *Strange Interlude* might take six hours to per-
form and that it was promised to Katherine Cornell. If she turned
it down, the Theatre Guild could have the play. Cornell chose
instead Somerset Maughm's *The Letter*, "earning herself a permanent niche in O'Neill's gallery of unfavorite actresses" (Gelb,

1960:633). Langner prevailed upon the Guild to produce both *Strange Interlude* and *Marco Millions.*

Lynn Fontanne was cast as Nina, against O'Neill's better judgment. She had played the Anna Christie role in that play's earliest version, entitled *Chris Cristopherson.* O'Neill was not pleased with Fontanne in *Chris* and thought that " 'she will give a very adequate performance but she will be far from my Nina' " (Sheaffer, 1973:271). By contrast, he was very pleased with the casting of the males: Tom Powers as Charles Marsden, Glenn Anders as Darrell, and Earle Larimore as Sam Evans.

Jo Mielziner was chosen to design the sets and found O'Neill well informed about scenic design: "O'Neill was always extremely interested in the technical problems of design and lighting and often made perceptive comments about them" (Gelb, 1960:657).

Phillip Moeller, the appointed director, had been a founding member of the Washington Square Players, which grew into the Theatre Guild, on whose board of directors he sat. O'Neill and Moeller never became close, but Moeller directed the world premieres of five O'Neill plays. Sheaffer (1973:273–74) describes him in this way:

> A shy, high-strung bachelor of aesthetic tastes and something of a dandy—he favored opera capes and used a long cigarette holder—Moeller suggested a dillettante; he actually was among the few creative directors around Broadway, one with an individual approach. Where most directors prepare in advance as thoroughly as possible, familiarizing themselves with the script, thinking out the stage "business" and blocking all the scenes, he would come to the first rehearsal, in Teresa Helburn's words, "strangely and deliberately unprepared." He kept himself "fresh for the first impact of the play" when read by the cast, and as the rehearsals progressed he relied on the inspiration of the moment. He was more like an imaginative participant with the actors than the instructor over them. "We used to say rather wistfully," Miss Helburn recalls, "that it would be nice if Phil would read a play before he produces it." But this time, since *Strange Interlude* was so formidable an

assignment—it was allotted seven weeks of rehearsal instead of the usual four—Moeller not only read
the script in advance but immersed himself in it.

O'Neill and Moeller spent the final prerehearsal weeks cutting the script. *Strange Interlude* was originally projected, by
author and producers, to be performed on two successive evenings. Under Moeller's guidance the script was cut sufficiently to
permit it to be given "Bayreuth fashion—that is, in one day, with
a long dinner intermission" (Sheaffer, 1973:273). The production
had only seven weeks of rehearsal to come together because the
Guild was then performing in repertory and could not take plays
on a pre-Broadway tour.

Once into rehearsals, the most absorbing question became
the nature and execution of the asides. The Gelbs (1960:650) write,
"During rehearsals O'Neill told Langner, 'If the actors weren't
so dumb, they wouldn't need asides; they'd be able to express the
meaning without them.' " Langner's (1951:236–37) published version of the same story was placed more carefully in context:

> Every now and then 'Gene would retire to the
> lounge with me, and give vent to his feelings about
> some of the acting in language he certainly did not
> learn in school at Stamford. He was never too
> pleased with his actors in rehearsal, and once told
> me that he adopted the technique of asides which
> showed what the characters were thinking in
> *Strange Interlude* because the majority of actors
> were incompetent to do so. This, however, can be
> taken with a grain of salt, like some of Shaw's
> remarks on the same subject. No author ever suc-
> ceeds in getting a complete realization of the part
> he has created, and he blames the actor because
> the actor is unable to achieve the impossible.

Despite O'Neill's specific stage directions in *Welded* that those
asides be indicated "by their tone," he appears to have left the
staging of the *Strange Interlude* asides to Moeller. In a postproduction article, Moeller (1928:VIII,4) related the options he faced in
staging the asides:

> The methods which I dismissed included, among
> others, a special zone of the stage which should be

the realm of those heard silences. Another was a
very complicated and difficult system of lighting
which should either accent or dim the character
speaking the unheard thoughts, or those not
exposed to hear them. I knew that the technical
difficulties involved made these devices practically
impossible, and I also sensed that this sort of teas-
ing the attention of the audience would very soon
become almost unbearable. Another easier method
which I gave up later was to differentiate clearly
the quality of the voice between the audible and
the supposedly inaudible part of the dialogue. I
soon realized that this, too, would be in the nature
of turning off and on the obviously and momentarily differing timbres of expression. I knew that
as soon as the audience became too acutely conscious that they were "on" to this they would be
watching and worrying about the swiftness of their
own adjustment and, because of this too insistent
preoccupation, inevitably losing some of the value
of the play. No, something else had to be invented,
some other way found.

    And suddenly it came to me, incidentally, on
the train up from Baltimore . . . I was deep in the
script and the problem of *Interlude*. Suddenly the
train stopped. Unconsciously this may have been
the hint, this may or may not have been the way
my mind got it. "Why not, for a moment," I
thought, "stop the physical action of the play and
allow the mental commentary to tell us its hidden
secret simply, directly and without any obviously
elaborate and intricate preparation?"

According to Sheaffer (1973:274), "that was the way the drama
was rehearsed and performed, with the other characters immediately freezing whenever one of them gave vent to a private aside."

    O'Neill agreed to the staging of the asides, but not to the dis-
covery of laughs. He wanted all laughs cut when "they interfered
with the emotional build of a scene. Moeller adored the comedy
and every time 'Gene solemnly cut out an amusing line, Phil would
plead vociferously for its return" (Langner, 1951:236).

As was the case with rehearsing a new O'Neill script, additional cuts were a major consideration. Teresa Helburn defended O'Neill against the charge that he was unyielding with regard to cuts and changes:

> To suggestions of changes he usually answers "no," but not arbitrarily, nor is that the end. He evidently considers them all for some time seriously and he frequently returns the next day having found a way to meet a suggested change that has dramatic value without damaging the fabric of his play. It is the same about cuts. He almost never makes them on the spur of the moment. He listens to the director's ideas but he takes the script home and brings it back the next day cut or not cut, as the case may be, according to his leisured judgment (Gelb, 1960:651).

When O'Neill proved less than responsive to ideas from the actors, Miss Fontanne adopted her own pragmatic method of cuts: "I respect authors, I really do, but I have a great sense of what will 'go,' and I didn't care much for the writing in *Strange Interlude*. There was a woodenness at times, and so much of it was repetitious. I asked O'Neill to cut certain of my lines and he wouldn't do it, so, without telling anyone—Moeller, Helburn, Langner, anyone—I cut, cut, cut and nobody ever realized it. I relied on the fact that the play was so long that not even O'Neill would remember what he'd written" (Sheaffer, 1973:275). No professional stage manager would have missed such cuts, but Fontanne went on to give a highly praised performance as Nina, without ever taking O'Neill's "Woman play" at his evaluation. In Sheaffer's words, "She did not consider Nina worthy of such intensive scrutiny. 'I thought she gave herself to those soldiers because she wanted to. She liked a lot of sex. She didn't feel sorry for them. I didn't ever feel that O'Neill made her a tragic figure. I don't think he knew the first thing about women' " (1973:275).

For a production with six different sets, the scenic design went for naught. Brooks Atkinson (1928:28) wrote that "limitations of space in the John Golden Theater are said to be responsible for the inefficient lighting of Mr. Mielziner's utilitarian sets." Dudley Nichols (1928:11) commented that "the settings were by Jo

Mielziner but few people had time to consider them, so engrossing was the action. Acted as it was last night, this play might almost take place on a bare stage without any loss of interest."

Critical interest was reserved for the asides and, on occasion, the staging of the asides. Gilbert Seldes' (1928:350) detailed description of the staging of the asides was at variance with every detail of Moeller's description:

> The extremely difficult business of introducing the uttered thoughts of the characters in the midst of their conversations was handled with amazing deftness. It would have been easy merely to create a convention; whenever the speaker turns to the audience and other characters look fixedly into space that means an interior expression. The monotony of such a convention is precisely what killed the old aside. Mr. Moeller created a style of utterance for these monologues; sometimes a variation in expression, or in pace; sometimes a look or a movement. This variety of means helped O'Neill enormously.

Some critics took umbrage, not at the staging of the asides, but that the asides themselves usurped the responsibilities of the actors. Charles Brackett (1928:24) complained that "unwilling to trust anything to his actors, he is trying to do their work for them too." Alexander Woollcott (1928:48) concluded: "I think that most actors would tell O'Neill with some asperity that such illumination was their business and none of his, and, by this dispensing with their aid, he would be calmly throwing away his only reason for turning to the dramatic form in the first place." *Commonweal* entertained the possibility that an actor would claim that "with a little skillful rewriting of the main dialogue, the play could convey in conventional form everything which Mr. O'Neill has now placed in the asides" (*Strange Interlude*, 1928:1098).

All comparisons between the stream-of-consciousness technique as practiced by novelists James Joyce and Virginia Woolf and by playwright O'Neill served only to heap hot coals on O'Neill's head. Brooks Atkinson (1928:28) asked the relevant theatrical question:

What distinguishes *Strange Interlude* from the old three-decker novel? When the "aside" merely elaborates the spoken thought it deadens the actor until *Strange Interlude* looks like a slow-motion picture. And one irreverently suspects that there may even be an even deeper thought unexpressed than the nickel-weekly jargon that Mr. O'Neill offers as thinking. When the "aside" shows contrast, and when it releases a smoldering passion that cannot burn in the normal dialogue, it is impregnated with the very stuff of drama. Even the pedant would not dispute its legitimacy, as no one disputed it in the entire history of drama until the naturalistic technique of the well-built play laid a deadly hand on playwriting early in the century. Mr. O'Neill has restored the "aside" without giving it an entirely new meaning. He has not, one suspects, always used it wisely.

The production photos of *Strange Interlude* look very postured, presumably the very quality which Brooks Atkinson called "slow-motion picture." Atkinson thought that O'Neill failed to give meaning to the asides, but it appears that Moeller's staging made the asides too conspicuous an element, despite his meticulous attempt to achieve the least unsettling effect. The staging pleased O'Neill, however, who inscribed in Moeller's script, "To Phil: the most sympathetic and comprehending director I have ever worked with—with all my gratitude for his invaluable collaboration in making this play live in spite of the dramatist" (Sheaffer, 1973:291).

Strange Interlude proved to be the greatest commercial success O'Neill ever experienced, but "the dress rehearsal was the last time the author ever saw the play" (Sheaffer, 1973:286). By 1932, O'Neill had concluded that "as for *Strange Interlude*, this is an attempt at the new masked psychological drama . . . without masks—a successful attempt, perhaps, in so far as it concerns only surfaces, but not where, occasionally, it tries to probe deeper" (Gelb, 1960:662).

1963 Production

Cast List

Charles Marsden	William Prince
Professor Henry Leeds	Franchot Tone
Nina Leeds	Geraldine Page
Edmund Darrell	Ben Gazzara
Sam Evans	Pat Hingle
Mrs. Amos Evans	Betty Field
Gordon Evans (age 11)	Richard Thomas
Gordon Evans (age 21)	Geoffrey Horne
Madeline Arnold	Jane Fonda

During the late 1950s, the membership of the Actors' Studio brought considerable pressure to bear on directors Cheryl Crawford, Elia Kazan, and Lee Strasberg to produce public performances. Cheryl Crawford (1977:229) writes:

> All three of us were hesitant, remembering the Group Theatre's vicissitudes. Kazan and Strasberg had different points of view. If there had to be a theatre, Kazan wanted it to be a small non-profit one, something like the English Club Theatre or America's own off-Broadway. By contrast, Lee felt that we should be involved in something on a large scale that would represent the apex of the Studio's work. He didn't care if it was profit or non-profit, but he wanted it to be big-time . . . These different approaches were finally reconciled by compromise.

The subsequent history of the Actors' Studio Theatre consisted of "big-time" productions on Broadway, a "compromise" much closer to Strasberg's idea than that of Kazan who left to head the Repertory Company at Lincoln Center.

The establishment of the Actors' Studio Theatre was formally announced in spring 1962. According to Cheryl Crawford (1977:231): "It would be a branch of the Studio, functioning under its tax-exempt umbrella, using only Studio actors and directors."

On April 2, 1962, The Committee to Secure the Long-Range Stability of the Actors' Studio Theatre drafted recommendations, including the following:

The Production Board would delegate to each director of a full production the authority to prepare, assemble and present the play as he sees fit, and would be available to advise and assist him in the path of overall Producing Policy for which the Board would be responsible.

The other plays should be directed by directors who have been associated with the Studio, and we would encourage them to continue their association with the Production Unit over a period of years.

We foresee the Studio's relation to the Production Unit as that unit's "Floating Company." The casting of all plays should be done basically and continuously from the bona fide membership of the Actors' Studio, only going outside to cast when the Production Board agrees with the director that the part cannot be properly cast by a Studio member who is available and willing (Actors' Studio Theatre file, Rodgers and Hammerstein Library).

The "floating company" was Strasberg's solution, as David Garfield (1980:216) writes:

to facilitate the involvement of as many of the major Studio "names" in the Theatre's productions as possible. Under this arrangement, members committed themselves to the Theatre for a limit of five months, floating in and out of active service, as it were. By making participation so flexible and therefore attractive to the Studio's leading players, Strasberg sought to avoid some of the pitfalls of the usual "permanent" year-round ensemble which has to tailor its repertory to the range of talents of a small number of actors who are willing and financially able to be tied down for long periods of time. Such long-term commitment, Strasberg observed, "usually eliminates the best people that you want." The "floating company" was his accommodation to this American reality and he believed that the "shared kinship" of Studio members would over-

come any problems such a loose-knit structure
might create.

Whatever the aesthetic principles on which it was founded, the
Actors' Studio Theatre was to be an inhouse operation.

It was generally accepted that an O'Neill play would be a
suitable premiere production. Rip Torn was the first to suggest
Strange Interlude. The production rights to all of O'Neill's plays,
however, were being held by the Repertory Company at Lincoln
Center. "Torn, however, found out that despite this arrangement
José Quintero was preparing an authorized production of *Desire
Under the Elms* at Circle-in-the-Square. He went to Quintero and
got himself cast as Eben in that production and talked the director into approaching Mrs. O'Neill to give the Actors' Studio The-
atre permission to stage a production of *Strange Interlude,* which
Quintero would direct" (Garfield, 1980:222). (The visit actually
netted Torn two jobs; he replaced Ben Gazzara in *Strange
Interlude.*)

Although working for the Actors' Studio Theatre, Quintero
was able to name David Hays as his designer. Hays said of the
Strange Interlude set: "we just used a turntable; the curtain was
down between each scene and the turntable happened to be a
handy shifting device. When the curtain went back up, there was
a new set. The reason for the turntable was just to cut down on
stage crew. You turn your furniture on the turntable and then bring
in various flying pieces." Hays had to be reminded that a number
of the set changes took place with the curtain up.

When asked what Quintero had wanted from the set, Hays
answered: "José didn't want them terribly realistic, but he needed
his furniture and so forth. It was a kind of soap opera, that play
(not really, it has implications), so the rooms were a little bit gos-
samer but still realistic. It was a little less realistic than Jo Mielziner's sets were in 1928 but still realistic: realistic wallpaper,
furniture, potted plants and proportions; the walls were a little
bit fragmented but not so much as to make it look unrealistic at
all."

Casting the production was the first indication that, despite
its prescribed guidelines, the Actors' Studio Theatre was subject
to the exigencies of the commercial theater:

> For many Studio members, the decision to cast
> Betty Field (Mrs. Amos Evans) and Franchot Tone

Strange Interlude, 1963. L to r: José Quintero, Jane Fonda, Geraldine Page, Pat Hingle, Ben Gazzara. Photo by Friedman Abeles.

(Professor Leeds), two non-Studio actors, was seen
as a breach of faith in the Studio family, even
though Tone, as a Group Theatre alumnus, had
spiritual ties with the workshop. (Strasberg further
justified bringing in Tone by pointing to the short-
age of older character actors in the Studio.) There
was also resentment that certain actors were cast
more for their "name" value than for their suitability. Resented, too, was the exception granted in
the case of Ben Gazzara (Darrell) and Jane Fonda
(Madeline), who were hired even though they could
only work for four months despite the understanding that everyone would be required to devote five
months to the Studio. These violations of the
agreed-upon organizational and functional principles not only indicated a looseness in the Theatre protocol, but a dangerous tendency to be too
readily accommodating when it seemed momentarily convenient (Garfield, 1980:223–24).

In spite of recommending that the Production Board delegate to each director "the authority to prepare, assemble and present the play as he sees fit," the rehearsal period for *Strange
Interlude* fell far short of that artistic autonomy:

There were also indications from the start that the
lines of artistic control had not been clearly defined.
José Quintero, since he brought the play to the Theatre, naturally wished to realize it in his own way.
As a non-Studio director, he did not want any interference from Strasberg or the Production Board.
By agreeing to do the play under the implicit condition that neither Strasberg nor the Production
Board would interfere, the Studio in effect had
compromised its own creative authority before the
fact, thereby sowing the seeds of inevitable conflict (Garfield, 1980:223).

Strange Interlude was cast in a manner that stretched from
old friends of Quintero's to Studio imposition by Strasberg. Geraldine Page (Nina) was a Circle-in-the-Square veteran and Quintero had hoped to use Franchot Tone in both *Iceman* and *Desire*.

William Prince (Charles Marsden) called himself "an interloper because I was pushed on José. The fact that Lee chose me to play this part was a concession. I don't know if Lee cast anyone else in the play. I never did know exactly how it went, but I was called for an interview with José at the Algonquin and he asked me if I'd like to do Charles Marsden. I said I'd love to. There were no auditions for it that I know of. I was completely nonplused." Geoffrey Horne (Gordon) was hired in a more unorthodox fashion: "I never auditioned. I was cast without my knowledge, so to speak. I was filming in Spain. I got a call or a letter, 'Do you want to play Gordon Evans in *Strange Interlude?*' "

Stage manager Richard Blofson said of the casting:

> I don't remember any auditions. José definitely cast it, all of the major parts. Those actors had all worked a hell of a lot. They brought their experiences of theater to this production, not just the experience of Strasberg's teaching. It wasn't just coming from the Studio, as a Studio production; these were a bunch of professionals, at the highest level of the profession, working with a director most of them respected very much. I don't think the Studio had a lot of influence on this production.

Rehearsals began on the stage of the Hudson Theater. Blofson said that "the theater was dark so it was available. A thousand-watt worklight and bare walls and a doorman." The first day of rehearsal did not show off Quintero at his prepared best. William Prince remembered:

> On the first day of rehearsal, after eight or nine hours, we never finished reading the play. We were using the published version. Then Quintero said, "Well, I'll have to make some cuts." I think I had said, "There must be a version around." The next day I ran into Karl Nielson, the stage manager of the original production and he directed me to Samuel French for the prompt book, two prompt books really. We stopped work for a day or two. José went through it and recut a version and we started again. We asked Equity for a fifth week of

rehearsal and were refused, so it was back to the
grind. He even made cuts after that.

Quintero used the original prompt book, but according to Blofson there was "no reference to the 1928 production."

Geraldine Page also recalled the first day of rehearsal: "José
said to the company that we were going to have to cut, although
Carlotta didn't want any cuts. He said, 'I want you all to bring
in what you think your own part could lose if it had to.' Everybody tried very diligently to cut his part, except Bill Prince and
he had the longest role."

The rehearsals were not an orderly procession toward a mutually agreed-upon goal. Blofson said that "there was not a sweet
genial atmosphere during rehearsals. The play is intense, José was
intense. I think that, internally, maybe he would go off somewhere
else and tear his hair. Yes, I know he did. He was concerned."

The sheer magnitude of the text to be learned was dispropor-
tionate to the rehearsal time. William Prince recalled that "Geraldine Page just disappeared for three, four, five days to learn lines.
She just said, 'There's no point in coming until I learn my lines.' "
Blofson corroborated: "Geraldine Page did miss rehearsals until
she'd learned her lines, but I don't remember that being a
problem."

Franchot Tone's drinking was highly disruptive. Geraldine
Page recalled that "José and Franchot would go into a tavern and
Rip had to haul them both out." William Prince added: "I remem-
ber once they called up Franchot and he said he wasn't coming
in. José said, 'Tell him we will sit on the stage and wait for him.
He's trying to make me fire him and I won't do it.' "

The presence of Rip Torn was divisive. Garfield (1980:223)
writes that "when rehearsals bogged down, Quintero and Rip Torn
had furious arguments over what corrective action should be taken.
Torn, by virtue of his position on the Production Board and as
the initiator of the *Strange Interlude* project, functioned as a sort
of unofficial executive producer."

The impact of the *Strange Interlude* rehearsals depended upon
the individual. William Prince was an objective viewer: "I was
always sort of an outsider, not only with the Studio people but
with José as well. I just went my way. Probably storms were
swirling all around me and I was just blandly going ahead not
being aware of it." Prince had had to make great concessions to

the soap opera he was doing at the time to be allowed to play in *Strange Interlude*. He was delighted to be back on the stage and warmed to working with Quintero:

> He's a man of feeling, he feels his way through plays. He doesn't say, "Now do this, now go here." It's all "What do you like doing?" I remember rehearsing a scene with Franchot Tone. Suddenly, from the back of the theater, came this tortured "*Speak* to each other." We were shocked, nobody said a word. We started the scene again. Later on he said, "Good things today, good things." That torture had come from the depths of his soul. It was very effective.

Geoffrey Horne knew Quintero quite well before the production: "José and I had a drink one night and we discussed *Strange Interlude* and he said, 'You know, I don't love this play the way I love other things.' He wasn't thrilled. He liked working in a smaller way, I guess. I don't think he was terribly comfortable with all this stuff." Horne's memories of rehearsals are like those of William Prince; not large, abstract directorial principles, but very basic acting points focused in such a way as to be memorable:

> José never said anything to me about my performance. At one point, I was doing what a nervous actor does, doing it with my hands and he jumped up on the stage and, without stopping the scene, put my hands down like this. I got that. Then, in the next scene, I was seated. Geraldine came over to me and put her hand on my shoulder and I looked up at her. José did not stop me from talking but turned my head out. He taught me more in that moment about how someone can steal a scene away from you, even unconsciously. You look up at the hand and all the focus goes right there. Who are they going to look at? Not me. He was saying, "This is your moment, take your moment." Those are the things I remember his telling me and they were invaluable. I've never forgotten them.

Quintero has directed Geraldine Page over the years in *Yerma* (1952), *Summer and Smoke* (1952), *Strange Interlude* (1963), and

Clothes for a Summer Hotel (1980). In addition, they knew each other at the Goodman Theater in Chicago for a year in the late 1940s. Page recalled that "he saw me do my work in the third year, when I was in all the plays. I had the feeling then that José had a lot of faith in my range. In the beginning, I thought that we were very close in the way that we thought."

Strange Interlude marked a midpoint for Page and Quintero. When asked if, in the early days, Quintero was up there acting with his cast, Page responded that "there was none of that, none, none, none. In those days he would ask questions: 'What do you think about this? What do you think this person is doing? What does your character want?' And he would listen to you pour out all your thoughts about it and then he would ask: 'And you don't think maybe it would also be this?' And he would add some wonderful element that would just make the whole scene work." When asked for specifics, Miss Page quickly responded:

> One time in *Yerma* I came into rehearsal and he asked me, "Where are you going?" I said, "I'm on my way to the fields to give my husband his lunch." He said, "There's your bundle." And there was a big green cloth tied in a knot. It had in it a bottle of wine, an apple, a knife, some flowers and some fortune-telling cards. I went over to one of the pillars which was a tree and poured some wine. I cut the apple with a knife until the juice ran down my arm just as Yerma came in. Well, that was the whole play: my character handing this juicy apple to the barren one. He had just prepared that and then let me figure out what to do with it.

By 1980, in *Clothes for a Summer Hotel*, "he got up, acted it out, and said, 'OK, next scene.' He was no longer a collaborator. He'd never give us enough time to work it through, to retain anything."

During *Strange Interlude*, Geraldine Page took direction from both Quintero and her husband Rip Torn:

> I told Rip that José had spent three days telling Bill Prince how to button his coat and we have nine acts. Rip gave me a lot of notes and told me that we were playing the first act backwards, that I was coming in from all that experience and running

around when they should be relating to me. At one point José said, "See how much better Gerry is doing," but I was doing what Rip had told me. There was a lot of "Sturm und Drang." My most vivid memory, aside from sitting around listening to those endless, flowery speeches, was his telling Bill Prince how to button his coat.

Richard Blofson said of Quintero's direction that "José was extremely private in the individual direction: the arm around the shoulder, walking upstage talking. I don't remember José acting out the parts or any symbol demonstration. I remember a lot of discussion and a lot of trying and a lot of space for the actors. José was back watching, in the house. It was very much a collaboration between José and the actors. He did allow a style to develop. He had a lot of flexibility."

The evolution of how the asides came to be staged was fairly consistent in the telling. William Prince remembered that "we played around with the asides a lot. We decided that one would not turn away or aside, that, in fact, the thought process continued. The person who had the aside was still while the other people continued being natural." Geoffrey Horne recalled that "José's notion was that we were all to be very relaxed and breathing but still, as opposed to frozen, with one person speaking straight out front. I remember that the movement involved was very simple, very limited. People went on breathing, being natural, as if everyone was enjoying the day while this was going on, as if the inner thoughts were being shared with the audience."

Geraldine Page offered a quick demonstration; eye contact with her interlocutor, a quick turn out to deliver the aside and then back to eye contact, "as if taking the audience into your inner thoughts while you're going on and everybody do it in full voice and everybody else ignore the aside and take it as a continuity. We choreographed movement that would appear to be natural but it had no dialogue." Richard Blofson concluded that "José was very loose about it, he had not conceived a rigid framework for the asides. He may even have had it in his head, but he let it evolve. The speaker turned away to deliver the aside, and then went back to the listener. It was not frozen and dead, there was life going on, whatever inner life the other actors had kept going."

David Garfield (1980:223) writes of the rehearsal period that "Strasberg, who in his capacity as the artistic director of the Theatre theoretically had a say in all matters of production, was reduced to working with some of the actors behind the director's back." William Prince disagreed with Garfield: "I know of no rehearsals behind José's back. We got close to dress rehearsal time when Lee announced that he was going to come. He came and José didn't come, he just didn't show up that day at all. The two men never met that I know of. It was José's production and there was never any thought of its not being his production. It was José's completely."

Geoffrey Horne categorically denied that Strasberg acted in such a manner: "Lee, whom I'd known for years, never interfered in any way. I don't know where he [Garfield] got that information. I don't know of anything from Lee or Cheryl or from anyone at the Actors' Studio that, in any way, interfered with José's work at all. In fact, there wasn't enough interference in that there was not a producer there. None of the people *would* have gone to Lee."

Horne allowed that Rip Torn had interfered a great deal, but maintained that no producer had done so and recalled the following incident:

> There was a big meeting at the Actors' Studio one day after the production had opened. It was a meeting of the Production Committee. They were seated up there and we were all out here. I was angry about something. I don't know why I did this and to this day I haven't figured out what I was thinking of. I asked, "Where is the producer of this play? Cheryl is busy with other productions and Lee is going to Moscow." Cheryl got furious and left the meeting. Well, it all got back to Lee who was irate. He spoke out at the next meeting and directly answered my question. He said that he had been asked not to be there, by the director I think he said. They probably did not meet much.

Blofson said of Garfield's statement, "That's crap. Unless it was done totally without my knowledge. I know nothing about that." When asked if Strasberg had interfered in the production,

David Hays quipped, "It wasn't until *Godfather II* that I even knew what the hell Strasberg looked like."

The production opened to generally good reviews. In the 35 years since the play's premiere, the theater-going public had long since absorbed the Freudianism, asides, and stream-of-consciousness that had originally made the play sensational. English critic Anthony West (1963:25) described how the 1963 production took advantage of that passage of time:

> In the 1928 production, the play was handled as if its presentation was part of a promotion designed to build O'Neill up as America's answer to Goethe, Victor Hugo and other examples of obsolete European greatness. Now the Actors' Studio has got away from all that. Under José Quintero's inspired direction, the members of the company play the emotion behind the scenes with a wonderful directness and simplicity. Since there is no laboring after impressiveness on the stage, the piece can speak for itself.

American critics, less concerned with world theater history, honed in on Quintero's staging of the asides. Richard Watts (1963:27) wrote:

> José Quintero wisely underemphasized the controversial O'Neill "asides." In the original production the stage action was frozen while the characters expressed their secret thoughts, and it served to underline the fact that their meditations added little of significance to the story. By letting the asides flow casually in and out of the action, Mr. Quintero removed the emphasis on their comparative barrenness and helped them to serve their essential purpose of giving breath if hardly depth to the dramatist's detailed examination of the subconscious element in motivation.

Newsweek ("Overwhelming," 1963:97) wrote that "amazingly, the production devised by José Quintero makes the famous technical gimmick thoroughly unobtrusive. The dialogue slips from overt speech to pretended thought with utter smoothness." Both

L to r: Rip Torn, Pat Hingle, Geraldine Page, William Prince. Photo by Friedman Abeles.

Watts and *Newsweek* give the impression that Quintero had glossed over a small technical difficulty that had no further impact on the production.

Michael Smith and Harold Stern both felt that Quintero's choice impaired the production. Smith (1963b:20) wrote that "Quintero chooses to play the asides as if they were regular speeches; they are often spoken straight at the character being talked about. While this approach minimizes their difficulty it also minimizes their effectiveness; a bold (if unsuccessful) experiment is turned into an unobtrusive, unnecessary task." Stern (1963b:?) wrote that "as the play is staged, it is often difficult and occasionally impossible to tell when the dialogue ends and the stream-of-consciousness begins."

Walter Kerr (1963b:?) acknowledged that the words and thoughts often got blurred, but, unlike Stern, he was able to justify it:

> Director José Quintero has carefully untucked the once celebrated device of offering us both the character's words and his secret thoughts—in alternation and with shifts of voice. The shifts of voice are gone, and even the alternation is difficult to spot; the open thoughts and the secret thoughts are simply run together as though they constitute the uninterrupted flow of a single personality, a continuum in which the concealed and the spoken are virtually simultaneous in time. There is no problem of plausibility in this, partly, I suppose, because the subconscious has by this time become an old friend; but also because the characters who are not speaking at any given moment quite clearly possess private censors. That is to say, they hear what their own psyches will permit them to hear—and the fact that we, out front, are hearing everything is simply our right as omniscient observers. A problem has been solved by making no problem of it.

During the run of *Strange Interlude,* Columbia Records recorded the entire production. On the recording, the distinction between private and public utterance is very clear, but that was, to a certain extent, the technical achievement of working in a studio: "Each wore special microphones for the 'asides' or inner voices of O'Neill's troubled people. Goddard Lieberson said, 'We're recording the natural voice on one tape and the inner voice on another' "(Gardner, 1963:34).

Harold Clurman and Henry Hewes examined the acting implications of Quintero's staging of the asides. Clurman (1963b:275) wrote:

> Where O'Neill sharply separates the actual dialogue from the inner thought sequences the director takes so little account of this division that the presumably silent speculations are frequently more vehemently expressed than the active speech. But there is still subtler stylization in O'Neill's text. He maintains a certain loftiness of tone so that the stamp of a grandiose (Greek Drama?) elevation will mark the whole. The acting in the new production is lack-luster naturalism.

Hewes (1963b:36) wrote:

> In *Strange Interlude* O'Neill was using for the first time a technique in which actors spoke aloud their private thoughts before and after speaking the dialogue the other actors are assumed to hear . . . Such a device can be performed in two ways. Either the actor can speak each of the private thoughts with an emotion that simply reinforces the statement in them, or he can speak the thoughts with an emotion appropriate to the character's motives and situation, with little or no regard to the words themselves. The Actors' Studio production uses both techniques, but the play becomes most vital and interesting when the second approach is operating. And indeed it is the second approach that best suits Method actors.

This "second approach" would support Clurman's statement that "the presumably silent speculations are frequently more vehemently expressed than the active speech."

Both *Newsday* (Oppenheimer, 1963b:3C) and *Variety* (Hobe, 1963:72) bemoaned the lack of illusion in David Hays' sets: "sets which seemed to me ill conceived and badly lit, with shadows of the actors projected on the walls for no apparent reason and a visible revolving stage that destroys illusion," and "the David Hays scenery, using a turntable stage which turns in sight of the audience, is needlessly distracting and timetaking, and some of the semi-transparent drops also lessen illusion."

Harold Clurman (1963b:275) rejected Hays' attempt to stylize the sets: "What 'style' we now find is provided by sets that revolve and drops that change in view of the audience—an increasingly fashionable device and, in this case, a silly one, particularly when the sets are as tatty and occasionally ugly as these are."

Hewes (1963b:36) was willing to take the sets on the metaphoric level:

> David Hays has designed the settings imaginatively with translucent walls, through which we can see the characters before they enter, and his scene changes, accomplished excitingly before our eyes by a revolving stage and raised and lowered backdrops which are often not in place until after the ensuing scene is started, are a delightful and dramatically effective departure from the illusionistic theatre convention of letting the background establish itself and thereby seem to evoke the action. Here it is the reverse, with the characters seeming to recall the backgrounds, to leave us with a sense that the inner lives of people come first.

Both Geoffrey Horne and Geraldine Page agreed that no such effect was intended. Horne concluded that "I think it was more a practical solution to a problem than anything theoretical or philosophical. We wished to make the sets fly more gently and not so abruptly."

When asked if Quintero had asked for sets that commented on the way the mind works, Hays answered, "No, but a designer like myself would almost subconsciously find that happening to his work. When you choose the level of reality you're going to work in, you very often do it at a subconscious level. You're not even aware of it yourself." He did maintain, however, that his set and Quintero's staging were more of a piece than those of the 1928 production: "If you have a slightly less realistic set and your people drift into their asides, in a sense that's all a little unrealistic. In the earlier production, though, there was a realistic set and then, in order to get the asides, they broke it and went into another thing altogether. They didn't have a smooth interlap but a sharp break. They had two things going on."

Although the production opened during a newspaper strike, it got off to a good start. Cheryl Crawford (1977:233) writes:

> It made an operating profit of nearly $42,000 in the first nine weeks. Unfortunately, the Hudson Theater was the only one we could get at the time, and we leased it for only three months, assuming, since it was usually not in demand, that we would be able to extend our stay if we wanted to. But the owners asked for a huge increase in rent to permit us to stay. We moved to the Martin Beck Theater at a cost of over $10,000; to make matters worse, because of that theater's arrangement, we had to pay four musicians who did not play. Much of our early profit was expended in this transfer. That was the unhappy result of not having a permanent home.

William Prince concluded, "A switch of theaters and no publicity. It was badly run really. The newspaper strike took so long and somehow they didn't get with it with radio or television. They had tremendous houses and word of mouth and it should have run much longer."

Strange Interlude opened within two months of *Desire Under the Elms* and was received in much the same fashion; the performances were determined by Quintero's staging choices. Where Moeller had chosen to stop the action to demonstrate how the mind worked, Quintero chose to keep the action moving. The effectiveness of this pivotal choice depended upon the beholder. Whoever accepted the proximity of private and public utterance welcomed the faster pace. Whoever desired to see the difference spelled out between private and public utterance balked at the blurring of the two.

5

Marco Millions

Writing

First draft completed October 1924; revision completed January 1925; final version completed May 1927.

Premieres

Original: January 9, 1928; New York, Guild Theater.

Quintero: February 20, 1964; New York, ANTA Washington Square Theater.

1928 Production

Cast List

Christian Traveller	Phillip Leigh
Magian Traveller	Mark Schweid
Buddhist Traveller	Charles Romano
Mahometan Captain	Robert Barrat
Corporal Albert	Van Dekker
Princess Kukachin	Margalo Gilmore
Donata	Natalie Browning
Tedaldo	Morris Carnovsky
Nicolo	Henry Travers
Maffeo	Ernest Cossart
Dominican Monk	Albert Van Dekker

Knight Crusader	George Colton
Papal Courier	Sanford Meisner
Kublai, the Great Kaan	Baliol Halloway
Chu-Yin	Dudley Digges
Ghazan	Morris Carnovsky
General Bayan	Robert Barrat
Paulo Loredano	Phillip Leigh

In 1921 while researching Ponce de Leon material for *The Fountain*, O'Neill became interested in the character of Marco Polo. *Babbitt*, which Sinclair Lewis had published in 1922, greatly influenced the characterization of Marco Polo as a Venetian Rotarian. The Gelbs (1960:529) write that the characterization was also suggested by the financier, art patron, Otto Kahn, "who had often urged O'Neill to write a play about the American businessman, portraying him as a hero and a man of genius, and O'Neill took a wicked, if subsidiary, delight in presenting him with a rather different conception of the hero-genius, Marco."

O'Neill's working title was "Mr. Mark Millions," but that gave way to *Marco Millions*, O'Neill's approximation of the Italian "Il Milione." As the play continued to expand in conception, O'Neill wrote, "It's a tremendous big thing to stage, with lots of crowds, silent and otherwise, to be trained perfectly—or they'd fall flat . . . In fact, it involves everything a theatre can be made (let us hope) to give, and it will take *some* directing" (Gelb, 1960:561).

O'Neill's first draft was twice the length of a standard play. He revised it, but was reluctant to cut it further until he knew what organization would produce the play. In conception, the project was too overwhelming for the triumvirate at the Greenwich Village Theater. O'Neill hoped to interest Max Reinhardt and Morris Gest, who had just spent $500,000 to produce *The Miracle*, but without success.

By November 1924, O'Neill had sought out David Belasco: "Only a few years earlier, Eugene had scorned Belasco's offerings as typical of the 'Broadway show-shop,' just as Belasco had once assailed the Villages presentations as 'vicious, vulgar and degrading,' but the times and the theatre had changed" (Sheaffer, 1973:160). On November 22, 1924, O'Neill wrote to Belasco, " 'I now have a play to submit to you . . . It has these defects from a production standpoint: it is costly to put on, involving a forestage, music, many scenes, large crowds, etc.— and also *it seems to last two nights*—to be two plays in fact.' " Belasco agreed to take an option if the play were cut to " 'one long evening' " (Sheaffer, 1973:163). In January 1925, O'Neill sent his revision to Belasco who, in February, agreed to produce the play the following year. By April 1926, however, he dropped his option. The play was then refused, in turn, by Arthur Hopkins and Gilbert Miller. The stage was now set for O'Neill's meeting with Lawrence Langner in Bermuda in March 1927 (see Chapter 4).

The Theatre Guild agreed to produce *Marco Millions*, provided the play were substantially cut. Designer Lee Simonson, a member of the board, "estimated that the play, as written, would cost $30,000 which was considered exorbitant." As originally conceived by O'Neill, "*Marco* would have required mechanical apparatus that was out of the range of the Theatre Guild's resources" (Gelb, 1960:633, 645).

By 1927, O'Neill had reached a critical period of his career. Commercial producers still refused to stage his plays, and the art theaters he had helped to develop lacked the resources to stage the plays he was now writing. The Theatre Guild seemed to be the obvious producing unit for O'Neill, but he and the Guild had been flirting with each other for seven years without ever coming to terms. O'Neill told the Guild that " 'you have either to do it up to the last gasp of cost and magnificence . . . or else very simply. Half-way measures would be ultra-fatal,' . . . but he suggested a number of script changes, including the omission of full scenes, that would 'cut down cast, costumes enormously' and hoped that his response 'shows how far I am willing to go—and how desirous I am to work with the Guild' " (Sheaffer, 1973:249).

O'Neill's willingness to compromise (and Langner's eagerness for the rights to *Strange Interlude*) carried the day. In May 1927, the Theatre Guild accepted both *Marco Millions* and *Strange Interlude* unconditionally. O'Neill now had at his disposal the most creative, efficient producing unit then available to an American playwright. Although O'Neill had contracted for two productions, this guarantee only served to enhance his philippics against the process of producing plays on stage. In July 1927, O'Neill wrote to Joseph Wood Krutch:

> There can be no such thing as a really good production in the American theatre, and I gave up all hopes of ever getting one years and years ago; I am

> tickled to death if a play of mine is done ade-
> quately. I expect bad productions. In a theatre run
> as a commercial gamble . . . where more than five
> weeks rehearsal is a dangerous financial risk, where
> directors, actors and actresses have no chance for
> any real training and no background or tradition
> of artistic feeling for their own calling, where—
> but why go on? You know the facts as well as I
> do—it is simply a proof of congenital imbecility to
> expect a good production . . . you can't build tem-
> ples out of rotten wood. When we can afford time
> in the American theatre, then and only then will
> things begin to pick up (Sheaffer, 1973:268–69).

O'Neill and the Theatre Guild proved to be good for each other. In his remaining years, O'Neill had 10 plays produced. All of them, with the exception of *Lazarus Laughed*, were produced by the Guild.

The Theatre Guild assigned Lee Simonson to design the set, which had to display "a constant change of scene, each more exotic than the other" (Sheaffer, 1973:150). Rouben Mamoulian was assigned to direct the production, fresh from his triumph in staging the original *Porgy* for the Guild: "O'Neill, who always tried to get 'rhythm' into his plays, had been impressed by the ebb and flow, the rhythmic pacing of *Porgy*, and was pleased to have Mamoulian" (Sheaffer, 1973:272). The three principal roles— Marco, the Princess, and the Great Khan—were cast from the company with Alfred Lunt, Margalo Gilmore, and Baliol Halloway.

Rehearsals were held at what was then the Guild Theater at 245 West 52nd Street. O'Neill shuttled back and forth from *Marco Millions* rehearsals to those of *Strange Interlude*. His habit was to slip in and out of the theater to watch unobtrusively, but Sheaffer (1973:272) reports an interesting exception: "He once interrupted *Marco* when Henry Travers, playing Marco Polo's father, resorted to a broad piece of business for an easy laugh. The playwright was immediately on the stage asking him to desist. 'Oh, I wouldn't do that when we open, Mr. O'Neill'—but the other cut him short. 'Don't tell me you wouldn't. *I know actors.* My father was one.' " The anecdote is a fascinating, but inconclusive, insight into O'Neill's expectations of rehearsals. The actor's response was perfectly valid; the purpose of rehearsals is to try out everything and then pare it away to the essentials. Was O'Neill intolerant of the process by which actors achieve their ends? Did he demand results too early? Or was he correcting mugging which would have grown bigger if left unchecked? It is impossible to say from this anecdote.

Marco Millions was O'Neill's first Broadway opening in four years. Critics who wanted a state-of-the-union message found the play's satire thin and dated. The sets, however, received special notice. Lee Simonson had designed "a three-fold division of permanent setting, his use of simple inserts to indicate the many changes in locale required by the text," according to John Mason Brown (1928:175). Brown (1928:175–6) had high praise for the unit set:

> The groupings of Mongolians are heightened by the ever-colorful and often superb costumes of Lee Simonson and backed by some of the most effective settings Mr. Simonson has ever designed. Seen without their colors these sets would immediately confess that their lines are not distinguished: but lighted as they are at the Guild they present a steady sequence of highly contributive backgrounds. By his ingenious use of permanent set pieces, Mr. Simonson not only makes the production possible, by solving the difficulties presented by the globe-trotting of the script, but lends the play a unity which considerably strengthens its picaresque form.

Joseph Wood Krutch (1928:104–5) described the inserts and the style in which they were painted:

> He has solved the apparently unsolvable problem of suggesting the magnificent exoticism of the Orient by designing stage pictures of surpassing beauty which depend for their effect, not upon an effort to reproduce the scenes naturalistically, but upon their success in utilizing the artistic conventions of the various countries. Thus, that which represents the throne room of the emperor and which is perhaps the best, presents us with a huge frame of filigreed jade behind which lies a back drop upon

which are sketched in Chinese fashion the peaks
of a mountain range. No naturalistically constructed scene could achieve the desired effect.

The expressions "stage pictures of surpassing beauty" and
"backed by some of the most effective settings" convey the impression of a painted background in front of which the production
took place, rather than an integral portion of the production. The
removable panels sound flexible, but proved not to be so in production, according to the Gelbs (1960:645): "Even simplified, the scene
shifts were distracting, for the action, instead of flowing smoothly
and rhythmically, was chopped up by a lowered curtain and overlong waits." Percy Hammond (1928:28) wrote of those overlong
waits that "warped a little by its eight intermissions it lags here
and there."

Barrett H. Clark (1928:170) was the critic who most clearly
perceived why the set was not integrated into the production:

Of one thing only I must complain; the waits
between scenes. Considering the amount of labor
involved, the Guild did as much as could be done
without a revolving-stage or "Wagons." But why
not the revolving-stage? American managers always
tell me that the thing is not practical. But I know
it is and I know besides that only by linking together
the many scenes of a play like *Marco* by some such
means is it possible to create the proper effect . . .
Macbeth and *Hamlet*, like *Marco Millions*, are
divided into several scenes not for the convenience
of the audience, but because the dramatist wished
to produce certain effects; they aimed at continuity.
When the producer gives the audience a total of
thirty or forty minute intermissions in a play that
ought to require less than two hours in the playing, he is doing his best to break down what the
playwright has carefully built up. When I read
Marco in manuscript three years ago I went
through it in an hour. Stretched out to two and a
half hours, it seems thin.

1964 Production

Cast List

Christian Merchant	James Greene
Magian Merchant	Jack Waltzer
Buddhist Merchant	Graham Jarvis
Mahometan Captain	John McCurry
Corporal	John Phillip Law
Princess Kukachin	Zohra Lampert
Marco Polo	Hal Holbrook
Donata	Crystal Field
Nicolo Polo	Lou Frizzell
Maffeo Polo	Michael Strong
Tedaldo	David J. Stewart
Dominican Monk	Barry Primus
Papal Courier	Scott Cunningham
Prostitute	Virginia Kaye
Dervish	Jim Ray-James
Kublai, the Great Khan	David Wayne
Chu-Yin, a Cathayan Sage	Joseph Wiseman
Ghazan, Khan of Persia	Harold Scott
General Bayan	Stanley Beck

In 1964, Quintero had joined in the birth of the Repertory Company at Lincoln Center, headed by Elia Kazan and Robert Whitehead. Barbara Gelb (1964:II,3) wrote that "under the influence of the same spiritual narcotic that has caused Elia Kazan to devote himself to the vision of a repertory theatre, Mr. Quintero is pinning his future almost exclusively on the Lincoln Center. He has a contract to direct four plays there over a flexible period of time." Quintero had contracted to direct *Marco Millions* and both *All God's Chillun Got Wings* and *A Moon for the Misbegotten* were being discussed.

In an interview by Barbara Gelb (1964:II, 1–3), Quintero discussed *Marco Millions* from a spatial point of view: "It's different from O'Neill's other plays. Most of them are confined physically. This one goes all over the world. It is a magician's show." He

Marco Millions, 1964. L to r: José Quintero, Zohra Lampert, David Wayne. Photo by Martha Swope.

stressed the nature of the play's repetitions: "I haven't cut a single scene or character. People say O'Neill's plays are repetitious, but he wrote like a composer, building theme on theme, and variations on theme. In *Marco*, he says a thing in detail; then he says it in a condensed form; then he says it in pantomime; he knows exactly what he is doing when he repeats himself." Three days later, Leonard Harris (1964:27) interviewed him and he paid tribute to Carlotta for teaching him the musical structure of the plays: "Mrs. O'Neill as a critic knows more about her husband's work than almost anyone. She made me understand the repetitions he uses. 'It is almost like music,' she said, 'rhythm and tempo, the theme played by a single instrument, then by three, then by half an orchestra, then by the strings, then by the full orchestra.' "

Quintero's reputation for staging O'Neill was a major, but not the sole contributing factor to his selection by the Repertory Company at Lincoln Center, as Barbara Gelb (1964:II, 3) stated:

> The choice of Mr. Quintero as the director to alternate with Mr. Kazan was based not only on his experience with O'Neill but also his extensive experimentation with arena-style directing off-Broadway. For Mr. Quintero, the challengingly open stage of the company's contemporary theater poses few technical problems; he has learned how to use suggestion of scenery and baths of light to make up for lack of conventional trappings. In *Marco* which calls for lavish settings in Venice, Cathay, Persia, India and Mongolia, he will tap (with the help of his long-time associate, the designer, David Hays) "every piece of lighting equipment on the theater's switchboard."

The company's theater was *not* the Vivian Beaumont Theater, which was not completed in time to open the first season of the Repertory Company. *Marco Millions*—along with the other two productions of the first season, Arthur Miller's *After the Fall* and S. N. Behrman's *But for Whom Charlie*—was produced at the ANTA Washington Square Theater, a no-longer-standing temporary home designed by Jo Mielziner for the company's first two seasons. After all three productions had opened, John Chapman (1964b:II, 1) wrote an evaluation of the new theater: "The pit is impressive. The open stage, which can accommodate no scenery beyond hand props and occasional pieces of furniture, is at the bottom . . . Ringed about the stage in a little over a half-circle are steeply tiered rows of seats, as in a Roman amphitheater. This is the only theater in New York where every seat is a good seat . . . And the acoustics are faultless. If you can't hear an actress, it's her fault."

This was the space in which David Hays had to create exotic illusion. Hays said that "Bob Whitehead asked me to do *Marco Millions*, although I assume that he got a nudge from José." When asked what specifics Quintero had requested for the set, Hays responded:

> He said one thing particularly to me. He said, "We've got an open stage here and we have no tunnels. We have nowhere to go. You get downstage on that apron and you can't get off it. My actors are going to come down, look at the audience, say their speech and then turn around and go right back where they came from." He said, "Try and fix that up for me." I went and designed what I thought we needed here which was a turn-table pushed by actors. Jo Mielziner was particularly kind because he had a complicated set in there for *After the Fall* and, from the very start of the season, he accommodated his set to our needs. The floor of *After the Fall* was the revolve turn-around adapted, ready to be taken apart so that ours could go in. We had a steep slope looking down so you were very aware of the floor which became the chief design element. At the Guthrie, for instance, it's a three-quarter but the stage is raised somewhat over the first row; here it was raised less, more people seemed to look down on it. It was a real cockpit.

In 1928, Barrett H. Clark had insisted that what *Marco* needed was a revolving stage. Hays designed a revolve which was actor-operated, rather than mechanical. Hays was familiar with Lee Simonson's set for the 1928 production, but concluded that "you couldn't work that way, the stage demanded my set."

Stage manager Frank Hamilton described the set to which David Hays had to accommodate his own set: "The set of *After the Fall*, from which we all had to take off, had two entrances right and left onto the apron and then there was this enormous thrust. There were two stairways which came down to ten feet above the stage level on either side where the wings occurred and then could be added to in order to go directly across, bridge over or down to. They were different for each show."

Hays made two large additions to the stage. Henry Hewes (1964:23) wrote that "since Jo Mielziner's ANTA Washington Square Theater is one in which we all look down at the stage floor as much as we would ordinarily look across at a back wall, Mr. Hays has covered the thrust stage with a mosaic carpet that changes appearance with different hues of light . . . He has also constructed a ceiling of colored netting that becomes iridescent under lighting from above."

Barbara Gelb (1964:II, 3) wrote that, within this framework, "David Hays will flood the stage and much of the auditorium with rippling blue light, to evoke what he hopes will be a network of Venetian canals; he will try to create the effect of a gondola by revolving a segment of the stage, while Marco Polo seems to be propelling it with a long pole." To accomplish this effect, Marco began at nine o'clock and poled while the revolve, hand-operated, came 270 degrees in a counterclockwise fashion to 12 o'clock. Marco then jumped off onto dry ground—the permanent part of the stage—at Donata's rear-stage balcony.

Even more spectacular was the fully rigged wedding barge in which Marco conducted Princess Kukachin to become Queen of Persia. Henry Hewes (1964:23) called it a "total theater creation of an embarking ship, accomplished by raising filmy sails and by having crewmen climb suspended ropes and slaves slowly push the rotating forestage around—as if into the wind." The ship was accomplished with eight actors pushing the revolve and four actors inserting and then climbing two poles. Hays said that "the billowing of the sail was magnificent. The draftsman who took my sketches and drawings said it was like an engineering drawing of a fart."

There were witty devices to indicate changes of time: "Two runners carry a silken banner, printed with the image of camels, swiftly across the stage to show that Marco, his father and uncle have left Venice and arrived in the East" (Nadel, 1964:14). To indicate place, "he introduces each new locale with style and humor by having men spirit across the stage carrying appropri-

ate natural history banners" (Hewes, 1964:23). David Hays
described the effect of the revolve as these changes of time and
space were occurring: "We used the banners as the table turned,
with shields and banners, and, before he knew it, the actor was
walking in the same direction but heading out in the direction
he'd come from because the table was turning around."

The Repertory Company at Lincoln Center projected the
development of a permanent acting company from which the
productions would be cast. They recruited about 50 actors, aged
25 or younger. Crystal Field, one of the trainees, recalled that
"we were auditioned several times and then weeded out gradually. We were placed in a gruelling 9-month training program,
unpaid, and told that we would be the backbone of the company.
They weeded us down to15. I was one of the survivors. After we'd
gone through the training program, suddenly they brought in what
they called 'semi-names' and we became the extras. Most of us
got nothing."

The productions were finally cast in Broadway fashion with
middle-level actors and stars. Casuals were hired for one show.
Jimmy Greene, a veteran of many years of repertory with the
Association of Producing Artists (APA), said:

> The Lincoln Center Repertory Company was
> formed in order to do *After the Fall*. That's my
> impression. They cast *After the Fall* and then they
> said, "Now this is our repertory company." I never
> felt that they were taking the long view when they
> got that company together. It was a very mixed
> bag. For instance, Jason wasn't about to be in every
> show, to play small parts as well as big parts. It
> wasn't a healthy group of actors because you had
> a lot of names and well-established actors for half
> of the company: David Wayne, Joe Wiseman,
> Ralph Meeker, and Jason. The other half included
> a lot of young people in the early part of their
> careers. They had all kinds of classes, speech and
> dance and all that. The young people went to these
> classes and the more established people almost
> never went to the classes and a resentment grew
> about that. It was never really a family unit and
> they ended up doing *After the Fall* for a year and

a half and any idea of repertory went out the window. It was very different from the APA.

Crystal Field said:

> We had a company and the idea was to cast from the company, but there was trouble all along the line. The writers balked. They said, "I don't want this actor, I don't want that actor." And the directors probably felt the same way. When you cast a production out of a rep company, you've got to live with the actors you've got, and nobody wanted to do that too much. They just called these other people up and asked them to do the parts and join the company. They *tried* to cast everything as a company, they tried to have a rep company.

To add to the complexity, the season to be cast consisted of three plays, two of which were world premieres with the author present and one a revival of an O'Neill play that had failed badly when it premiered. *Marco* was the runt of the litter. Frank Hamilton said, "I think the casting of *Marco* was a committee decision with the idea of utilizing the company. Kazan, Whitehead, Harold Clurman the dramaturg, and José all had input as to what the company would be and José was the junior partner."

Quintero cast David Wayne as the Great Khan, Hal Holbrook as Marco, and Zohra Lampert as Princess Kukachin. He cast Mary Claire Costello from the training program as Donata. Crystal Field said that "Mary Claire had started out rehearsing Donata, but was not satisfactory to José, so John Phillip Law recommended me to José. I auditioned for it and got the job."

The production rehearsed for six weeks, noon to five, at the Birns Building, in the ballroom above Ratner's Restaurant on Second Avenue. There were occasional rehearsals at the theater on the *After the Fall* set, but, as Frank Hamilton said, "we had rehearsal-space problems because it was expensive to switch over, so we rehearsed in the rehearsal space until we got to the technical problems of the set."

The social satire of *Marco Millions* is a far cry from the anguish and guilt of *Iceman*, *Long Day's Journey*, and *Desire Under the Elms*, the O'Neill plays that had hitherto brought out the best in Quintero. Frank Hamilton said that "*Marco* was more

production-oriented than O'Neill-oriented. In the scene with the
two uncles, José spoke about their greed in an O'Neill fashion;
in that instance José did try to get those essences he always deals
with."

John McCurry recalled:

> Quintero came in and knew what he wanted and
> how he wanted it done down to the nth degree.
> The set was marked out for the first reading and
> he discussed the physical aspects of the play. We
> had to present movement on that small stage. We
> were to be trudging across the Siberian Desert with
> camels and warriors. That was the impression we
> had to give. He wanted the sense of tremendous
> size. It was like picking out just one microcosm in
> the whole thing; there were people in front of us,
> behind us, and all around us, but the important
> activity was the one we were engaged in on the
> stage.

This emphasis on production implies that Quintero orches-
trated the entire process. Actually, according to Frank Hamilton,
"when we got to the technical elements of the show José was very
quiet. David Hays did a lot of the work which another director
might have done. When it came to the working of it, David made
it work. José is the least technically oriented director I've worked
with. He works with people who know how it works and José lets
it happen." David Hays is an expert sailor and revelled in the nau-
tical elements of the Venetian gondola and the fully rigged ship.
Hays said that "our costume designer, Beni Montressor, was supposed to be Venetian and couldn't pole a gondola. I had to show
him. I showed Hal Holbrook how to stand in a gondola and pole
the thing along." Hays did not attend regular rehearsals, but he
did oversee the week of technical rehearsals. He determined what
had to be done and Quintero adjudicated and assigned tasks to
specific actors. Jimmy Greene recalled, "I thought at the time that
if David Wayne or Zohra Lampert got sick we'd put on the understudy and there'd be no problem at all, but if one of these actors
who's got five lines to say and 40 rope changes gets sick, we'd be
in a great deal of trouble."

John McCurry said of Quintero's acting direction that "he
wants you to do it your way. He would tell you what he wanted

and probably walk it through if he thought it was too difficult or, if he thought that his explanation wasn't full enough, he would try to show you, but he didn't want you to copy what he did; he was very insistent on that."

Crystal Field said, "José never acted out my part for me; he told me what he wanted and he was never in the space, always outside. That's what I loved about him, he talked a lot about the life of the play. He was an artist completely, and everyone's attitude toward him was that he was an artist, a great director, and we all felt that he was being screwed by taking the actors away from him."

In a three-play repertory situation, schedules were changed arbitrarily and priorities necessitated that an actor be reassigned at the last moment. Quintero had not worked in repertory and could not accustom himself to having actors withdrawn when he needed them. As Crystal Field elaborated:

> José had the most awful experience because they would say to him, "You can't have that actor now. We need him for the other play." It was utterly arbitrary, totally, completely. If he had been a stronger man he probably would have fought them on it. It was a horror story for José. It takes a while for José to get started. He doesn't really get started until nighttime and then they would say "stop." He had to work with the stage manager. You can work that way, but only if you're used to it. That's what happened to José. He couldn't have the actor when he needed him. That blew his mind and he'd go for a drink.

Frank Hamilton said of the complexities of scheduling a repertory company that "it was always a mess; understudies, one show running, another going into rehearsal, and a third auditioning. First priority is the show in production. But José is an emotional man."

David Hays said, "Well, I'm a company man. You keep your eye on the forest rather than just the trees. The other designers, Jo Mielziner and Boris Aronson, cooperated completely in sharing our resources. We worked toward the best possible aim. If the manager says, 'I've got to give you less time today,' I'll hang around

L to r: Unidentified, Joseph Wiseman, David Wayne, Zohra Lampert, Hal Holbrook. Photo by Martha Swope.

and say, 'You took it from me yesterday, I need it today.' That's
how you work it out."

Crystal Field described the production style that evolved during rehearsals:

> There was great freedom in the staging. There was
> no scenery as such; there were set pieces, everything
> was totally portable, evocative, skeletal. In a jour-
> ney, everything was carried. José would change the
> areas a lot so you never had the sense of a stage
> with perimeters. It was a space without walls and
> things came in. Suddenly you were in the moun-
> tains and you accepted it. He isolated the space
> with light and then used totally portable set ele-
> ments. This series of shields, for instance; they went
> up and then down to reveal the center piece. There
> was no stylized movement, that was to José's credit.
> He emphasized the dignity of the court, an Orien-
> tal world. He made Marco Polo a car salesman
> from the naive West. Hal Holbrook used his nor-
> mal speech. David Wayne spoke in Shakespearean
> speech, wonderful, but not phoney speech. It was
> stage speech, but very natural, with his own accent
> creeping in often to be real.

It becomes easier to evaluate Quintero's contribution to the
Lincoln Center project by comparing his work with that of Elia
Kazan. Crystal Field commented:

> Quintero's approach was very philosophical. He
> spoke about the scene the way Kazan would never
> do. He was very unlike Kazan. His way with psy-
> chology, especially for women, was wonderful.
> He's a very gentle man. I played Marco Polo's
> adolescent love. Kazan would have put some sex
> into it. We did it very romantically, I cried when
> he left. Kazan would have put adolescent sex into
> the scene, and then he would have taken you aside
> and talked about what you were doing and said,
> "Don't tell the other actor what you're doing."
> Then he'd talk to the other actor and say, "Don't
> tell her what you're doing." He gets a thing going

that way and the sparks fly. José doesn't look for sparks, he looks for a kind of inner passion. If Kazan had been doing the final scene, he would have brought out the shame Donata felt at being fat. Quintero's attack is not like that at all; it is much more romantic and idealistic, a vision of the world.

Frank Hamilton's gloss on Crystal Field's statement was "with young actors the trick of not telling the other actor what you're doing *can* work. Kazan dealt with sex, it's a big part of his life. All male/female relationships have that possibility with him, but José does not think of sex as one of the great driving forces of life. José is a very gentle man; he is a loving man."

A large problem during rehearsals was hearing Zohra Lampert. (John Chapman's statement about the theater's acoustics, "If you can't hear an actress, it's her fault," can have been directed only at Miss Lampert.) Crystal Field said that "Zohra Lampert could not be heard past the first row. That is unforgivable." Frank Hamilton observed that "the closest rapport José had was with Zohra. She didn't speak loud enough. She does, as an actress, get very *intime*. José didn't bother about that; that she had the essence was enough for him." Crystal Field had the final word on the subject: "At a meeting after we opened, I said that Zohra Lampert should be louder and I don't think José liked my saying that. Kazan redirected her and José was very upset at that. Kazan is much like Joe Papp in that what has to be done must be done and in any way he has to do it. Kazan had no influence during rehearsal, we were left alone as far as the play went."

Frank Hamilton added, "Kazan is technically brilliant. If you say to Kazan that tomorrow we're going to rehearse from noon to five, he will begin at noon, work till five, and accomplish exactly what he set out to accomplish. José will arrive a little late (he's very South American), he'll talk for a little while, and then you rehearse. He doesn't use his time particularly well."

Having seen all three productions of the opening season, Edward Sothern Hipp (1964b:E1–E3) compared Quintero's use of the stage with that of Kazan:

> The vast stage with its many levels, ramps, tiers and naked stretches, has, oddly enough, kept direc-tor Elia Kazan off balance. This, one would have

guessed, is exactly the kind of stage to bring unrestrained cartwheels from Kazan, a showman who has often met technical challenges with remarkable triumphs. Here in Washington Square in a depressed, dramatically appealing playhouse Kazan was given an assortment of stages on which to work. He had the benefit of a mightily impressive array of powerful overhead lights. And he had the complete attention of a new band of dedicated artists, proud to be counted in an ambitious organization. However, it seemed to me that he fell far short of his potential in both *After the Fall* and *But for Whom Charlie* while José Quintero, with *Marco Millions*, gave O'Neill's vicarious voyage to Cathay more color, ingenious groupings and graceful movement than it deserved. Conceding that such an achievement is easier with an episodic play rolling from Venice to the Orient than with a modern drama, I still think Kazan might have made better use of the playhouse's equipment and devised some ways of getting the Miller and Behrman characters on and off the stage without long parades.

Because the revival was not expected to reveal a neglected masterpiece, the critics looked to the production for its theatricality. Norman Nadel (1964:14) wrote that "he has not made *Marco Millions* an important play nor corrected its faults. He has minimized them, however, with an imaginative and exotic staging and he has provided the explicit contrast of spiritual and materialistic values which the play requires." Walter Kerr (1964a:11) asked the relevant question in writing of the play's "loose, journeying, semi-spectacular form. What can the flexible new stage of Lincoln Center Square Playhouse make us see in the play we might have missed before?"

Only John Chapman (1964a:80) felt that "José Quintero's staging of *Marco Millions* is quite desperately stylized. It might have come off better on a proscenium stage." Louis Chapin (1964:12) spoke for the overwhelming majority when he found the stage uniquely appropriate for the play:

> *Marco Millions* is a play which chafes at the
> proscenium of the conventional theater, which
> deals in modern terms with the turning of a Renais-
> sance world and which glows richly and almost for-
> gotten behind Eugene O'Neill's later work. It is,
> in fact, impressively suitable for the revolving,
> light-blessed arena stage at the new ANTA
> Washington Square Theater.

Michael Smith (1964:12) disliked the staging and related it
to Quintero's roots at Circle-in-the-Square:

> Quintero has staged the play symmetrically,
> organizing the actors on an axis straight up the mid-
> dle of the stage. Throne-room scenes are always dif-
> ficult to block, since everybody is upstaged by the
> ruler and their total failure on this occasion leads
> to questions about the new stage. At Quintero's
> former home, Circle-in-the-Square, an actor all the
> way downstage facing upstage is visible to about
> half the audience; at Lincoln Center he is visible
> to almost no one.

If the 1928 production of *Marco Millions* had given the
impression of two-dimensional Chinese drawings, *Newsweek*
("O'Neill Magic," 1964:56) rhapsodized on Quintero's 1964 production that "the aftereffect of *Marco Millions* is an awed sense of
having travelled far in spirit and in space. Out of airy nothings,
director José Quintero contrives miraculous illusions of gondolas
gliding on the canals of Venice, sailors singing in the shrouds,
caravans tracking the desert." Quintero's production was more
rhythmic in that it moved faster from place to place, but also that
the space in which it moved was three-dimensional rather than
a backdrop. A comparison between the two productions prompted
Edward Sothern Hipp (1964a:92) to write that "stage direction
has advanced dramatically in thirty-six years."

In the complex politics of Lincoln Center, that Quintero had
directed the play successfully loomed less large than the question
of why it had been selected in the first place. Quintero had not
selected the play, but stood only to lose by the question's being
asked. His status in the Kazan-Whitehead regime was undermined.

He was not offered a production in the second season. Kazan and Whitehead were replaced at the end of the second season and Quintero never again directed for the company.

6

Hughie

Writing
Begun December 1940; first draft completed April 30, 1941; second and final version completed May 19, 1941.
Premieres
Original: Not produced in O'Neill's lifetime.
Quintero: December 22, 1964; New York, Royale Theater.

On November 29, 1940, O'Neill wrote in his notebooks that he had gotten a "new idea for series of monologue plays—short— "By Way of Obit"—for book more than stage, perhaps—scenes, one character, one marionette (life-size) The Good Listener—I do brief outline for five of them" (Floyd, 1981:346).

O'Neill wrote to George Jean Nathan on June 19, 1942, explaining that in each play the main character would discuss a recently deceased person with "a person who does little but listen. Via this monologue you get a complete picture of the person who has died—his or her whole life story—but just as complete a picture of the life and character of the narrator. And you also get by another means—a use of stage directions mostly—an insight into the whole life of the person who does little but listen" (Sheaffer, 1973:521).

Carlotta described the projected cycle of one-act plays:

> "Gene started writing these plays as a diversion.
> He was writing so many serious things at the time
> that this was something to play with. It required
> no responsibility and it amused him." One dealt
> with an old Irish chambermaid O'Neill had known
> when he and Jamie lived at the Garden Hotel.
> "They would wake up in the morning with hang-
> overs," Carlotta said, "and the chambermaid
> would be scrubbing up the bathroom. She would
> tell Gene stories and gossip and Gene would
> encourage her to talk" (Gelb, 1960:843).

A chambermaid play was listed among the projected plays,
but *Hughie* is the single surviving play. When O'Neill gave the
script to Langner in the summer of 1944, he mentioned a companion piece, in need of revision, that might constitute a full evening of theater. This much-needed companion piece may have
been the chambermaid play.

The stage directions for *Hughie* contain, among other anoma-
lies, long passages of interior monologue for the desk clerk intended
only for someone reading the play. O'Neill wrote to George Jean
Nathan, in fall 1941, that *Hughie* was designed "more to be read
than staged" (Sheaffer, 1973:522). O'Neill no longer had the energy
to project how the play would be staged. The Gelbs (1960:844)
maintain that:

> O'Neill did not intend *Hughie* or any of the other
> plays in the series to be given conventional stage
> productions. He told Carlotta that he was think-
> ing of some new technique, possibly utilizing a
> filmed background and soundtrack. But he did not
> pursue the idea. He shrugged off the problem, say-
> ing: "It would require tremendous imagination. Let
> whoever does it figure it out. I wouldn't want to
> be around to see it."

Sheaffer (1973:523) reinterprets O'Neill's disclaimer: "Actually, O'Neill doubted *Hughie*'s theatrical viability only if it were
staged conventionally. Anticipating the mixed-media of later
decades, the visionary playwright told Carlotta that ideally the

playlet should be produced with a soundtrack for the interior monologue and stage directions that would accompany the live dialogue, in addition to a background film of the city."

Hughie had its world premiere in Sweden in 1958 at the Swedish Royal Dramatic Theatre with the King and Queen of Sweden in attendance. The English-language premiere took place in London in 1963, in a production with Burgess Meredith and Jack MacGowan, on a triple bill with O'Neill's *In the Zone* and *Before Breakfast*.

1964 Production

Cast List
Erie Smith   Jason Robards
Night Clerk   Jack Dodson

Stuart Little (1964:15) wrote that "Robards, Mann and Quintero first considered doing the play eight years ago when Robards was playing Hickey in the famous Circle-in-the-Square production of *The Iceman Cometh*. The Circle first announced the American premiere of *Hughie* in 1958, but later rescheduled it for 1960. It was to have starred Myron McCormick, on a double-bill with *The Emperor Jones*." Arthur Gelb (1960:23) wrote: "According to the producers, *Hughie* and *The Emperor Jones* are being done as companion pieces because they are both studies of men who appear cocky and confident in their worlds but who can be gradually seen to crumble as their true selves are revealed."

Jason Robards denied that such earlier productions for *Hughie* were ever scheduled: "We never discussed my doing *Hughie* in the late '50s. *Hughie* came up in 1964 out of some desperation José and I had to do a play again. We'd both had bad times in plays and we had to do something good again, so we decided to try to get *Hughie* on. Ted Mann had the rights so we had to do it with him. I had to get José and Ted together so that we could get the show on. Joe Levine put up the money." According to Stuart Little (1964:15) the ensuing production was "brought together rapidly. For some time they had been looking for another play to pair with *Hughie* to make a conventional length evening. Seventy-two one-act scripts were submitted to Robards for review. 'The play seemed to demand to be done by itself,' Quintero said, and a twelve-performance schedule was worked out." Robards said that we were going to double it with a play that Jim Bridges wrote, but Mrs. O'Neill didn't want it done with any other play.

David Hays was given a quick call to design the set: "My experience with *Hughie* was that on Thursday afternoon I was told to do a set and could I have it ready for Monday. It was one of the best sets I've ever done. We had no time for meetings. I did a set and they liked it and that was that. That was very much a job I had to do by myself."

The first thing Hays did after receiving the commission was to go to the Royale Theater, where he discovered that the stage was exceptionally wide. He then went to 47th Street and explored a hotel (no longer standing) that he felt would evoke the correct environment:

> It was all there. It went from 47th to 48th Street. It had the cage, it had the coloring, it had a one-inch stripe that went all the way around the lobby and about five and a half feet off the floor, every column and every wall, and the sconces. I rearranged that space into what the Royale had. All we did was make our scenery and lean it up against the walls. It was wall-to-wall scenery. It took the entire stage space of the Royale. It went from one wing (stage left) which was short to the other wing (stage right) which was extremely deep. We put the switchboards out in the loading dock so they weren't backstage where they would usually have been. We put columns up, we put up a ceiling, we put the elevator cage up. I mean it was a set that was built and brought in like anything else, but it was like we wallpapered the particular configurations of that theater with the flats.

The cage imagery that so dominated the production was Hays' discovery: "The cage was partly in the hotel I saw, but then I isolated it a little more, I brought it out, the way steps wind around those old Central Park buildings which used to have square stairwells." Hays then brought Quintero and Robards to look at the hotel. Robards recalled, "It was a through-lobby. That's where we got the set. It was right. The play takes place in limbo, no sides. José wanted no definition on sides."

The only other role, that of the night clerk, was offered to Jack Dodson at the eleventh hour:

> It was Thanksgiving of 1964. José phoned and asked me if I wanted to be in his play. I was a little reluctant because I had decided I wasn't going to do any more off-Broadway productions. And I hemmed and hawed a bit and he said to me no, it was for Broadway. It would be just Jason and I in *Hughie*. I was startled because there hadn't been any indication that the play was going to be done at all. I asked when he was going to do it and he said, "We start Monday." This was like Friday. There had been no announcement about the play for several years. My prior knowledge of *Hughie* came from what I read in the paper. I had never discussed it with José and I had never envisioned myself in the part. I was surprised to have it offered to me because I had done five plays for José at the Circle and not one of those resembled that character. I did not feel that I was like that character physically, but of course he wasn't casting it according to O'Neill's description anyway, in either case, either Jason or myself.

Ironically, Jack Dodson had been a night clerk in a hotel: "Not that kind of hotel. Generally speaking, a night clerk has a good bit to do, lots of paper work, and in this play the night clerk has nothing to do. I couldn't rely on my own experience because I had been darn busy all night long. My personal image was always those guys you see selling tokens in the subway at three o'clock in the morning. It's that kind of existence; the cage, the dreariness, the monotony."

Dodson arrived for rehearsal at the Royale Theater on the Monday morning set by Quintero, assuming that he had the job:

> José was there and we sat at a table. We read the play and José said, "Thank you, Jack, I'll call you." I had thought that it was all set. I started out of the theater and got into the alley, and they called me back. José said, "You're playing the part. We start tomorrow." It had been a cold reading; he

Hughie, 1964. L to r: Jason Robards, Jack Dodson. Photo by Friedman Abeles.

didn't say anything. I later assumed that this was
because Jason did not know me. This had been for
his benefit and they sent me out in case Jason said,
"I can't stand the son of a bitch. Get rid of him."

When asked if he does maintain a veto power over Quintero,
Robards quickly responded:

I have *never* gone against José's casting choices. I
feel that, as a director, that's part of what he brings
to a show. I can't very well go in and say, "I don't
want him." That's terrible, I won't do that. He has
a right to make his mistakes and his good strokes.
Most of the time he casts well. That's the biggest
part of the job, casting; 80 percent. With any director. Who knows what they see? This is what I, after
42 years in this business, know. You cast it wrong
and it doesn't get realized. That's just a theater
axiom.

There were two weeks, "approximately 12" rehearsals,
according to Dodson. On the first day Quintero did not have a
blocked-out script. He did not precede rehearsals with a long
preparatory discussion. He had, however, selected for Dodson
those interior monologues of the night clerk (Dodson had skipped
all of them at the previous day's first reading), which he proposed
to use in the production. Dodson recalled that "All of them are
not usable. I guess we used about half of them." As the staging
of the interior monologues evolved, Dodson said:

I just did them as asides. There was a light change
with each. There were a couple we altered after
we got it in front of the public. I realized that they
didn't know what to make of my saying of the foot-
steps, "if only he'd shoot it out with a gunman some
night," so I changed it to "if only that cop would
shoot it out." The audience didn't know who was
out there. There was the sound of a cop running
his nightstick along railings, but that's a sound a
modern audience would not identify as quickly as
one in the '30s would have.

The interior monologues were the stage directions with which Quintero took liberties. He made no attempt at any mixed-media style. When Arthur Gelb (1960:23) asked Quintero to comment on O'Neill's stage directions for *Hughie* and O'Neill's statement "Let whoever does it figure it out. I wouldn't want to be around to see it," Quintero replied that "he would simply do what Mr. O'Neill had in mind."

In general, during the rehearsal period, according to Dodson:

> Quintero would talk and relate things from his life and experiences, from his knowledge of O'Neill. His way with metaphors communicates concepts very well without ever being explicit about anything. In terms of anecdotes, his very rich imagery, his command of the language is superb, so you're never at a loss to understand what he's about or what he wants to accomplish, although he's never terribly specific. He's not a director who ever says "louder and faster" or "pick up the pace" or that kind of director.

Specifically, Quintero discussed the importance of silence in the play and the pauses. Both items are familiar Quintero concerns. Uncharacteristically, Quintero discussed the concept of the production with clear reference to the design that Hays had initiated. Dodson recalled Quintero's "use of the elevator which became almost like a third character in the play. We were in cages. They didn't explicitly look like cages. Jason's was the elevator, my cage was the desk. They had a mesh backing behind the clerk's desk and a mesh door, the same steel mesh that was used in the elevator shaft, implying these two cages and traps. José always referred to the line in the play about beating up to my cell and grabbing some shut-eye, that that represented death to Erie."

The cages do not appear in O'Neill's stage directions. "Who cares?" shrugged Robards, "That was *our* idea." Was it unusual for Quintero to work with such a specific visual concept? "I don't know," Robards responded, "you'd have to ask José." And then, with another no-nonsense shrug, "That play; I learned it and put it on in about 10 days. I had no awareness of any great, artistic ideas. I had to learn a ton of words and get 'em out without flubbing. That's what it comes down to, doesn't it?"

There were only two hardback chairs on the set and, according to Dodson, "What furniture there was was so spare as to be nonexistent, so there was no place in this lobby for this man to find any comfort at all, but he keeps trying and he finally sat on a bundle of newspapers downstage right by the water cooler. If there had been any comfort in that lobby to be found, Erie would never have gone up to his room."

Dodson often found it easier to define Quintero's production by setting it in opposition to the subsequent 1974 Broadway production of *Hughie*, which Martin Fried directed with Ben Gazzara starring. (That production coupled *Hughie* with an original one-act play.) Dodson found that production's set design "all wrong because it had stuffed couches and magazines and a radio. It was very homey and comfortable so that Erie could come in and plop down and bullshit the night away whether anybody was there or not, but that barren empty stage which was José' s concept contributed so much to the mood of the piece, the desperate loneliness of these people."

Quintero left the hotel entrance off-stage as O'Neill had designated it:

> Off-stage you heard Jason's coughing. He entered off-right. It was interesting because we had no doors; it went off into infinity. When Gazzara did it, they had a right and left stage wall and there were two glass doors up right that opened almost onto the street so that when he made his entrance he almost popped onto the stage. It made me realize what an incredibly brilliant concept José had of this lobby going on beyond and that his entrance came from the darkness somewhere out there. You heard his echoing footfalls before he actually came on stage. Seeing the reality of those doors indicating the street robbed this piece again, as the furniture on the stage had done, robbed it of its loneliness and its emptiness. The Gazzara piece was more realistic.

David Hays was very matter-of-fact about the absence of doors in the set he designed: "Nobody had to go out; I never figured out why you needed a door anyway. I didn't make a choice. I didn't have a door because there was no reason for a door. There was no door in that hotel we visited. You walked through miles of lobby before you came to the desk which was in the middle. You approached with your heels clicking. It had to do with sound, that set; I don't mean to make sound, but the way sound looks in an empty room."

The production played to sold-out previews before its December opening. *Hughie*, all 45 minutes of it, was perceived as a skimpy experience for a full-priced Broadway evening. John Chapman (1964c:52) complained that "it's a curtain-raiser. But a curtain-raiser to what?"

Critics welcomed the cage concept. Walter Kerr (1964b:9) commented:

> David Hays' setting is an extraordinarily right container for these words: endlessly horizontal, interrupted only by blocks of cement, a ghostly mausoleum in which all sounds echo, and echo, and echo . . . There are two cages on the stage at the Royale, just as there are two characters in Eugene O'Neill's *Hughie.* If it is difficult to get one man to come out of his cage, it is next to impossible to pack the other into his. The cage that restive Jason Robards won't get into is the ancient grilled elevator that is waiting to take him upstairs to his silent room.

Whitney Bolton (1964:2) described the same tension: "And the night clerk is enticed from his cage only to have Erie go into the lift cage." Howard Taubman (1964:21) wrote that "David Hays' design of the wide, deserted spaces of the lobby makes a virtue out of what is fundamentally a hazard for a play of modest dimensions—the uncommon width of the stage."

As was the case with Quintero's *Desire Under the Elms*, the nature of the set influenced the acting style. Henry Hewes (1965:40) wrote:

> Indeed, the moment the curtain goes up to reveal an enormous, pale green hotel lobby, one realizes that Jason Robards, who plays Erie, will either have to ignore the challenge and distraction of so much space or somehow try to fill it with action. He chooses the latter course and finds himself

extroverting the role, almost as if he were demon-
strating for the benefit of the audience whose presence he acknowledged. Thus it is that José Quintero
whose direction of *Long Day's Journey* and *The
Iceman Cometh* contributed masterful examples of
the right way to underplay O'Neill's dialogue here
permits too much stress, too much pushing of the
obvious, as if he didn't quite trust the play.

Walter Kerr (1964b:9) felt much the same impact and
observed:

> There is, from the outset, a singular sense of over-
> emphasis, as though all points were to be made at
> once and made at full impact lest we should miss
> them and go home empty-handed. Mr. Robards is
> not permitted to begin by assuming that he can
> make the new nightman into another Hughie.
> There is no first effort at intimacy, no try at an easy
> footing. The actor is, instead, hustled to the cen-
> ter of the vast and booming stage and urged to
> boom out all his complexities at once. He must be
> obviously an overblown sport, obviously a boaster,
> obviously insecure—and all at the same time. It is
> as though every one backstage had whispered "vir-
> tuoso performance" before the actor had as much
> as got his makeup on and the reach for a round-
> house effort starts instantly. To approach the small
> piece as though it were a twenty foot tower which
> would require a stunt man to scale it is to damage
> the casual sense of expanding discovery O'Neill
> surely had in mind and thus to rob it of its climax.
> As staged, it is virtually all climax, a rush of top
> notes together which means that it must sustain
> itself at a single level of intensity instead of arriv-
> ing, progressively, at half a dozen.

When asked if there had been any other choice for the set,
given the Royale Theater, David Hays answered, "Sure, I could
have put a conventional set, a little bit of a set, in there. I could
have done it in front of the curtain there. It was my choice to use
the space."

Robards has done the play in many different houses since 1964. When asked if a smaller house is more conducive to the play, Robards answered, "No, I don't think it should be done in a long boxcar of a theater like the Broadway, but I've played it to 300 seats at the Donnell Library over on West 53rd Street and 2,500 seats at the Zellerbach, where it was fabulous. I think it's a wonderful play and it doesn't matter where we play it."

The reviews reduced *Hughie* to a modest Broadway run. It was not helped by the totally anomalous 12-performance schedule. *Hughie* played Tuesday, Wednesday, Thursday, and Sunday evenings at 9:00 P.M., Friday and Saturday evenings at 7:30 and 10:00 P.M., Wednesday at 2:00 P.M., Saturday at 2:30 P.M., and Sunday at 2:30 and 5:00 P.M., not a schedule geared to the Broadway theatergoer.

After closing, the production toured to Los Angeles and San Francisco. Robards and Dodson subsequently reconstructed the production four times and even videotaped it for television. The videotape made interesting use of voice-over and dream sequence, but Dodson was explicit that "the decisions regarding the filming were not José's."

When the production was revived in 1976, Robards described Quintero's direction:

> José gets to the heart of the matter. He gets right down to what's on the page. He doesn't confuse things. He doesn't read things into it that aren't there. It's simple and it's direct. Over the years, we've built up our own sort of language. We barely have to say anything to each other, we just know what we both want or feel. I'll bet people would look into our rehearsals and think we're not even working when we're really going at it full-tilt.

Because of its chamber-play size, Quintero's production of *Hughie* has been revived many times in very different-sized theaters. It has proved to be Quintero's greatest ongoing success. Jack Dodson was involved in at least a half-dozen versions of the production over the years and concluded:

> In the original production, the character of Erie was a more tormented, anguished figure who had more in common with Jamie Tyrone than in later

productions we did. When we did it originally, Jason played the tragic elements of Erie's character to a greater degree than he did later in the revivals. It was a very anguished period in Jason's personal life. He had a lot of things going on about which he was anguished and tormented so that there was a good deal of his personal torment involved in the interpretation of the piece. When we came back to do it in 1976, Jason had had his accident, been through that torment, had given up drinking and was pretty much at peace with himself. His whole psyche and approach to the piece was less anguished, with more emphasis on the humorous side of the character, a little bit more of the bullshit artist than the anguished liar. I think it was infinitely better in the revival than when we did it originally because I don't think it was meant to be that heavy a piece, not to be dealt with as heavily as we did it originally. The resolution of the piece, if that's the right word, the coming-together, the upbeat note that the piece ends on worked much better in the revival.

7

More Stately Mansions

Writing

Begun mid-April 1938; first draft completed September 8, 1938; second draft completed January 1, 1939; third draft completed January 20, 1939.

Premieres

Original: Not produced in O'Neill's lifetime.

Quintero: October 31, 1967; New York, Broadhurst Theater.

The American Cycle

In January 1934, O'Neill returned to Sea Island, Georgia, exhausted after producing *Ah, Wilderness!* and *Days Without End* back to back. In the final months of 1934, he began working on *The Life of Bessie Bowen*, a contemporary play set against the background of the automobile industry. The play was part of a projected *God-Is-Dead* trilogy. According to Sheaffer:

> O'Neill had long been undecided whether to write the auto industry story as a separate work loosely related to the other "God plays" or as part of a larger series about a family with an acquisitive strain. At last deciding to accept the challenge . . .

O'Neill set the unfinished "Bessie Bowen" aside and
in the first days of 1935 began a project that would
give him all the scope to grow he could possibly
want, a multiplay cycle that would span a large
part of the American past as it dramatized high-
lights in the history of a "far from model" family.
Not only was its overall theme the same as that of
"Bessie Bowen"—the debasing effect on human
nature of greedy materialism—but the playwright
intended to incorporate "Bessie Bowen" itself in the
final panel of his panoramic work (1973:441).

The word "Cycle" first occurred in O'Neill's notebooks on
January 1, 1935. He conceived a trilogy, the first play of which
was to be set during the American Revolution, the second in 1840,
and the third, "Bessie Bowen," in a contemporary setting. When
the Cycle grew to five plays, O'Neill gave it the overall title, *The
Calms of Capricorn.* By February 1936, however, the title was
changed to *A Touch of the Poet* and, according to Floyd
(1981:220), "he saw that his central character, Sara Melody
Harford, would require more background, so he introduced her
parents and those of her husband Simon in two earlier plays, *A
Touch of the Poet* set in New England in 1828 and *More Stately
Mansions* set in New England in 1832–40. On April 10, 1936, *A
Touch of the Poet* became the title of a single play and the name
of the Cycle became 'A Legend of Possessors Self-Dispossessed.' "
Midway through 1936, O'Neill had to add two more plays,
tracing Sara's mother-in-law Deborah back in time. The cycle had
grown to nine plays. By June 1939, just after revising *A Touch
of the Poet,* instead of beginning *The Calms of Capricorn* as
planned, O'Neill began *The Iceman Cometh.* He had embarked
on the great, final burst of creative energy that produced *The Iceman Cometh, Long Day's Journey Into Night,* and *A Moon for
the Misbegotten,* but, without realizing it he had, in effect, shelved
his cycle.

A year later, on July 17, 1940, O'Neill wrote to Lawrence
Langner that "the Cycle is on the shelf, and God knows if I can
ever take it up again because I cannot foresee any future in this
country or anywhere else to which it could spiritually belong"
(Floyd, 1981:222). He continued to make notes for the Cycle and

in 1941 expanded it to 11 plays, but told no one for fear of ridicule. O'Neill did not conceive of his Cycle in a vacuum. His projections for staging it varied as it grew larger and more unwieldy.

In March 1935, Langner (1951:286) learned from O'Neill that "we were not to expect to receive the first of them until the last was completed because he would be making changes in them until the very last one was done." Then, on July 3, 1935, O'Neill wrote to Robert Fisk of the Theatre Guild, "How to produce? Nothing decided yet. The best scheme might be at the rate of two per season, keeping the past ones going, in some sort of repertoire arrangement. A strictly no-star company" (Bogard, 1972:376). Croswell Bowen (1959:250) quotes O'Neill as saying, early in 1937, that the plan is to withdraw the first play before the second starts, even if it is a success. It—the Cycle—will be noncommercial.

On February 13, 1938 (Bogard, 1972:383N), O'Neill wrote to Teresa Helburn (1960:269) and referred to the nature of the company he had in mind:

> I'd like to wait until all nine are completed. This last is the ideal, of course. Then we could engage a repertory company for the whole cycle—show the actors and actresses we have parts that would make it worthwhile, out of pure self-interest, to tie up for several seasons under our conditions. No stars, of course, but show the young and ambitious their chance to become stars through this cycle . . . I'm very obdurate on this point. In fact, to be blunt, I won't allow it to be done any other way.

In 1941, however, when O'Neill saw Ingrid Bergman play *Anna Christie* on the West Coast, he asked her to join the company.

When Langner (1951:400) went to visit O'Neill on the West Coast, in May 1941, they:

> discussed many ideas for producing the cycle away from Broadway. One of these plans was to develop an O'Neill acting company in San Francisco and to produce the plays there, so that 'Gene would be able to attend rehearsals from his house at Tao House. At first, 'Gene seemed quite hospitable to this idea, but when I discussed it with him later

on, he remarked that he had come to California in order to get away from the theatre, and that it would not be a wise plan to bring it to his doorstep again.

The chronology of O'Neill's cycle, its hydra-headed escalation, its pendulum swings from commercial to noncommercial, East Coast to West Coast, unknowns to stars, makes depressing reading. Four-and-a-half years work produced only one complete play, *A Touch of the Poet*. There is no evidence that O'Neill ever acknowledged that he had lost contact with the theater of his time, merely that he lacked the strength to complete his Cycle.

On February 21, 1944, O'Neill burned two holographs of *More Stately Mansions*, but preserved the typescript, adding a page labeled "Unfinished Work. This script to be destroyed in case of my death: Eugene O'Neill" (Sheaffer, 1973:480).

In May 1956, Carlotta phoned Donald Gallup, curator of the O'Neill collection at Yale, and learned for the first time that the *Mansions* typescript had survived. At her request, Gallup sent the typescript to her. In spring 1957, Carlotta permitted Karl Ragnar Gierow to take the typescript to Sweden, photograph it, and prepare an acting text from it. He returned the typescript to Carlotta, who then returned it to Yale.

Gierow's shortened version had its world premiere in Stockholm on November 9, 1962. The present Yale edition of the play is the text of the Swedish production and represents "less than half of O'Neill's complete typed script" (O'Neill, 1964:x).

Because O'Neill did not settle on a final number of plays in his projected cycle, *More Stately Mansions* cannot be assigned a numerical position in the series. It does, however, follow immediately after *A Touch of the Poet*, which takes place on July 27, 1828. *More Stately Mansions* begins in 1832 and runs until 1840.

1967 Production

Cast List

Simon Harford	Arthur Hill
Sara Harford	Colleen Dewhurst
Deborah Harford	Ingrid Bergman
Joel Harford	Laurence Linville
Nicholas Gadsby	Fred Stewart

Benjamin Tenard	Kermit Murdock
Jamie Cregan	Barry Macollum
Mickey Maloy	Vincent Dowling
Nora Melody	Helen Craig
Cato	John Marriott

According to Cecil Smith (1967a:25), José Quintero first approached Elliot Martin with the *More Stately Mansions* project in Los Angeles in October 1966. Elliot Martin recalled that "I had been discussing several projects with José and he told me that he was in partnership with an agent at that time and that they were going to acquire the rights to do *More Stately Mansions*. Was I interested? I then acquired the basic rights from this agent. When José and I first began discussing the project, I was not the head of the Music Center in Los Angeles. When I got that job, I mentioned that I'd been working on this project with Quintero for Ingrid Bergman and they flipped out. They thought that would be a wonderful project to open in Los Angeles."

Barbara Gelb (1967:II, 22) wrote that "Mr. Quintero spent a year preparing a text." Elliot Martin said of the acting version:

> We then took the entire script, which was about an inch and a half thick, from Yale, and worked on the script for a month in Los Angeles. José, his partner and I edited and cut the script. So we ended up with what we called a José Quintero version. He did not work on it for a year, we had to do a crash program on this for a month in the summertime before we went into rehearsal. We ended up with three different versions of it; the first version was too big, the second version was also a little too big, and the third version was the right thickness, so to speak.

Martin was very specific that the acting version they prepared (less than half the actual text) was derived entirely from the Yale typescript and owed nothing to the Swedish acting version prepared for the world premiere.

Quintero wanted David Hays to design the set, but the lighting design had already been promised to John Harvey, a close friend of Quintero's then agent/partner. Hays refused to design just the set and stuck to his guns. Quintero then approached Ben

Edwards. The two had not worked together previously, although Quintero had wanted Edwards to design the set for the 1958 *Great Day in the Morning*.

Edwards said: "I saw a lot of José's productions, both at the old Circle-in-the-Square and at Bleecker Street. I know he likes a certain sort of freedom of movement. He talked about that. He likes to walk out of walls, he likes to have complete freedom of movement in terms of his actors."

When asked if Quintero used a lot of imagery in describing the effects he wanted, Edwards answered:

> No, very little, although he does use religious imagery. He talks the way I really like directors to talk. He talks about the play, he talks about movement, how he likes to direct. That's the trouble with a lot of directors; they don't do that. Only good directors do that. If you work with Kazan or Harold Clurman or José, you spend weeks and weeks of doing nothing but talking about a play, talking about what it's about. And from that it gives you the full guide or feeling of what you want to do with the set; otherwise you're just out on a limb, on your own, which is not my idea of working in the theatre. I feel that the director is the thing. Some of them talk about it in different ways, different ways of approaching the same thing, but you still talk about it.

The script called for nine scenes with six different sets. The same locale was never used consecutively; consequently, the scene changes were a paramount concern. Cecil Smith (1967a:25) wrote that Edwards' set design "included a broad forestage with steps and levels that move down, as Miss Bergman said, 'into the laps of the audience.' The design incorporates scene changes while actors are performing to give a constant flow to the drama from scene to scene." Edwards was pleased with this description of his design and commented, "That's fine. José and I talked about the downstage areas, where anyone could move down onto the apron and we had steps down onto the apron. José wanted a very flowing production whereby his actors who were downstage could still be talking and suddenly, boom, we move right into the next set, which is pretty much what we did."

Henry Hewes (1967:96) described the scene changes as "an interesting method of melting from one scene into the next by lowering a black gauze curtain that allows the actors to end scenes on a forestage while the setting is being changed."

Production stage manager William Weaver denied that the sets changed during the scene: "The scene ended, the black came down and a work light went on. There was always a wait between scenes, but the changes were made very quickly. There were a great many drops. In the office scene, the upstage wall was all cabinets and a bookcase which was flown. The garden scene had a fountain which came in on a wagon and the gazebo was brought in on a cable. Set pieces like the big desk and chairs were placed by the prop men."

Ben Edwards insisted that the sets *did* change during the scene: "Yes, they did change while the actors were on the forestage; otherwise there wouldn't have been much point in that set. Henry Hewes is right; it wasn't that much, it wasn't overdone and there may have been several times when it didn't happen at all."

When asked what were the implications of Quintero's desire for free stage movement, Edwards answered:

> We had some doors, but nothing in the set prevented anyone from walking right down to the footlights and moving around or sitting on the spaces, little constructions which had nothing to do with being inside a room, yet the room was there. He was never bound by walls, except a door or a window. He was never tied in. It says in the script, and you need it, that Deborah disappears in the garden house. Other than that, there's nothing there except space to walk and act. Ingrid came and sat down on the apron all the time.

Cecil Smith (1967b:15) wrote that the style of the sets shifted "between stark realism and almost misty abstraction, to define the opposing elements." Edwards acknowledged that "the office was the most realistic of all the sets. It was the most realistic scene; money, business, and sex. The mother's garden is another thing entirely. She has enclosed herself in that garden. It was her protection." He denied, however, that there was a production concept in which the hardness of the Irish-American mercantile world was to be opposed to the New England Brahmin gentility, but

added, "I'm not sure that you go through all that completely while
you're doing it, except it's always in the back of your head, it's
there."

In the acting version that Quintero had devised, the first scene
takes place in the Melody tavern at Con Melody's wake (the scene
is not included in the Yale edition). Edwards had designed the
1958 American premiere of A Touch of the Poet, a play which
takes place entirely in the Melody tavern. Edwards wished to
return to the set he had earlier designed for the tavern:

> I did a version of that set because I felt a certain
> continuity was in order. A lot of people had seen
> that play and, of course, this play was a sequel.
> José had seen A Touch of the Poet. I couldn't do
> the full set because Poet had been a full set, whereas
> Mansions was made up of fragmentary sets. It
> wasn't the same although it had the same windows
> and a piece of the back wall. I certainly discussed
> it with José because the characters are the same in
> both plays and, having worked so long on A Touch
> of the Poet, there was no way for me not to have
> discussed it.

When asked if he had taken advantage of the five O'Neill
sketches and plans published in the Yale edition of the play,
Edwards responded that "they were available, but I didn't pay
much attention to them. I looked very carefully, but at the time
I sort of thought that I knew what he was getting at. He had obviously gone to some effort to check on Thoreau's cabin, which was
10 by 15 and certainly came right out of Walden [Yale edition,
facing page 1]. I didn't use any of that, but I don't think O'Neill
meant anyone to use any of these. I think he did these for himself, thinking about the play."

Edwards said of O'Neill's sketch for the sitting room of Sara
Harford's home [Yale edition, page 42], "It's fascinating when you
look at it because it's so untheatrical in terms of work. If you put
a sofa in that corner and a table down there, the audience would
see none of the sofa. Even with a raked stage, you'd need an alpen-
stock to get up there." Of O'Neill's sketch of the Harford mansion [Yale edition, page 116]: "O'Neill couldn't possibly have
wanted his set to look like that. The set is only one living room.

I think he wanted to show what impressed him about the Bull-finch/McIntire architecture in New England, which he mentions in the stage directions. He is describing a room of the period and a designer has to use that as a basis, but you don't have to follow that. Like any playwright, he described all these things, but I think he meant them as a guide."

Normally Ben Edwards does sets and lights, but in this instance he was willing to do what David Hays was not. He designed the sets alone and John Harvey designed the lights, which, according to Cecil Smith (1967:25) were immensely complex; Elliot Martin calls it "ballet lighting." There were two follow spots. When asked if they were both focused on Ingrid Bergman, William Weaver responded, "No, there was a spotlight for Bergman and Dewhurst. When all three stars were on stage, it was a little tricky."

Bergman played Deborah, but Quintero (1974:279) writes that his first choice was Vivien Leigh, whom he had directed in the film *The Roman Spring of Mrs. Stone*. After reading the play, Miss Leigh told him, "I don't have the genius to play Deborah. As a matter of fact, I don't really think I would like to play again." She died six months later.

Actress Jackie Brookes, who stood by for both Deborah and Sara, said of the roles of Deborah and Simon that "the crucial thing is the business of moving into madness and the characters who have this shaky relationship with reality; maybe not so shaky, but actually stepping in and out of sanity. Interestingly enough, José told me that he offered the part to Vivien Leigh, who said (this is the gist of it), 'I can't play this, it's too close to me.' So she really knew what was going on in the story. And I always wondered, if she had played it, if she would have lengthened her life. She suggested Ingrid."

Elliot Martin denied that the role had ever been offered to Vivien Leigh: "Vivien Leigh, to my knowledge, well . . . we may have said wouldn't it be wonderful if Vivien Leigh could do it, but I don't think she was physically right at that time to do anything. José was very keen for Jessica Tandy, as was I, but we'd sent the script to her and we hadn't heard back from her."

Cecil Smith (1967a:25) quoted both Elliot Martin and Quintero on the casting of Ingrid Bergman:

Elliot Martin said, "I have always believed in one, great inviolate truth in theatre—the chemistry of casting. Here was an immensely important work of theatre, but to make it happen it had to be cast exactly right. The key role was Deborah. We made up an idealized list of actresses who could play Deborah. The first name on that list was Ingrid Bergman." Quintero said, "It was like you made up a list for Santa Claus, the things you would like to have, even the impossible things. Bergman was the impossible." Neither Martin nor Quintero knew that the contact had been made a quarter-century ago when the dark, death-ridden playwright had talked of massive unrealized dreams on the stage to a vibrant young actress who never forgot.

The contact of which Smith spoke took place in 1941 when O'Neill saw Bergman play *Anna Christie* on the West Coast and arranged to meet her. He offered her a place in the company he was projecting for his American Cycle. O'Neill said, according to Bergman, "I want a company that stays with me. After all, it is the same family that goes through many generations, and I want the same faces. In one play you will have a big part and in another you will have a small part. You will play a sister, an aunt, a young daughter . . . I want this company to stay together for four years. In four years we will have produced them all" (Floyd, 1979:294–95).

Quintero (1974:291) went to France to offer the role to Bergman and, according to him, she responded, " 'Of course I am going back to America to play Deborah. I have a commitment to Eugene O'Neill.' "

Elliot Martin concluded, "I sent the script to Kay Brown for Ingrid Bergman and Kay read it and called me up the next day and said, 'Look, I know Ingrid's going to love this and she's available. I'll send it right over.' She sent it to Paris and Ingrid read it and said that she was interested in doing it and could José and I fly over, which is what we did. We flew to Paris and discussed the entire play with her and that was it." Bergman signed a contract that committed her for six months, three months in Los Angeles and three months on Broadway.

More Stately Mansions, 1967. L to r: Ingrid Bergman, Arthur Hill, Colleen
Dewhurst. Photo by Tony Esparzo.

Jackie Brookes said of that casting coup that "once the magic name was mentioned everyone jumped at it, but no one stopped to consider if Ingrid Bergman had a tenuous hold on reality, if indeed she knew anything about that experience. Was she willing or able to deal with that? That is a very risky thing for an actor. Both Ingrid Bergman and Arthur Hill are very sane people."

Quintero then cast Colleen Dewhurst as Sara and Arthur Hill as Simon. He auditioned the other actors.

More Stately Mansions was the first drama to be produced at the 2,000-seat Ahmanson Theater in Los Angeles. Stage manager William Weaver recalled that "there was no place to rehearse at the theater. José Ferrer was doing *Man of La Mancha*. We rehearsed in various places in Hollywood. One of the places was a television station, we used a room there, then in some sort of Masonic place and then we went into the Ahmanson for a long series of previews before we opened."

Los Angeles *Times* critic Cecil Smith (1967b:16–17) was present at the first read-through, held at the Ahmanson Theater:

> Director José Quintero, apart from his cast, told me: "This is the most nervous time. Not the opening, not the first performance or the dress. The most nervous, the most frightening is the first rehearsal, the read-through. This is the moment when you know what you have. After that, it is how well you fulfill it. This," he said, "is when it is born." He glanced around at the actors. "They meet like strangers," he said. "Even those who know each other meet like strangers. It's this moment you think you've forgotten everything you know."
>
> To his cast Quintero said, "Most of us are strangers, and that is not the way I would like it but that is the way it usually is in the theatre. We have no time for worrying about does she like me, do I like him, why doesn't she like me, that's nonsense. And we are not in a constant audition for one another. The play is in four acts. I hope for two, but we'll see. What this play means we'll find out as we wrestle with it, bit by bit."

The actors worked from a mimeographed script. Colleen Dewhurst said, "I think we worked out a text as we went along."

Jackie Brookes said that "it wasn't wieldy from the beginning and cutting didn't exactly help it: It made it shorter but not any clearer or more dramatic."

William Weaver recalled the rehearsal period:

> We went more than five hours a day. We began in the morning, had lunch, and then worked quite a few hours in the afternoon, though we would sometimes break early. José did not specifically link *A Touch of the Poet* with *More Stately Mansions*. We knew of the connection. He didn't discuss the period, he didn't intellectualize. José did an awful lot of this play on private levels with the actors, and I was never aware of what he was telling them. He did many things secretly. Sometimes he would bar all of us from the theater after lunch. He would have the full crew called, full sets, props, everything; then he would come back from lunch and spend the entire afternoon with Ingrid and none of us was allowed in the wings or anywhere near. It was very odd. God knows what he and Ingrid talked about for hours alone on that great stage in that great theater. That would have been interesting.

Jackie Brookes said of the relationship that sprang up between Quintero and Bergman:

> My vivid memory is of him talking to Ingrid and talking into the part in a certain way and really experiencing what Deborah was; a very one-to-one feeling of what was happening, not necessarily man or woman, but the experience of madness. José knew a great deal more about this from an organic point of view than either Ingrid or Arthur, in terms of willingness to face it. Maybe because he wasn't going to act it he could do it, and yet it was clear that he knew, in the deepest sense, what this character was going through.
>
> When Ingrid listened to him (she adored him, she would have dived out the window for him) she would do what he asked her, but then she would go into the run-through and be unable to do it. It

would infuriate me that she would do it and then not do it. But then I realized that she couldn't do it. She could do it when she was being stimulated by José, but, finally, she couldn't make it her own. It was too much a part of her life to simply deal with the here and now. She couldn't do it without José's continual prompting. It was only as he coaxed it out of her that she could grasp it, but it never became hers, it was his. José was drawing on his own experiences and on that of Carlotta; he did experience that with her. Ingrid worked on that part through the entire run and she grew in the part. You can play any part that your imagination can grasp, but it has to grasp it. With Ingrid, I don't think she could *allow* her imagination to grasp it.

Cecil Smith (1967a:23–25) described Quintero's direction of Bergman thus:

During rehearsal, Quintero was never still. He roamed the theater, stopping to drop into a seat to watch for a second, then up again, darting between rows, pacing, listening. He would stop and wave those long, spider-thin arms at the actors. He would rush to the stage to show Bergman how to play a scene, the slumped body on the stairs, the gesture of despair. He would straighten her spine—"like this," he said.

She sat at the edge of the forestage, a tragic figure as Deborah speaking of her dead husband. "It appears I've spent my life with a stranger," and Quintero cried, "No, no. With a smile, a laugh. It is the biggest joke in the world."

"There is no regret?" she asked.

"No, it is a joke: Who knows what life would have been like? Now it is too late."

Arthur Hill received considerably less attention. William Weaver said, "I know that Arthur Hill didn't get much help from José. Arthur would come to me and ask, 'What am I going to do?' He finally just did his own thing." Jackie Brookes agreed: "I guess José just felt that Arthur would work." When asked if Quintero had simply been more interested in the women, William Weaver answered, "Yes, I think he was, particularly Ingrid. And Colleen and he were old buddies. His direction to her is all grunts." Jackie Brookes said that "with Colleen, it was simply her part. Ingrid and Colleen got along beautifully. The exchange of identity worked beautifully."

Both William Weaver and Jackie Brookes independently compared Quintero's direction to that of Guthrie McClintic. Weaver said that "José never gave line readings. He did act it out, but without the words. He was in and out of the space at rehearsals. He would do a Guthrie McClintic, from the auditorium seat up onto the stage." Brookes said that "José would kind of illustrate it, but not in the way that directors do that insults you, who do your part or parody it. He directed like Guthrie McClintic, being able to inspire you, to talk to you and inspire you, just whisper something in your ear. God knows Ingrid was in love with him."

The production opened on September 13, 1967. The publicity engendered by Ingrid Bergman's return to Hollywood made the opening a social affair of the first magnitude, dwarfing any real theatrical criticism. The review of Cecil Smith (1967b:15) in the Los Angeles *Times* merely repeated the production information from his earlier article. The production sold out for its six-week run in Los Angeles.

On the Sunday before the New York opening, the *New York Times* carried the traditional Barbara Gelb (1967:II, 22) article, which examined the play's history and previewed Quintero's method of production. The salient paragraph read as follows: "Mr. Quintero spent a year preparing a text. He is convinced that the play he has distilled from O'Neill's manuscript is essentially what O'Neill himself would have arrived at. (He says he has cut and rearranged the play, but the words are O'Neill's own.)"

The two areas in which Quintero had expended most of his energies, the adaptation of the text and the casting and direction of Bergman, proved to be the very grounds on which the critics pilloried the production.

The critics thought that Quintero had robbed O'Neill's grave and were not reluctant to say it. Edith Oliver (1967:127) wrote that "although Mr. Quintero claims that every word in it is by Mr. O'Neill, its present form may bear no relation whatsoever to the play that O'Neill might have completed. Doing it at all is a dirty trick on a dead man, and a piece of impudence."

John Chapman (1967:53) wrote that "as a sentimentalist, I think *More Stately Mansions* should have been erased—utterly and finally destroyed—as its author so definitely wanted it to be. This morose dramatist should have been allowed to take it with him."

Clive Barnes (1967:40), normally agreeable to almost any O'Neill project, wrote that "what we have here is José Quintero's adaptation and completion of a play by O'Neill that O'Neill in all sincerity destroyed. O'Neill was right . . . With friends like Mr. Quintero, the shade of O'Neill might think he needs no enemies."

Whitney Bolton (1967:3) called himself "a passionate admirer of Mister O'Neill since 1924, one who went with him in triumph as well as error. I have to say as a critic that I wish fervently this play had never been put before an audience . . . Never having seen Mister O'Neill's script, I certainly do not know where he left off and Mr. Quintero took on. I only hope that it was audacious of any one to write for and in the name of Eugene O'Neill."

In a long, thoughtful Sunday leader, Walter Kerr (1967:II, 1–5) agreed that the play was unfinished:

> The play is born a ruin: a great architectural emptiness derived from slaved-over blueprints, an eyeless, topless tower that cannot escape the earth in which it is so deeply embedded. The draughtmanship is finished. The earth has been dug. No one will ever live there . . . O'Neill had never completed the necessary business of relating dimensional people to the implied dimensions of his panoramic scheme.

Kerr concluded, however, with less rancor than his peers: "Should it, then, have been produced? I think so. Not all copies of the manuscript were destroyed. Now they never will be. Because the work exists and because it was a project for the stage, our information about it can only be increased by seeing it on the stage."

Not one critic would concede that Ingrid Bergman was cast for any reason other than her film stardom. Edith Oliver (1967:127) wrote that "Miss Bergman, dressed always in white, looks lovely and frequently as young as Miss Dewhurst which may account for some of the confusion in poor Simon's cleft brain. But she spends most of her time upstage of everyone else and no matter where she stands or sits, she is bathed in glowing, flattering light—a state of affairs that renders it impossible to accept her as anything but a star making a personal appearance."

Henry Hewes (1967:96) wrote that "the casting of Ingrid Bergman in the leading role of Deborah is another mistake for Miss Bergman appears incapable of seeming anything but a lovely, healthy girl, with no pretensions and no anxieties . . . The play's drastically shortened final scene, which would tax the powers of a more appropriately cast actress, completely frustrates Miss Bergman as she nominally goes through the motions."

Whitney Bolton (1967:3) wrote that "Miss Bergman looks beautiful, often is moving and looks about as much like a grandmother as does the eldest candidate in any given Miss America contest in Atlantic City."

Martin Gottfried (1967:56) dwelt on the difference between the aesthetics of Colleen Dewhurst and that of Ingrid Bergman:

> Ingrid Bergman and Colleen Dewhurst play the two ladies and they present as fine an example as I can remember of the difference between acting and performing. Miss Dewhurst, as the wife, is entirely brilliant, moving between unsureness of her husband to an assumption of her female powers; from a fear of the mother's strength to a delight in the competition. Miss Bergman does not act for a moment and unlike Miss Dewhurst you never forget who she is. It is Bergman and you know it. But Bergman is a magnificent "star"—that physical look and in personal grandeur, she is altogether magnificent. Even thrilling. The acting is old-style, heaven knows: a hand to the waist, a knuckle to the mouth and all the tired business. But she does it with such a golden presence that you are sometimes forced to notice only her.

Gerald Weales (1967:35) wrote of the staging that "Quintero has heightened the nineteenth-century feel of the play by placing the characters in formal patterns on the stage, not simply the thematic formality of the man between his two women but confrontation scenes that look as though they might be frozen for the kind of tableau once used as visual tag at the end of acts." William Weaver said that this was nonsense: "I think that's some critic's idea. I don't think José ever intended anything like that. His direction was real, it was not stylized."

Dissatisfaction with Quintero's staging was attributed to the incomplete script. Alan N. Bunce (1967:6) wrote that "too often the characters seem to be working their way painfully, haplessly, through empty scenes toward some important dramatic goal." Walter Kerr (1967:II, 1–5) concluded:

> Blame must be passed on to director José Quintero who has really helped no one. Having made his own cutting of the text and having asked designer Ben Edwards for the gloomy reaches and void-like portals of the settings, Mr. Quintero seems determined to reinforce what is already wrong—instead of making the day-by-day life of reading newspapers, baiting bankers and doing the evening sewing genuinely intricate, plausible, concrete in its detail, he has urged everyone toward overinflated melodrama, arranging them again and again like so many self-important statues in the moonlight.

In an interview with Barbara Gelb (1977:136), Quintero said of the *More Stately Mansions* production, "I wasn't as protective of O'Neill as I should have been." Gelb added, "But the drinking was getting worse and he needed the money." At a time when his concentration was limited, Quintero took on the problematic task of rewriting O'Neill. It was more desperation than hubris. He then became infatuated with only one element of the production, directing Ingrid Bergman, and trusted that Colleen Dewhurst would prevail as Sara (which she did) and that Arthur Hill could flesh out the underwritten Simon on his own (which he could not).

Part Four

BROADWAY POWER

The brutal reviews Quintero received for *More Stately Mansions*, a solid wall of rejection, accelerated his already well-advanced drinking problem. The financial success of *Mansions* (credit Ingrid Bergman) enabled Quintero to direct Tennessee Williams' *The Seven Descents of Myrtle* in 1968. Quintero was unable to cut the script or to deal with the intrusions of producer David Merrick. He quit and then rejoined the production, which failed on Broadway.

By the late '60s and early '70s, Quintero, drunk in the early afternoon, was a familiar midtown spectacle. In 1970, he directed a one-night disaster, *Ghandi*, off-Broadway, and in 1971 another one-night disaster, *Johnny Johnson*, on Broadway. Quintero had bottomed out. He sought professional help with his drinking and by spring 1973 was on the wagon.

Quintero, Dewhurst, and Robards barely scraped together a summer-stock production of *A Moon for the Misbegotten*. Not since 1956 had the pieces so fallen into place. The critical and financial success gained by *Moon* provided Quintero with the clout to work on Broadway for the rest of the decade.

Quintero attempted to turn the success of *Moon* into a film career. He spent a year preparing a screenplay entitled "The Wedding." Production was announced, with Robards starring and Quintero directing, but it was never filmed. Quintero went on to direct a production of *The Skin of Our Teeth*, which played for a month on Broadway in 1976. In the same year, he directed Liv Ullmann in *A Moon for the Misbegotten* in Norway, an association that triggered a new collaboration in the 1977 production of *Anna Christie*.

In 1979, Quintero finally had his anomalous Broadway production, a play *not* written by O'Neill, Williams, or Wilder: the American premiere of Brian Friel's *The Faith Healer*, an experimental, poetic play dramatized in four successive monologues. This was presumably the kind of play Quintero would have been staging in his own theater, if he still had one. On Broadway it proved to be a *succes d'estime*, but, even with James Mason starring, it was a quick commercial failure.

In 1980, Quintero staged *Clothes for a Summer Hotel*, the final Broadway premiere of a Tennessee Williams play, starring Geraldine Page. Touted as a reunion of the three talents from the 1952 *Summer and Smoke*, it proved to be a melancholy reunion.

Summer and Smoke had been a finished script. Quintero had as difficult a time cutting the unwieldy *Clothes for a Summer Hotel* as he had had with *Seven Descents of Myrtle* a dozen years before. In casting Page, Quintero had hoped to go back to the well of 1952. He was quickly disabused of that notion. It was a stormy rehearsal period and, although Quintero's personal notices were positive, the play died quickly.

In summer 1981, Quintero was offered a 10-week residence to teach film direction to graduate students at Columbia University. He was also offered the opportunity to direct a play of his own choosing. He chose O'Neill's *Welded*.

He moved to Los Angeles the following year (like O'Neill, he prefers a warm climate). Quintero told David Richards why he had forsaken New York City for Los Angeles:

> With Tennessee going, O'Neill not being done commercially as often as he should, with the Broadway theater restricting itself to the one-set, four-character play, I began to feel surrounded by shadows and a sense of death. Walk down 45th Street these days. It is like one big morgue—places that were once so alive! If you have any love for life at all, you're going to flee. But I think what finally sent me to California was the demolition of the Helen Hayes and Morosco theaters. That made a profound impression on me. This is perhaps childish, but theater is so fleeting, I liked to think that the great things that happened in those buildings would be retained there forever in the walls. Then when I saw that iron ball hit into them, well, it was like I had been hit in the belly myself. I somersaulted in the air and landed in California (1985:K10).

Using Los Angeles as a base, Quintero launched into a series of projects. He initiated the Chaplin-O'Neill Theatre to develop projects in workshop, but soon aborted the project. In fall 1983, he returned to the East Coast and joined the Brandeis University faculty as coordinator of a new graduate program in directing and as artistic director of the Spingold Theater. There he directed a production of *The Time of Your Life*, casting it with a combination of professionals and students, which led him to repeat many of his *Welded* mistakes. In winter of 1984, he barely scraped through the American premiere of *Rainsnakes* at the Long Wharf Theater's Second Stage in Connecticut.

8

A Moon for the Misbegotten

Writing
 Begun late October 1941; first draft completed early 1942; final version completed mid-May 1943.
Premieres
 Original: February 20, 1947; Columbus, Ohio.
 Quintero: December 29, 1973; New York, Morosco Theater.

1947 Production

Cast List

Phil Hogan	James M. Kerrigan
Josie Hogan	Mary Welch
James Tyrone Jr.	James Dunn
Mike Hogan	J. Joseph Donnelly
T. Steadman Harder	Lex Lindsay

On October 28, 1941, O'Neill wrote in his workbook, "Shaughnessy play idea, based on story told by Edmund in 1st act of *Long Day's Journey Into Night*—except here Jamie principal character and story of play otherwise entirely imaginary, except for Jamie's revelation of self" (Floyd, 1981:361). Sheaffer writes (1973:528) that "Apparently Eugene had come to view *Long Day's Journey* as too severe on Jamie and an incomplete family portrait because it did not adequately convey Jamie's deep feeling for his mother, the only woman he ever loved, the 'Cynara' to whom he had been faithful in his dissipated fashion. *The Misbegotten* was designed, in other words, as a kind of fifth act to the four-act-long *Long Day's Journey*." It was to be the final play O'Neill completed.

Phil Hogan (as Shaughnessy was renamed) was modeled closely on pig farmer John "Dirty" Dolan, a one-time tenant of O'Neill's father. O'Neill based Josie an Christine Ell, a sometime lover of his in 1919. There are no photographs of this remarkable woman, but the Gelbs (1960:362–64) are lavish in their description of her:

> Like Josie Hogan, Christine Ell was a large woman, five feet nine inches tall, wide-hipped and big-breasted . . . She was self-conscious of her bulk and made fun of herself. Also like Josie, she was convinced that she was basically unattractive to men . . . The pathos of her personality was always close to the surface . . . She personified what O'Neill once called "a female Christ." Although he was as much amused by her wit and her escapades as anyone, O'Neill was acutely aware of her inner agony. Several of her lovers have recalled the strangely virginal quality that belied the affected coarseness of her manner. There was a paradoxical delicacy of spirit concealed in her hulking body, of which she was both proud and ashamed.

O'Neill initially referred to the play as "the Dolan play," Dolan's being the pig farmer on whom Phil Hogan was based. The play then became *The Man of Other Days* as long as it focused on Jamie. As Josie's character developed in O'Neill's mind, he changed the title to *The Moon Bore Twins* and finally to *A Moon for the Misbegotten*. O'Neill forced himself to work on the play from late October through the depressing days of Pearl Harbor. He finally finished a disappointing first draft, but the escalating tremor in his hands provided him with many days in which he could not write so that he did not complete the play until the following year.

In early summer 1944, the Langners visited the O'Neills in San Francisco and O'Neill gave them *A Moon for the Misbegotten* to read. On the following day, O'Neill and Langner reached a verbal agreement for the Theatre Guild to produce *Moon*. (They also agreed that, after the war, O'Neill's plays would be produced by the Theatre Guild in the following order: *A Moon for the Misbegotten*, *The Iceman Cometh*, and *A Touch of the Poet*.) Langner and O'Neill agreed on Robert Edmond Jones to design *Moon*. They decided to approach Barry Fitzgerald for the role of Phil Hogan, but he had radio commitments and James Dunn, whom they wanted for Jamie, had film commitments. Langner (1951:403) saw immediately the difficulty of casting Josie: "In addition to the physical requirements of the actress, she must be tremendously experienced in the theatre and must have exactly the kind of emotional acting experience that it would be difficult for a girl of her stature to obtain. I made a mental note of all the very big girls I knew—emphasizing the Irish quality which was needed." Trips to Hollywood, New York, London, and Dublin failed to produce a Josie Hogan. *Moon* proved so difficult to cast that, contrary to schedule, *The Iceman Cometh* was produced first. Eventually, James Dunn was cast as Jamie, James M. Kerrigan as Phil Hogan, and an unknown New York actress named Mary Welch was cast as Josie.

Mary Welch (1957:68) was initially told by the casting official that she was too normal for the role, 50 pounds shy of the size they wanted, that "Josie is the lead and only woman in Mr. O'Neill's play. She is a great mother-earth symbol and the actress who plays her should have a range from farce to Greek tragedy." Miss Welch persisted, however, and was granted an interview with O'Neill, whose first concern was not her size, but her Irish ancestry. The New England setting, notwithstanding, O'Neill wanted his cast to be as Irish as possible. When O'Neill responded favorably to Mary Welch, he was told by the Guild that she was too normal.

The Gelbs (1960:850) speculate that "while O'Neill created Josie as though she were a character in a novel and he knew that it would be impossible to reproduce her on a stage with physical accuracy, he felt that his description would at least make potential producers think twice before deciding to cast a typical ingenue in the role." Indeed, O'Neill dismissed the physical demands he had written into the play and insisted that "she can gain some more weight, but the important thing is that Miss Welch understands how Josie feels. Those other girls, who are closer physically to Josie, somehow don't know how tortured she is, or can't project it. The inner state of Josie is what I want. We'll work the other problems out in clothes and sets. I think the emotional quality is just right" (Welch, 1957:82). Welch continued to audition and to eat heavily and was finally awarded the role provided she gain the specified weight.

The production was still without a director. O'Neill had insisted on an Irish director, but all those under consideration were committed to Hollywood contracts. (Fortunately, O'Neill knew better than to direct his own play. When Barrett Clark [1947:162] asked him why he didn't direct *Moon* himself, O'Neill responded, "The trouble is I can tell the actors what to do, but they won't do it.") At the eleventh hour, Arthur Shields arrived from Hollywood. A veteran of the Abbey Theatre, where he had played with his famous brother Barry Fitzgerald, Shields was handed a *fait accompli*, a cast he himself had not chosen.

Arthur Shields reported of his prerehearsal meetings with O'Neill that the play "should have a minimum of action, and Mr. O'Neill agreed with me. The hardest thing in the theatre is to get actors *not* to do something. Langner, the players, everybody wanted to break it up, to do something, especially during Tyrone's long speeches in the third act" (Sheaffer, 1973:594).

The combination of personalities was compromised all the way down the line. Mary Welch was totally committed to the play, while Dunn and Kerrigan had great reservations about the play's subject matter and language. The first read-through was so disarming to O'Neill that he uncharacteristically agreed when Langner suggested that the production needed a pre-Broadway tour.

As rehearsals progressed, the Theatre Guild was concerned about Mary Welch while O'Neill was concerned about James Dunn, whom he had cast on the basis of seeing him in the film *A Tree Grows in Brooklyn*. The Gelbs (1960:882) quote Lawrence Langner:

> During rehearsals O'Neill kept complaining that Dunn wasn't playing the role with enough gentlemanliness; he kept telling me that his brother was a gentleman. I told him that his brother may have been a gentleman, but the way he'd written James

Tyrone, that quality didn't exactly come across, and
that Dunn was playing the role as written. O'Neill
couldn't accept this. I felt that he idealized his
brother and would not be able to accept any actor
in the part.

According to Mary Welch (1957:83), O'Neill was ill during
the three weeks of rehearsals and was able to attend only three
rehearsals: "His first major note was that we were playing the
tragedy of the work too early. 'A *Moon for the Misbegotten* is
almost farcical in places in the first act, though it becomes almost
Greek in its tragic structure in the fourth and final one.' " When
asked what the 1947 production was like, Armina Marshall
Langner replied that "it was a good workman-like production,
but it didn't have fire. It was mild because she was a mild actress."

The production opened in Columbus, Ohio, on February 20,
1947, to uneven notices, although the Boston *Post*'s Eliot Norton
made the trip west and was deeply moved by it. The production
traveled to several midwestern cities, ran into censorship problems in Detroit, and closed in St. Louis. The Theatre Guild
intended to remount the play with a different cast, but O'Neill
would not permit the play to be staged again. In 1951, heavy med-
ical expenses caused O'Neill to authorize Random House to publish *A Moon for the Misbegotten*, but the edition sold dismally and
by 1952 "O'Neill himself had come to 'loathe' the play" (Sheaffer,
1973:660).

A Moon for the Misbegotten did not reach New York City
until May 2, 1957, at the Bijou Theater on West 45th Street, in
a production directed by Carmen Capalbo with a cast composed
of Wendy Hiller, Franchot Tone, and Cyril Cusack. Brooks Atkinson thought that the production was the best that the play could
hope for, while Walter Kerr found the play's depths as yet
unplumbed.

In spite of its inauspicious beginnings, *Moon* was frequently
staged in universities, summer stock, and regional theaters. Josies
varied from the most bovine apprentice to the tall, slender elegance of Salome Jens in Ted Mann's highly successful 1968 Circle-
in-the-Square revival.

1973–74 Production

Cast List

Phil Hogan	Ed Flanders
Josie Hogan	Colleen Dewhurst
James Tyrone Jr.	Jason Robards
Mike Hogan	Edwin J. McDonough
T. Stedman Harder	John O'Leary

By 1973, Quintero had already directed two separate productions of *A Moon for the Misbegotten*. In 1958, when Gian Carlo Menotti opened his Festival of Two Worlds in Spoleto, Italy, he invited Quintero to represent the United States with an American play. Quintero quickly chose *Moon* because, unlike his Theatre Guild predecessors, he had already found his Josie, in the person of Colleen Dewhurst, whom he had first directed in the 1958 Circle-in-the-Square production of *Children of Darkness*. In his memoir, Quintero (1974:193) describes Dewhurst's embodiment of Josie Hogan:

> It happens to be Colleen's favorite character and the closest and dearest O'Neill heroine to me. Josie is probably the one role that the stage has offered Colleen that life has not . . . It took O'Neill to write a woman as strong and large as nature, bearing as deeply as she could with the rough talk of a lying harlot, the virginal seed of a miracle. A woman who "is all woman," for Colleen to feel that at last she was properly cast.

Quintero cast Richard Kiley as Jamie and Farrell Pelly as Phil Hogan.

In 1965, Quintero was invited to open the Buffalo Studio Theater and staged his second *Moon*, with James Daly playing opposite Colleen Dewhurst. Ted Mann wanted Dewhurst for his 1968 *Moon* at Circle-in-the-Square, but she would not do it without Quintero.

In 1973, Jason Robards was recovering from a near-fatal automobile accident. "My agent Clifford Stevens called and said, 'We've got to get something for you and a guy I know named Marshall Migatz runs the Lake Forest Theater just outside of Chicago and wants you to do *A Moon for the Misbegotten*.' I said, 'For three weeks? I don't have a job, I'll do it.' So we tried to get Colleen and José." Robards concluded deprecatingly, "I just never thought of doing that play. I thought it was a Freudian soap."

Colleen Dewhurst recalled that she and Quintero "weren't anywhere, weren't doing anything and we were broke. So we said, gee, this might be a super time to do *Moon*" (Chase, 1974:II, 1). It was Migatz who suggested Ed Flanders to play Phil Hogan. Quintero knew Flanders only by reputation and was surprised to learn that Josie's father was to be played by an actor 10 years Miss Dewhurst's junior.

Migatz wished to cast the two subsidiary roles, Mike Hogan and T. Stedman Harder, from the Chicago area and suggested that Quintero see some local actors. Ned Schmidtke was teaching acting at the Goodman School of Drama. Migatz had seen him in a showcase and thought him right for Harder. Schmidtke went out to the Festival Theater and auditioned for Quintero by reading the scene on stage with the stage manager: "Then José came up on the stage with me and he started to play the role of Josie. I did the scene again and this time he kept interrupting and pushing me around the stage while I was trying to do the scene, which was kind of different. I didn't know it all that well, I had it sort of memorized. And that was it. Then he just sort of looked up at me through his eyebrows for a long time and nodded."

Quintero subsequently cast Chicago actor Don Modie as Mike Hogan. It is characteristic of Quintero's manner of casting that while Schmidtke was an academic who had read the Gelb biography of O'Neill, Modie, Schmidtke recalled, "had never heard of Quintero, knew that Jason had made several westerns, and wondered if O'Neill had written 'any other stuff.' His eyes were wide."

The production was to be rehearsed in Los Angeles so that Robards' surgery could be completed. The day before the East Coast contingent was to fly to Los Angeles, Migatz suffered the fate that Robards had been spared; he died in an automobile crash. Out of respect for Migatz, the board of directors chose to go ahead with the production.

Dewhurst recalled that "we just kind of met in a room in Los Angeles and began to rehearse. Jason's wife Lois took over trying to cue us, get our costumes organized, everything. They had trouble paying us because the contracts were all in Mr. Migatz's briefcase, and had been confiscated by the police" (Chase, 1974:II, 3).

A Moon for the Misbegotten, 1973-74. L to r: Ed Flanders, John O'Leary, Colleen Dewhurst. Photo by Martha Swope.

Schmidtke and Modie arrived for rehearsals at the Mark Taper Forum a week after the principals. Schmidtke's responsibilities were seen to quickly: "I remember that José and I were a bit at odds at the beginning, but not for long. I played the scene one day and José had absolutely nothing to say. He made a few little adjustments in blocking to make Jason and Colleen's business clear, but he didn't have that much to say to me."

Schmidtke spent most of his time watching:

> Jason had a wonderful sense of it right from the beginning. Colleen was concerned about her age. She thought she should be younger. She was therefore concerned that they pick just the right clothing. They took a long time choosing what she was going to wear and how it was going to look. Lois helped her pick it out and Jason brought stuff from his own closet. It was self-designed. We went to the Hollywood shops. It was done by trying things on and trying to make them work. I wouldn't swear that nothing was built. There were times when you almost felt, "My uncle's got a barn, let's do a play."

Quintero had worked with Robards for over 20 years and with Dewhurst for 15, but newcomer Flanders fit in immediately. Flanders told George Gent:

> "Once we got down to rehearsal . . . everything worked out beautifully. This is a warm experience—working with supertalented people who don't have to talk each other to death about the motivation behind every word and action . . . José was such a big help. He's one of the most sensitive, most vulnerable persons I've ever met. His pores are this wide," he said, stretching his palms a foot apart. "But José listens, and then he just drops a line, and pow! it all falls right into place" (Gent, 1974:20).

Although Quintero had staged *Moon* twice before, he began this production with an uncut script. According to Colleen Dewhurst:

> You must understand that José cut an hour out. Only José knows how to cut O'Neill. He knows

when O'Neill has given all the lessons in his play, what he wants repeated over and over again. Like many great playwrights who are, in some ways, terrible writers but wonderful playwrights, he over-writes because he's afraid; he forgets the actor, so the actor has to sit up there and talk it to death instead of the playwright, but José knows when to let the repetition come in and when to take away 40 pages because it can be done with a look.

Ned Schmidtke provided an in-depth look at the manner in which the script was cut:

The script had not been cut and we just sat one day and cut and then we came back the next day, rehearsed the scene and discussed what had been cut out. O'Neill *does* tend to overwrite and the same point was made a number of times. Jason would come in and had pages turned down because he'd gone through it the night before and found every place where he said the same thing or brought up the same idea in other words. They would then track it all the way through the play and then decide whether it had to be said all those times or whether three would be enough, and of these three which was the most interesting in terms of stag-ing. In *reading* the play, all three might have their own separate, specific function. In front of an audience, though, going by one time only, which of these three sounds only like the same thing repeated and which can be dramatically different so that, even though it's the same idea, dramati-cally it moves the play forward?

The problem in cutting is that O'Neill has repeated the idea to introduce it in a slightly differ-ent context; the leitmotif has a different contrapun-tal effect because of other elements going on in the scene. If you cut one of them, the idea is still there, but you have it in only one context. It does not reverberate as O'Neill intended.

They wrangled a lot about the cutting because they knew that masses of the script had to go to

make it work, but they wanted to leave the sense
of it intact. I don't remember exactly what terms
José used, there was a lot of mumbling going on.
A lot of the discussion was very brief although the
thought process was very long. Jason would say,
"I don't know why I have to say that, because I
said it before," and there would be a long pause
during which you could read the thought process
going across José's face because he would look dis-
gruntled. Then he would look happy when he
would capture a thought like a butterfly. Then it
would disappear and leave him and he would shake
his head and then he would stand up and walk
around in little circles and then sit back down and
say, "Well, yes, we'll try it without." They made
Brando's pauses look like nothing.

The rehearsals contained very little discussion of motivation
or methodology, Ned Schmidtke recalled:

I did watch Quintero direct the other people, but
there's so little that he says in rehearsal. He cries
a lot, I remember that; that was his way of saying, "That was beautiful." He would walk around
the actors but he wouldn't say anything; he would
walk around like a camera, he would get down and
look at their faces, and Ed and Colleen and Jason
all seemed very comfortable with that.

You ask me what I saw at rehearsal? Well,
with Lois, Jason's wife, acting as stage manager and
most of the people having worked together before
and all this mumbling going on, I finally quit going.
When I went out there I thought, "I will go to every
rehearsal, this is too good an opportunity to pass
up." But I found that so much of the conversation
went on at such a low level or in a kind of shorthand that I couldn't begin to pick up on that I
thought, "I've seen this. I saw this yesterday and
the day before," because the most salient element
was the way the people related. That was the scene;
it was a very tight group of people.

The Spoleto and Buffalo rehearsals had been talkathons, but the presence of Robards in Lake Forest precluded the need to talk matters to death. Dewhurst recalled:

> When we did *Moon* in Italy and up in Buffalo, José would say, "If only Jason could do this," because the men had great difficulty with the breakdown. With the other men there were hours spent in discussion. José finally said, "You are literally, disgustingly throwing up all over this woman, over her face, her hands, her body." With Jason, he never had to say anything, Jason never asked a question. It was perfectly logical to Jason. It just went like a shot. With the others you knew it was going to be a long day. Mostly they wanted it cut.

Robards said of rehearsals, "Ed, Colleen, and I, we never had to talk about *Moon*. José just said, 'Don't sit so early, it makes me think you're going into something else,' or 'Let's keep this next section of 10 pages on stage left, and see where it goes.' That's the kind of thing he does."

Robards, who had so thoroughly dismissed *Moon* before rehearsals, never experienced any miraculous conversion to the play. Robards is all work:

> You just learn the lines and try to get out there and not be embarrassing. I tried not to be self-pitying and hammy and tried to read it true and not be embarrassing with some very embarrassing material, corny material in many ways. I tried to take the curse away from it. It is a good *play*, it has good dramatic structure and as you get on with it and play a good play you learn more about it, so that your initial feelings are not the ones you end up with. It's *good* to have some initial reservations that you can overcome.

How much preparation for playing Jamie in *Moon* was playing Jamie in *Long Day's Journey*? "I never thought of it. You start from scratch; it's a totally different play, different time, different people. How do you solve the problems of *this* play and get it presented? How do we get it off the page and make it behavior?

That's all. Get all those black typewritten letters and commas and dashes and present it as behavior? That's the job; it's make-believe."

When the production moved to Lake Forest, Jane E. Neufeld became the stage manager of record. She specified that "the show had a life of its own, in that it arrived at Lake Forest mostly rehearsed, without actually having been in production. This production of *Moon* was outside the normal summer stock process." As stage manager, Neufeld was responsible for preparing a production script and rehearsing the understudies, but found it just as difficult as Ned Schmidtke to overhear what was transpiring at rehearsals.

The set, costumes, and lighting were executed by the resident staff at Lake Forest. Neufeld described the physical circumstances of the Lake Forest production:

> The set was very similar to the Broadway set; the scrimming of it was stronger and the lighting more orange and straw colored. When it was redone, it was done first class. The whole concept of the show was the same. There was a little set on there, a solid house with the downstage walls scrimmed so that you could see through. The porch was the most important element. The stage at Lake Forest is a very wide proscenium, maybe 50 feet wide, with a sloping, sweeping curve, not very far out, but it doesn't make for a straight proscenium situation. There were more than 600 seats.

Ned Schmidtke said, "I remember that at the curtain call, opening night in Chicago, José came on stage and said, 'It's wonderful, it's beautiful. We will all be together in New York in the fall.' "

Dan Issac made the journey to Lake Forest and in his review stressed the Irish nature of the play: "O'Neill always had a huge problem trying to write a naturalistic stage language that would be both poetic and American. He finally solved the problem here by giving it over and writing for a character who was an *Irish*-American. Even lines freighted with big meaning have a special poetic quality . . . The speech is poetic simply because the Irish love colorful alliterative language" (1973:60). Issac's review was later credited as being the impetus for bringing the production to Broadway. Reviews alone, even excellent reviews, are only a first step to moving a production. The Chicago production dispersed with no set future.

Quintero, Robards, and Dewhurst attempted to put a package together themselves: "José and I are about equally good at business," Colleen says, "and we were trying to figure out where we could borrow money—Jason said he had some—and how we could tie up the rights; though where we'd have gone with it we didn't know. If someone had paid us to come from Chicago to Saskatchewan for two weeks, we'd have done it" (Chase, 1974:II, 3).

Unbeknownst to the people in the Chicago production, producer Elliot Martin had already purchased the touring and Broadway rights to *Moon* as a vehicle for Jack Lemmon. By the end of the summer, Lemmon had decided against the project and Martin tried to assimilate the Chicago production. Martin, however, could not raise the necessary capital. Although Roger Stevens was willing to guarantee the production against loss for three weeks at the Kennedy Center in Washington, DC, the production could not get into New York until Martin yielded controlling interest to producer Lester Osterman. Osterman took on the production, to a large extent, because he could book it into his then-dark Morosco Theater for five weeks and tour it afterward. The scheduled bookings were projected to do no worse than break even. Osterman read the play and, determining that his usual investors would not be interested, invested his own money.

Ben Edwards became involved with designing the Broadway production "before it became a reality, before there was any money to do it." While the production team waited for the money to be raised:

> I talked to José quite a bit about *A Moon for the Misbegotten*. Out in Lake Forest, the stage dictated what he had done. He wanted me to provide the freedom of space that he needed. I never saw a picture of the Lake Forest set. He never gave me specific dimensions that he wanted, only "I want to be able to walk here, to have freedom of movement." That's all. He roughed out and showed me the stage they had used out there in Lake Forest. It was a very flat stage with no depth. He had eliminated the interior/exterior, by necessity. He had an

interior that was all tied in with the exterior. That
was about all the conversation until I began to work
out the way that you could have the interior and
everything all in one. It was a very simple set, for
many reasons. One, it *was* simple and two, there
was no money. If we had wanted anything more
complicated, we would never have gotten it.

Edwards had never seen O'Neill's sketch for the house in *A
Moon for the Misbegotten*. When he was shown the sketch he said,
"It's the same house for *Desire Under the Elms*. You take the facade
off and you're inside." It was that very process of taking off the
facade that distinguished Edwards' set from the Lake Forest
original:

I don't like to see actors behind scrims. It's all right
for a quick scene in a musical, but I don't believe
that out there in Lake Forest they played those
interiors behind a scrim. I had a skeletal house. You
could walk in and out. When you were outside,
you lit outside and dimmed the inside. You changed
the lights when they went inside. There were many
light changes. There was no point in lighting up
two little pieces of furniture. They were completely
visible, only not lit. They weren't accented. I concentrated the light on where the action was happening, down on the apron mostly.

With production assured, Quintero proceeded to recast the
two subsidiary roles. As Harder, he chose John O'Leary who had
played the role in the 1965 Buffalo production. To recast Mike
Hogan, Quintero budgeted an hour on Wednesday afternoon
(rehearsals were to commence on Friday morning, with Thanksgiving Day intervening). Quintero had to interview six actors, who
had been submitted by agents. He met Edwin J. McDonough in
Lester Ostermann's office where they chatted for five minutes.
O'Neill specifies that Mike Hogan is 20 years old and about four
inches shorter than his sister; at the time, McDonough was 30 and
stood at least six inches taller than Dewhurst. Quintero explained
with great charm, "I have this problem that the first image of Colleen must be that she is *huge*—and, next to you, she is not huge."
For whatever reason, Quintero waived that objection and the cast
was complete.

L to r: Colleen Dewhurst, Edwin J. McDonough. Photo by Martha Swope.

The production went back into rehearsal on Thanksgiving Friday, 1973, at the Dance Theater Workshop on West 19th Street. Quintero took 15 minutes to put McDonough into the production. He stressed Mike's hatred of the farm and of his father, the brunt of which he directs at Josie. Quintero acted out the scene, indicating the level of Mike's rage. He first brandished a rake and then the suitcase with which Mike flees. McDonough asked Quintero if Mike should have an Irish accent; Quintero said to try it. The direction ended there. McDonough subsequently asked O'Leary if that was typical of Quintero. O'Leary answered that if José is getting what he wants, he doesn't say anything.

The rehearsals consisted for the most part of the three principals, Quintero, and Jane Neufeld, who stressed that the New York rehearsals contained almost no discernible direction:

> Rehearsals were held to review the situation, keep the muscles in tone. The few moments of direction that I remember were: "Maybe . . . could you . . . perhaps." You didn't know what anyone was talking about. *They* did. And those moments weren't many because, if there had been any preliminary great directorial work, it would have been done in Los Angeles. By this time, in effect, they were doing a refresher of the show that had been done in Lake Forest.

After approximately eight days of five-hour-long rehearsals, the production played the 1,100-seat Eisenhower Theater at the Kennedy Center in Washington, DC, during the three weeks prior to Christmas. It sold well (it had been added to the subscription) and received strong, though not overwhelming, notices. Dewhurst said, "sold out, but again I wouldn't permit myself to think too far. Sometimes for a second or two, I'd wonder if we'd be able to extend in New York, get maybe eight weeks, then I'd say uh-uh, the little group that loves O'Neill will come to the theater and that'll be it" (Chase, 1974:II, 3).

When Robards was told that the five New York previews were sold out, he said knowingly to Quintero, "the previews to *Hughie* were sold out, too." Clive Barnes of the *New York Times* attended a Thursday matinee preview, in which Robards' laryngitis barely permitted his voice to reach beyond the proscenium. The producers had not even arranged a party for Saturday's opening night, so

Robards and Dewhurst gave a party at Delsomma's on West 47th Street.

At 11:00 P.M., publicist Seymour Krawitz announced that the *New York Times* review had arrived. Colleen Dewhurst covered her ears and screamed, "I don't want to hear it." "You want to hear *this* one," Krawitz rejoindered. "This notice is a publicist's dream: 'This is a landmark production that people are going to talk about for many years to come.' "

The reviews of *Moon* most resemble those of *Long Day's Journey;* all judgment and no description. The judgments were overwhelmingly positive, even superlative. The headlines resembled each other. Richard Watts (1973:9) wrote, "A superb play, superbly done." Walter Kerr (1974:II, 1) wrote, "It's a rich play, richly performed." Clive Barnes (1973:22) threw up his hands and asked, "But how can you write about performances you are going to talk about for years?" His description of Quintero's direction is all rhetoric: "Mr. Quintero plays his cards unerringly. You could take a temperature chart of his staging, and it would be the same as the play itself. He never exaggerates, falsifies; indeed he never cheats on the playwright's scoring." The critics described the plot and placed the play in the context of O'Neill's oeuvre; they offered copious value judgments, but failed to describe how the production worked. John Simon (1974:53) wrote that "José Quintero's direction seems minimal, but, with these actors, that is enough." This incorrectly implies that any competent director could have taken the same actors, shown up at rehearsals, and achieved the same result.

There can be no Brechtian modelbook for Quintero's production of *A Moon for the Misbegotten*. The only element of technique to be examined is the principle by which Quintero cut the text, a marked improvement over his *ad hoc* method of cutting *Strange Interlude* a decade before. The production jelled because of two factors: the personal relationships Quintero had built up over a generation with Robards and Dewhurst and immediately with Flanders; and the confluence of these four careers in summer 1973. After a series of divorces, bouts of alcoholism, and two automobile accidents, four talented people—survivors—pooled their resources, overjoyed to be alive and working together.

9

Anna Christie

Writing
Revision of *Chris Cristopherson,*
begun summer 1920; final version com-
pleted September 18, 1920.
Premieres
Original: November 2, 1921; New
York, Vanderbilt Theater.
Quintero: April 14, 1977; New York,
Imperial Theater.

1921 Production

Cast List

Johnny-the-Priest	James C. Mack
1st Longshoreman	G. O. Taylor
2nd Longshoreman	John Hanley
Postman	William Augustin
Chris Christopherson	George Marion
Marthy Owen	Eugenie Blair
Anna Christopherson	Pauline Lord
Mat Burke	Frank Shannon
Johnson	Ole Anderson

In May 1918, when O'Neill was almost 30 years old and still
unproduced on Broadway, he conceived and began writing a play

based on Chris Cristopherson, an old Norwegian seaman-turned-bargeman, whom O'Neill had known when both had lodged at Jimmy-the-Priest's. O'Neill called the play *Chris Cristopherson*, after its protagonist.

In *Chris Cristopherson*, the eponymous bargeman who has come to hate the sea attempts to dissuade his respectable young daughter, Anna, from marrying Paul Anderson, a midwestern second mate. Anna is a thoroughly bourgeois young woman, and Anderson is a portrait of O'Neill's own reluctance to shoulder responsibility. The scenes between Anna and Paul are undramatized exposition. Chris and Paul do not even have a scene together. Anna finally accepts Anderson's marriage proposal after he agrees to work hard for his captain's papers.

The play was first offered to producer John Williams, holder of the option on the unproduced *Beyond the Horizon*, who turned it down. Arthur Hopkins was then approached, but he never bothered to read it. It was finally optioned by George C. Tyler, an old family friend who had produced some of the elder James O'Neill's plays. Casting difficulties postponed its production and it might have fallen into limbo, but on February 2, 1920, John Williams successfully presented *Beyond the Horizon* on Broadway. Tyler decided to produce *Chris* immediately to take advantage of *Horizon*'s success. Tyler cast Emmet Corrigan as Chris and Lynn Fontanne, who had recently come to America from England, as Anna. Anna, as she was drawn in *Chris*, was a proper young stenographer who had been reared in England. O'Neill found Lynn Fontanne's manner "a little too grand for Anna, but he was overruled" (Gelb, 1960:418).

A combination of family illnesses drove O'Neill back to Provincetown before the final rehearsals of *Chris*. The production opened in Atlantic City to adequate reviews and small houses. O'Neill refused to travel to Atlantic City, but agreed to rewrite the final scene: "He belatedly realized that he had so concentrated on the old bargeman that he had scanted the young couple and failed to individualize them" (Sheaffer, 1973:9). He had pinpointed the structural flaw, which would eventually transform the play into *Anna Christie*. Tyler and O'Neill agreed to close the play in Philadelphia and start from scratch.

Chris Cristopherson was O'Neill's first out-of-town experience. He had seen some of the rehearsals and none of the performances, but he had already developed the relationship he would maintain for his entire career between his writing and its staged representation:

> It was one of his conceits that he did not really need to see one of his scripts acted to know how they would play; he believed—and surprisingly often he was right—that he could tell exactly how and where work must be done. (Whenever he was proven wrong he blamed the actors for throwing the picture he had visualized out of focus; he resented the fact that actors were people, rather than puppets; he was affronted when they displayed mannerisms, attitudes, and sometimes even opinions that he himself had not evoked. He always wrote his characters as if he were a novelist, allowing no leeway for deviation. Casting was inevitably a horror to him, for he felt that he was yielding, inch by inch, the characters he had created, and losing them to flesh-and-blood aliens, with lives of their own) (Gelb, 1960:418).

O'Neill's revision of *Chris Cristopherson* took only several months. Although he entertained working titles such as *The Ole Davil* and *Tides*, he finally named the play after its new protagonist, *Anna Christie*.

O'Neill sent a copy of the play to critic George Jean Nathan, who expressed concern over its unduly optimistic denouement. O'Neill wrote the first of many *apologias* for the play's conclusion: "The happy ending is merely the comma at the end of a gaudy introductory clause, with the body of the sentence still unwritten . . . My ending seems to have a false definiteness about it that is misleading—a happy-ever-after which I did not intend" (Sheaffer, 1973:67).

Early in February 1921, Tyler "approached the Theatre Guild to co-produce the *Chris* play with him or take it over completely, offering terms that Eugene thought 'most generous,' but the Guild found them excessive" (Sheaffer, 1973:50). When Tyler's option ran out, Arthur Hopkins agreed to produce and direct *Anna Christie*:

> Hopkins had been among the first on Broadway to discard the ultrarealism of David Belasco and favor

the imaginative new stagecraft dreamed into being by Adolphe Appia and Gordon Craig . . . Hopkins mounted productions that were at once commercial hits and artistic triumphs. Their genuine brilliance was due not only to their stellar portrayals but to the scenery and lighting of Robert Edmond Jones, a true artist in his field (Sheaffer, 1973:65).

Hopkins (1948:123) writes of his rehearsal technique with Jones:

> Jones as designer, and I as director, agreed at all times that our contribution should not be individual, but support parts of the whole pattern. This resulted in a harmony of background and action otherwise unattainable. After the movement of the play has been set, Jones sat through rehearsals to check his work with mine and to play his light plots in relation to the arranged positions. Thus, before a production was set up, it had been completely envisioned by both of us so that the arrival of the scenery, costumes and properties rarely revealed a problem which we had not foreseen.

That summer, O'Neill invited Robert Edmond Jones to Provincetown to discuss the sets for *Anna Christie*, "three of whose four acts take place aboard a battered coal barge, and O'Neill invited him to Peaked Hill, where the sea had obligingly cast ashore just such a barge . . . Jones spent a few days sketching it, and no sooner had he finished, when, mysteriously, it began to burn" (Gelb, 1960:476). Jones designed two interiors (the saloon and the cabin of the barge) and one exterior (the barge at anchor).

Hopkins (1937:179) had been guiding Pauline Lord's career for several years prior to *Anna Christie*: "Gene had a new play called *Anna Christie* which he wanted me to read. As soon as I read it I telephoned Polly, saying 'I've got your play. Come down and get it.' She read it and was enthusiastic." O'Neill (1952:79) describes Anna as "a tall, blonde, fully-developed girl of twenty, handsome after a large, Viking-daughter fashion." Pauline Lord "was thirty-one, delicate, almost fragile, with a tiny waist, small hands and feet, a pale, oval face, and tragic brown eyes. She had been acting since she was sixteen—rarely in the conventional

ingenue parts, more often as tragic victims . . . Like O'Neill, she
was shy and withdrawn in company; she admitted to friends that
she could act well only when she was unhappy or nervous. O'Neill
was delighted with her" (Gelb, 1960:476–77). Hopkins cast George
Marion as Chris (he repeated the role in the Garbo film) and Frank
Shannon as Mat Burke.

In eliciting from Pauline Lord a legendary performance, Hopkins showed the patience and understanding of the process of acting
that was totally denied to O'Neill. Hopkins (1948:61, 94–95) num-
bered Pauline Lord:

> among actors who have worked with me who
> showed nothing encouraging in the first days of
> rehearsal . . . As unknowns they would have been
> in danger of dismissal. They were like distance
> horses in a race, out-paced for three-quarters of the
> way, but moving ahead to pass all others at the fin-
> ish . . . Polly is not a fast-blooming plant. Her roots
> are deep and not quickly reached. Without their
> nourishment her work is lifeless, but all of the time
> there are notes in that haunting voice that are
> unmistakable soundings of the rich flow that is to
> come. And then, one day, near the end of rehear-
> sals, the flow is freed and the full promise of the
> soundings is revealed.

Hopkins (1937:179) writes of the rehearsal period that "Gene
saw the play for the first time at the final dress rehearsal and was
pleased." Sheaffer (1973:64) notes that "after attending a few
rehearsals . . . he told friends that if it failed, he could only blame
his script." Whatever the number of rehearsals he attended, O'Neill
was pleased. He was cooperative with Hopkins (1937:179): "I told
Gene I thought the play was a half-hour too long. He told me to
make the cuts." *Anna Christie* was O'Neill's first thoroughly professional production.

The reviewers praised Hopkins, the American disciple of
Craig and Appia, for his thoroughly realistic production. There
were sharp attacks on the play's conclusion, however, spurring
O'Neill (1921:VI, 1) to write to the *New York Times*:

> [This is] not a defense but an explanation. In the
> last few minutes of *Anna Christie* I tried to show

that dramatic gathering of new forces out of the old. I wanted to have the audience leave with a deep feeling of life flowing on . . . of a problem solved for the moment but by the very nature of its solution involving new problems. Since the last act seems to have been generally misunderstood, I must have failed in this attempt . . . A kiss in the last act, a word about marriage, and the audience grows blind and deaf to what follows.

No amount of correspondence with the *Times* could alter the play at the Vanderbilt Theater into the one in O'Neill's head. He came to despise it. Several years later, he told Malcolm Cowley that " 'in telling the story I deliberately employed all the Broadway tricks which I had learned in my stage training.' He added scornfully that it had all been 'too easy' and that he would never write such a play again, although he could turn out a dozen *Anna Christies* if he wanted to" (Gelb, 1960:482).

O'Neill's contempt for the play did not preclude its financial success, neither did he refuse the Pulitzer Prize nor seek to suppress subsequent productions. He had unintentionally created an actress's play. He might have dissipated this fate by naming it *Tides*, but *Anna Christie* was destined to become a "vehicle" to carry Garbo, Ingrid Bergman, Gwen Verdon (in the musical *New Girl in Town*), and Liv Ullmann.

1977 Production

Cast List

Johnny-the-Priest	Richard Hamilton
Longshoremen	Edwin J. McDonough
	Vic Polizos
Larry	Ken Harrison
Postman	Jack Davidson
Chris Cristopherson	Robert Donley
Marthy Owen	Mary McCarty
Anna Christie	Liv Ullmann
Mat Burke	John Lithgow

After directing Liv Ullmann in *A Moon for the Misbegotten*, in Norway, Quintero once again established an extremely close

Anna Christie, 1977. L to r: Robert Donley, Liv Ullmann. Photo by Martha Swope.

relationship with a female star. She expressed a desire that Quintero direct her in an O'Neill play on Broadway. He thumbed through the *oeuvre* and found the ideal Nordic heroine in *Anna Christie*. This was the first time in Quintero's O'Neill career that the star preceded the play. The choice of *Anna Christie* was almost inevitable, but the ensuing production always found itself in the position of having to defend the choice, not a good sign.

In a Toronto interview, George Anthony (1976:M3) wrote of Liv Ullmann that "she is, by her own admission, a bad judge of scripts. 'I go for the people, not for the scripts. If there is someone I admire, someone I want to work with, I do it.' Hence her choice of *Anna Christie* as a stage vehicle is not her choice at all. 'I choose José Quintero, the director, because I love him. He is a beautiful person. *Anna Christie* is his choice, not mine. But perhaps it will become mine too as we get into it.' " Ullmann later told Richard Eder (1977a:C15) that "when he talks it is as if it were the best play in the world. You really believe you have gold in your hands and should use it as something very precious."

Quintero brought the package to Alexander Cohen, who agreed to produce it with pre-Broadway tryouts in Toronto, Baltimore, Washington, DC, a limited run in New York, and then San Francisco and Los Angeles. Ben Edwards was called in to do the sets.

In the early 1920s, O'Neill had been experimenting in *Beyond the Horizon* and *Anna Christie* with alternating interior and exterior (it was not until *Desire Under the Elms* in 1924 that he attempted to show interior and exterior simultaneously). O'Neill's stage directions for *Anna Christie* call very specifically for three different sets: Johnny-the-Priest's bar in Act One, the stern of the barge *Simeon Winthrop* for Act Two (an exterior, very important for Anna's discovery that she has been cleansed by the sea), and the interior of the cabin on the barge for Acts Three and Four. Quintero and Edwards decided to strive for simultaneity in the barge scenes.

Johnny-the-Priest's bar was divided into two sections, as O'Neill specified: the barroom and a small backroom (what the Irish call a "snug" for ladies). The indication of a curtain, from upstage center to the front of the stage, served as the dividing line. The production was to play Act One, then an intermission, combine Acts Two and Three, intermission, then Act Four. There was to be only one set change, in the first intermission. Edwards designed a unit set for Acts Two, Three, and Four that, when properly lit and indicated, would serve as the interior and exterior of the barge. Because the production was booked into large musical houses in each city, the modest barge had to take on epic proportions.

When asked what specifics Quintero had requested, Edwards answered:

> We didn't talk as much as we did on the other productions. The only specific that José asked me for was that the barge have a sail. Now the barges on the Thames have sails, but I don't know that any American barges have sails. José did not specify that the barge be built wall-to-wall. It was a sort of symbolic barge in many ways. We knew the theaters to which we were going. They were large musical houses, but the proscenium opening isn't so much different in a musical house. The stage is not so much different. It may be deeper. The seating capacity is larger.

When asked about the simultaneity of interior and exterior, Edwards reiterated his consistent theme in designing for Quintero: "It goes back to having worked for José before. I know that you can have that little cabin, but you can't box José into that cabin. He would be absolutely claustrophobic as a director and couldn't deal with that and doesn't want to deal with that. That is not his style."

The decision was arrived at mutually:

> I think that, right from the beginning, we analyzed it and said we can play it all in the same space, except the bar. The bar was still on the deck; you could come way downstage. In the bar, even with the indication of a separate area for ladies, José didn't abide by those lines of demarcation either. If you were on the bar side and he felt like moving you over to the ladies' side, he did it, back and forth. It worked fine. The demarcation was there only, for my part, in deference to the script, so that when Anna and Marthy were having their very intimate conversation, people in the bar were paying

no attention, as if they were not seeing them. We used no curtain, just the indication of one. No one ever entered the bar from the no-man's land downstage. José was free to move downstage whenever he wanted, but no one ever entered from downstage, nor exited from down there.

At the Circle-in-the-Square, with the audience all around, the very nature of the stage required that freedom. I think that we agreed mutually that the whole sense of the background of the sky and the barge was more part of *Anna Christie* than shutting them up in an enclosed room where you couldn't see more than the cabin. We could have done a large cabin just as well.

Having cast his eponymous heroine, Quintero set out to select the remaining principals. John Lithgow was cast as Mat Burke, the Irish stoker. The role of Marthy Owen is strangely unbalanced in the writing. O'Neill gave her two marvelous scenes in the first act and then dropped her completely, although her relationship with Chris could serve to parallel the Anna-Mat relationship. (The film of *Anna Christie* and the musical, *New Girl in Town*, were both reconceived to expand Marthy's presence.) Quintero offered the role to singer-dancer Mary McCarty, who described her brief meeting with Quintero to Tom Burke: " 'José simply said, "I've seen everything you've done." I was amazed he'd seen me in *anything*. Then "How would you feel if I offered you Marthy?" I said, "I'd find that very interesting, but I know I haven't got a chance of getting it." José said, "But I've already decided" ' . . . Ask Quintero and he states of her, 'I always saw Mary as a singing actress. I could always feel her dramatic power, even in *Chicago*' " (Burke, 1977:C5).

Old Chris proved the most difficult role to cast. It was offered to Jason Robards, who wanted no part of the play, and no other star could be found who was willing to say "Dat ole davil sea" 14 times. The role was finally given, after several auditions, to character-actor Robert Donley.

On Monday, January 3, 1977, the cast (including Edwin J. McDonough, whose first-hand account of the rehearsals follows) and production staff gathered for the first time. The first hour was given over to journalists and photographers. Ben Edwards displayed a mockup of the set and his wife, Jane Greenwood, showed renderings of her costumes.

After the press had gone, the cast prepared for the first reading. Quintero picked up a script from the common pile and, with a flourish, indicated that there was not a single prepared note in his script. "I am prepared," he announced, "in that I am vulnerable to the experience." The cast was seated at two rectangular tables. Quintero said very little during the first reading. Afterwards, his remarks were concerned almost exclusively with the power of the sea over those who live by it. He had never thought of *Anna Christie* as a great play, but, after studying it for some time, had come to respect it a great deal. "Sailors have committed themselves by generations to a way of life . . . One does not have membership in the sea for a year . . . The sea can carry you onto the deck or off it. The sea is bad, beautiful and seductive . . . One wishes to be buried among one's own . . . The sea decides . . . For the breed of sailors, there is a code of which they are a part . . . For sailors, God is a tangible sea." Quintero pointed out that, as soon as Chris says, "Dat ole davil sea, she ain't God!," the sea throws up Mat Burke. Quintero acknowledged the presence of melodrama and urged that it be played to the full.

On Tuesday, January 4, the director, cast, and stage managers began to work in earnest. A dozen chairs were placed in a circle and the cast reread the play. Quintero interrupted at will to specify the points he wanted made very early in the rehearsal process.

Quintero called the first act in Johnny-the-Priest's saloon "the epitome of nonbelonging." Larry, the bartender, "grabs onto anything to do with sex." In examining the father-daughter relationship, Quintero said of O'Neill that "God gives some men the ability to see through the vulnerability of others." Quintero acknowledged that, although O'Neill had always inveighed against his own parents, he was an unsuccessful parent himself. Quintero maintained that "O'Neill was not unfeeling toward his children, but *too* feeling." Quintero spoke of a letter that O'Neill had written to his daughter, Oona, when she announced her engagement to Charlie Chaplin, in which O'Neill "blamed himself for her marrying a man old enough to be her father, but he never saw her again."

In preparing for the reunion of Chris and Anna, Quintero related that, after he had announced to his parents that he was going into the theater, his father announced "I had a son, José, but now he is dead," and did not communicate with him for eight years. After Quintero's success with *Summer and Smoke*, he made his first return visit to Panama, only to find his father standing on the other side of the ship's gangplank. Quintero described the quaking in his knees and said to Liv Ullmann, "One expects rejection, put up pretenses," and to Robert Donley, "Imagine the guilt Chris must have felt at abandoning his child. Chris must play all his alterations with fear underlying." Quintero asked Ullmann, "What made Anna write the letter to Chris in the first place? Imagine how bad her conditions must have been, and now this dump!" For the meeting of Anna and Marthy, Quintero said that "misery reaches out to misery."

In the second act, at Provincetown, "Anna has found her soil." When Mat tells of the storm he survived and how he saved the ship, Quintero said, "We involve other people in our occupation, we share our passions." To make his point, Quintero suddenly grabbed Lithgow and, taking the part of a harried director, frantically described a mythical production that arrived for a tryout in Boston with none of the sets properly constructed to fit the stage.

Quintero said of Mat Burke's third-act determination to marry Anna that "although it is in the new country, Mat comes in an old-country fashion and asks the father's permission to marry Anna." This was Quintero's first public statement of the characterization he wanted of Mat Burke. The text reads exactly the opposite: "I'm marrying your Anna before this day is out, and you might as well make up your mind up to it whether you like it or not" (O'Neill, 1952:128). Burke most emphatically does *not* come in an old-world fashion to ask Chris for the hand of Anna.

In the fourth act, Quintero stressed the importance of the oath that Mat extracts from Anna and the sacred nature of the cross his mother had given him. Quintero spoke of his visits to Panama, during which his convent-reared mother would address a holy object, as if it were human, imploring its blessing to protect her son in New York City. The stories were funny and effectively conveyed the conviction of believers in the efficacy of religious objects.

Most of Quintero's directorial choices were crystallized in the second week of rehearsal. In the first act, Quintero went to great lengths to demonstrate the nature of a bar such as Johnny-the-Priest's. He first strode cavalierly toward a table and sat with his legs crossed. He explained that such an entrance was more appropriate to the Plaza, where people wish to be seen. Johnny-the-Priest's, by way of contrast, offered the anonymity its customers sought. Quintero spoke about his own drinking problem. Beginning with the back-to-back successes of *Iceman* and *Long Day's Journey*, he had experienced the terror of failure, of being found out. The burden of responsibility, the need to continue his successes, necessitated his leaving the apartment earlier in the day "to work on the rehearsal set." In fact, it was the need for a prerehearsal drink to restore his confidence and get his energy going and then, subsequently, the need for one or more drinks during rehearsal. The pretense of stepping out for a breath of air was maintained, although it fooled no one. The only safe place for such clandestine drinking is a bar like Johnny-the-Priest's. Quintero's body expanded and contracted to show the temporary emotional surge that drink offers. He then mimed the drunkard's anticipatory stare as the bartender pours a shot, even lapping up drops that were spilled. Quintero's retelling of this decline transformed personal experience into raw material for the actors. It was totally professional, never maudlin or self-indulgent.

In Act Two, Mat Burke, after days of exposure to open sea and bolstered by a drink of whiskey, makes a pass at Anna. In the stage directions, O'Neill (1952:109) specifies that "he presses her to him and attempts to kiss her." Quintero staged this sequence as an attempted rape, with Burke tearing away at Anna's sou'wester. This was Quintero's only attempt to show the darker, brutal side of Burke. The scene was often theatrically effective during rehearsals, but it eventually became soft and non-threatening.

At the top of Act Three, O'Neill (1952:122) specifies that Anna is holding a newspaper, but "frowningly concentrated on her thoughts," while Chris "pretends to be engaged in getting things shipshape." O'Neill had already provided Anna with an activity adequate to her restless mood, but Quintero had other points to make. The third act is set inside the barge's cabin but, because Quintero was working on the same unit that before was the exterior (Acts Two and Three were played without an intermission), he had to indicate that the act began inside the barge's cabin. Quintero had Chris read the newspaper and Anna string beads. Anna restlessly threw the beads to the floor and Chris then swept them up. Quintero demonstrated for the entire company that Chris would sweep the beads up in a contained fashion, always upstage toward the back wall rather than out to the audience, to convey the sense of the interior of the cabin and its confinements.

The action of the third act did subsequently move outside the cabin, but characters never moved through the invisible side walls or downstage wall, always through a working door upstage right. Quintero seldom explains the conventions of a set to his company, but on this occasion he made it clear that if characters entered from stage right, they were outside until they walked through the door of the cabin. Quintero never staged the characters who were outside too close to the furniture inside, which would have blurred the convention of interior/exterior.

In rehearsing the Mat-Chris confrontation in Act Three, John Lithgow suddenly picked up the newspaper Chris had been reading and threatened him with it. Quintero applauded and exclaimed, "I thought you'd never find the paper. I put it there two days ago." Quintero wished to tell actors some things, but wanted them to discover other things for themselves.

In a *New York Magazine* interview, Dan Issac (1977:79) wrote:

> I then asked Quintero how he directed Liv Ullmann
> in a prostitute's role. He grew very animated and
> he answered the question. "Well, there is a stock
> prostitute—hip-swinging—and I didn't want that
> kind of prostitute. I wanted somebody who has
> been absolutely drained and has absolutely no
> respect for her body. And I said to Liv, 'Do you
> know where your body has been?' And I grabbed
> her—of course, not hard. This was make-believe.
> And in pantomime I backed her against the wall.
> 'Now everything hurts. And now you've had some
> liquor in order to forget those hands all over your
> body.' "

The original of this story took place during the second week of rehearsals. A scene had been completed and, during the break, Ullmann asked Quintero, "Does old Chris know that Anna's become a whore?" Quintero took a breath and said, "Such women have a stamp on them and men like Chris recognize the stamp. Mat immediately takes her for a whore and makes a pass at her." Quintero then went into painstaking detail to specify how that stamp was imposed; the time she spent on the farm with her cousins pawing her until, finally, the time when they grabbed her and would not let her go, the way they tore at her, the blood as they penetrated her. Then, backing Ullmann to the wall of the rehearsal room, Quintero threatened her, "And if you tell anyone, it will be worse the next time." Doubtless Quintero had been thinking about the material, but this half-hour performance was totally spontaneous. The half-hour performance on drinking had been prepared. Both were mightily effective.

The New York rehearsals, in a large studio on the third floor of the Minskoff Building, lasted three weeks. By the end of that time, some members of the cast agreed that two casting choices were wrong. Mary McCarty was *not* a singing actress. She brought sentimentality to a hard-edged character. In her fight sequence with Anna, Marthy says angrily, "Is that so? Well, I'll tell you straight, kiddo, that Marthy Owen never . . ."(O'Neill, 1952:82). Eight times a week Mary McCarty dutifully stopped at the word "never," having nothing more to say; not once did she suggest the "walked the streets," which an actress would have provided. Audiences, however, loved her performance and she was nominated for a Tony Award as Best Supporting Actress.

As Larry the bartender, Quintero had cast an actor whom he had known on the West Coast. Larry presides over the entire first act and initiates a great deal of the dialogue. Chris, Marthy, and Anna react to the mood he imposes upon them. This actor struck observers as being so incompetent as to warrant his being replaced, but Quintero resisted all moves from the Cohen office to do so.

On the final day of rehearsals, Quintero thanked the cast for not sounding a single uncooperative note. The production, at that time, seemed to be dominated by the theme that the sea is a determining God in whom the participants believed. The production did not have a clearly expressed structural throughline, such as: This is a confrontation between a woman who hates men and a man for whom women are either whores or saintly mothers. There were no obstacles established for the protagonists to overcome. The production, as it left New York, had Mat and Anna falling in love at the end of the second act, so that the obstacles of Acts Three and Four became paper tigers. The final tableau depicted the three principals toasting each other and threatened to be exactly the happy ending that O'Neill had dreaded.

Tryouts began in Toronto, where the company first donned its costumes and Mat Burke's characterization came more into focus. Mat survived the shipwreck wearing what Martin Gottfried

(1977:37) was to call "Brando's old underwear shirt." It was exactly the wrong image for Lithgow, serving to elongate his six-foot-four-inch frame. David Richards (1977:C2) commented that "far from being a thick and lumbering bruiser, the actor is thin and gangly. The layers of grime and the brawling accent can't entirely hide his refined sensibilities. As a result it is hard to excuse Mat as a klutz, if that's an excuse to begin with." Mat called on Anna in the third act wearing a Buster Brown suit that made him look seraphically innocent at a time when Lithgow's Mat desperately needed to demonstrate a dock-side roughness. When Lithgow's large frame is contained, as it was in *The Changing Room*, he is an arresting figure. When he is allowed or encouraged to spend his energy freely on stage, it spills over in all directions and dissipates itself. Instead of a brooding, rooted, violent Black-Irish stoker, Lithgow's Mat always appeared on the verge of song and dance. Quintero had encouraged the cast members to make suggestions about the production. In Toronto, cast members did mention to Quintero, in private, that Mat Burke was so soft in conception that it provided the production with no dramatic thrust. Quintero listened politely, but Mat's characterization forever remained what it had been on the second day of rehearsal, when Quintero announced that Mat had come to ask the old man's permission to marry Anna.

No production of an O'Neill play would be complete without at least one line that provokes unexpected laughter. The fourth act of *Anna Christie* contains the following exchange:

> Burke: God mend you, is it making me out to be the like of yourself you are, and you taking up with this one and that one all the years of your life?
> Anna: Yes, that's just what I do mean. You been doing the same thing all your life, picking up a new girl in every port. How're you any better than I was?
> Burke: Is it no shame you have at all? (O'Neill, 1952:170)

The enormous laugh of recognition that greeted Mat's line in Toronto was arguably the audience's strongest contemporary response to the production, yet Quintero was thrown by the laughter. He tried to kill it and, at one point, even cut Mat's line, before conceding that the laughter was legitimate.

The major revision in Toronto, Quintero's final major choice of the production, was to alter the final tableau. As initially staged, the three principals stood together toasting the future. Quintero now let the toast spend itself, acknowledging that the resolution was only temporary. Each of the three principals then took a moment to collect his/her thoughts in a separate portion of the stage. The movement was what Quintero does best: silent and suggestive. Alan Rich (1977:68) described the impact of the final tableau:

> And, as Quintero stages the last scene, cleverly undermining O'Neill's contrived "happy ending," by having his characters move apart and thereby leaving space (both physical and psychological) among them for Anna's further degradation, we are left finally with the feeling, beyond anything O'Neill himself could bring himself to suggest, that perhaps there is something more than flat melodrama to this play, some unwritten subtlety that will keep time moving forward beyond the final curtain.

The New York opening received mixed reviews. The headlines showed the production's focus all too well: "Liv Ullmann's *Anna Christie*" (Barnes, 1977:C3). "What's a Nice Girl Like Liv Doing in a Play Like This?" (Gottfried, 1977:37); "Liv in Limbo" (Kalem, 1977:84); "Liv's *Anna*" (Kroll, 1977:89); and "To See Liv Is to Luv Her" (Watts, 1977:28). Dan Sullivan (1977:?) was finally moved to accept the play on its own terms: "*Anna Christie* is— right?—Garbo in a raincoat and some crazy old man raving about dat ole debbil sea. Camp. O'Neill at his hokiest. So why at the Imperial Theater does it touch greatness? Because José Quintero and his cast believe in it." Martin Gottfried (1977:37) would not accept the play on any terms: "Still, to be fair to the revival that opened last night, it isn't at the Imperial Theater because of the play. It is there because of Liv Ullmann and she may be reason enough. This is a vehicle, pure and simple, and Miss Ullmann's stage intelligence, physical beauty and awesome sexuality make it easy to forget that vehicles have no business in the modern theater."

A number of Ullmann's personal reviews focused on the difference between her screen and stage performances. Only Harold

L to r: John Lithgow, Liv Ullmann, Robert Donley. Photo by Martha Swope.

Clurman (1977:539) questioned her suitability for the role: "Anna's sickness is the ache of a soul, an unromantic existential pain which is exemplary and not due to the accident of present circumstances. Ullmann, whatever her immediate ailment, strikes one as healthy at the core."

Critical responses to John Lithgow's Mat Burke were mixed. Critics who wanted a stage Irishman loved his work. Howard Kissel (1977:10) wrote that "Lithgow was a wonderful choice to play the suitor because, however rough his language or crude his actions, he projects a believable, redeeming innocence." Boston's Eliot Norton (1977:12) wrote that John Lithgow is a "happy, hilarious and sometimes frightening leprechaun of the sea."

It remained to Walter Kerr (1977:II, 5 & 36) to pinpoint the lack of the production's cutting edge, which precluded its coming into focus:

> I suggest that Miss Ullmann seems as isolated as she does and so unexpectedly at odds with the role because inadequate casting elsewhere and José Quintero's fidgety direction have combined to leave her without opponents sturdy enough or even steady enough on their feet, to demand her direct response . . . How is the actress to show us a secretly burdened, world-weary woman rather than a tot who pulls the bedclothes over her head during a quarrel with her father when the very weights that have oppressed her are never made visible on stage? The faces that have long since badgered and betrayed her and that may yet send her back to a life she detests—male greed, arrogance, opportunism, obtuseness—need vigorous dramatization in the persons we meet, above all in lover and father. But they are nowhere to be seen, not credibly, not with a challenging ferocity . . . Anna cannot conceivably blame any part of her plight on men like these; neither can she profitably do battle with them.

On the strength of the *Times* review, Alexander Cohen cancelled the tour and the production dragged through the summer doldrums to increasingly smaller houses until Ullmann's contract expired at the end of July.

Anna Christie marked a sharp change in Quintero's direction of O'Neill. In *Moon* four years earlier, he directed a play for the third time with a cast with whom he was intimate. In *Anna Christie*, he chose a play that needed toughness and he cast it soft, working with most of the cast for the first time. His direction was conspicuously more explicit than it had ever been: giving specific character notes at the second reading, explaining his staging conventions, and entering the playing space more often than had been his custom. Liv Ullmann is an actress who wants a good deal of direction. When asked by Richard Eder how Quintero compared with Ingmar Bergman as a stage director, Ullmann answered, "When he's directing a play instead of a movie, Ingmar is full of joy and laughter. Quintero, on the other hand, shows he's suffering and brings you with him. Bergman directs you like a conductor with a violinist. Quintero comes up and plays the violin beside you" (1977a:C15).

With *Anna Christie*, Quintero ceased being the platonic collaborator who paced the periphery of the rehearsal space; he finally entered the space to become a more active participant in shaping the production.

10

A Touch of the Poet

Writing*

Begun October 1935; first draft completed early spring 1936; second draft completed September 1937; final revisions early 1939.

Premieres

Original: Not produced in O'Neill's lifetime.

Quintero: December 28, 1977; New York, Helen Hayes Theater.

The out-of-town collapse of *A Moon for the Misbegotten* in 1947 influenced O'Neill to delay production of *Poet*, "even though Robert Edmond Jones had already drawn preliminary sketches for the set and plans had been formulated to have either Spencer Tracy or Laurence Olivier portray Con Melody" (Gelb, 1960:884–85). (Bogard [1972] repeats this casting information and, like the Gelbs, gives no source. Langner [1951] makes no such reference.)

O'Neill was fully aware of the difficulty of casting Con Melody. He told George Jean Nathan that "what this one needs

---

* For the background to O'Neill's American Cycle, see Chapter 7.

is an actor like Maurice Barrymore or James O'Neill, my old man. One of those big-chested, chiseled-mug, romantic old boys" (Sheaffer, 1973:576).

In 1950, Langner (1951:409) requested that O'Neill agree to a production "with a certain director of whom he approved. 'I don't believe I could live through a production of a new play right now,' he replied, and to my protestation that we would do everything possible to make things easy for him, he answered, 'No, that's my last word on the subject.' "

The play finally had its American premiere in New York on October 2, 1958, at the Helen Hayes Theater on West 46th Street. Harold Clurman directed the production that was produced by Robert Whitehead under the auspices of the Producers' Theatre. The production received excellent notices and ran for 284 performances. It is famous in theatrical circles for the lack of chemistry among Eric Portman's British Con, Kim Stanley's Actors' Studio Sara, and Helen Hayes' sweetness-and-light Nora.

1977–78 Production

Cast List

Mickey Maloy	Barry Snider
Jamie Cregan	Milo O'Shea
Sara Melody	Kathryn Walker
Nora Melody	Geraldine Fitzgerald
Cornelius Melody	Jason Robards
Dan Roche	Walter Flanagan
Paddy O'Dowd	Dermot McNamara
Patch Riley	Richard Hamilton
Deborah Harford	Betty Miller
Nicholas Gadsby	George Ede

In 1973, Quintero had contracted to direct Jason Robards in a Theatre-in-America television production of *A Touch of the Poet*. Robards knew the 1958 production well because he was a close friend of cast members Kim Stanley, Dermot McNamara, and Farrell Pelly. Robards and Eric Portman lived in the same building. Robards thinks "*A Touch of the Poet* is the best play O'Neill ever wrote, a fabulous play."

The filming schedule in New York coincided with the five weeks *A Moon for the Misbegotten* was to play on Broadway.

José Quintero and Jason Robards, September 1977. Photo by Martha Swope.

Robards began to rehearse Con Melody by day and play Jamie Tyrone by night, but quickly acknowledged the impossibility of the task. He withdrew from the project and Quintero quickly followed suit.

Not until 1977 did Quintero again contract to direct Robards in *A Touch of the Poet*, this time for producer Elliot Martin. Once again Quintero went to Ben Edwards to design the set. Edwards had designed the 1958 production, and in a *Theatre Crafts* article he (1967:25–27) discussed it:

> Several years after the production a director asked me why the scenic approach I chose for the play— and the director Harold Clurman agreed on—so carefully followed Eugene O'Neill's description of the set . . . I knew the director's question wasn't why I had followed Mr. O'Neill's description of the set but why I had not changed it. Why had I not added levels? Why had I made it a version of a "box set" rather than throwing it on a "more interesting angle"? Why no stairs in full view, up to "dramatic elevations"? He was, in fact, not asking questions but saying: "Had I been the director and not Harold Clurman, I would not have approved your design of a bare box set."
>
> For *A Touch of the Poet* I felt that to be too abstract would attract too much attention to the set. I usually start designing with some image in mind conjured consciously or unconsciously. This image need not have anything to do with what the set will be physically . . . In the case of *Poet* the image was of no specific thing. It was mostly a memory of a few seventeenth-century tombstones I had seen on a hillside on my first trip to Massachusetts. I can't say why this seemed to relate to the play for me. When it came to more concrete things, I remember that I visualized the tavern as being almost empty, as if all the tables had gone but a few—as if the tavern had only a few customers left, which was actually the case in the play.
>
> The set was covered in black velour, with only a suggestion of painted wood plaster detail. The

floor, however, was quite real—wide boards rak-
ing, in perspective, upstage to the center door and
four windows along a plain back wall.

I had a special feeling about these windows.
I wanted them to give the impression you get when
you have noticed the exterior of a shut-up old frame
house late in the afternoon. The house is all dark
and in shadows, but the bleached white putty
makes each window stare out of the shadows. Not
a spooky effect but one of emptiness. I can't say
why I wanted this look—but it seemed right. It
looked right.

Steve Lawson (1978:42) asked Quintero how he approached
a play like *A Touch of the Poet:* "You begin with the set: you talk
with your designer. . . . I guess because O'Neill only calls for one
room, in my mind there was a feeling of deception, of being
caught—attacked from above, from the entrance, the kitchen, the
bar."

Ben Edwards said:

To be perfectly honest, when I first started, José
said, "I liked your set. You can do it all over again
if you want to." That's what he said, but I didn't
think that he would be content with my reproduc-
ing my original set. I said, "Oh, José, I don't think
so because . . . We'll use elements of it, of course,
but I think you'll want more freedom somehow."
He seemed more pleased with that. We even went
further. José wanted, at the beginning, to have Cregan crossing the stage and entering the tavern. He
entered the tavern, but the door was way over on
stage right and he actually went through the wall
and came into the tavern.

Edwards designed a set in which, like the opening image just
described, Quintero could have his actors walk through walls when
convenient. He designed a dining room, the main playing space,
on a level above a hallway downstage and another hallway stage
right that separated the dining room from the bar. Edwards said
of the hallways that "in theory, these were the walls that were
no walls. José didn't abide by these walls very much. Although

there were two-step platforms to indicate a doorway, there were times when it was more advantageous for him to have the actors step through the walls. That's the way José directed the play. I don't think it bothered the audience. If it had been at Circle-in-the-Square, it would have been the same, no walls at all. They just disregarded walls." Unlike his 1958 set, Edwards added a visible staircase to the second floor. When asked if the difference in the two sets reflected the difference of designing for Clurman and Quintero, he answered, "Yes, I think so—I know so."

Stage manager Mitch Erickson said of Edwards' set:

> Ben is such a minimalist designer. He designed the barest of sets and everybody thought, "Pretty soon this will be dressed with muskets and pewter tankards and signs with the price of food and grog because it is an inn." Nothing. It was never dressed. It was left deliberately stark. Ben feels that gives the play its epic strength, it doesn't reduce the play to modern or petty detail. It's more upscale, enlarged, epic if that's the word. It stresses the play's classical derivation. The whole nonrealistic approach stems from José's work at the Circle where doors were out of the question.

While Edwards worked up the set, Quintero assembled the cast. Kate Reid was to play Nora, but had to drop out; Siobbhan McKenna was willing but unavailable. Luckily Geraldine Fitzgerald became available. Quintero cast Milo O'Shea as Cregan and Kathryn Walker as Sara. He then cast Betty Miller as Deborah Harford, Richard Hamilton as Patch Riley, and Dermot McNamara as Paddy O'Dowd, all of whom had worked for him before; auditions were not needed.

Dermot McNamara recalled the first day's rehearsal at the New Amsterdam Theater on 42nd Street:

> Quintero went into a lot of stuff about Con's alcoholism and Irish alcoholism. And then a big thing that none of us expected was class distinctions in New England, which I always remember because even the Americans in the cast were not aware of them because they don't think there are class distinctions in this country. We heard a lot about that

A Touch of the Poet, 1977-78. L to r: Richard Hamilton, Dermot McNamara, Katherine Walker, Milo O'Shea, Jason Robards, José Quintero. Photo by Martha Swope.

and about the period and the railroads. With me and the other rough fellows, we didn't get much of that talk.

McNamara, who is an Irish immigrant, said of Quintero that "his soul is very Irish" and described the specifically Irish fashion in which Quintero set up the opening scene:

> He went into great stuff about the horrible Irish night that must have happened the night before the play starts, which I loved. Horrible things were said the night before and they all have their hangovers the next day and, of course, in great typical Irish fashion (or even in English fashion) the Major was not about to mention any of this. Nothing had happened. That's the way, very rightly, José set up that morning. They didn't want to talk about it. He was being terrible nice to that unfortunate wife of his and terribly grand and trying to maintain the British part of him and to come away from that frightful Irish peasant that he really was, that drunken lout that had a veneer of a British major over it.

McNamara had also been in the 1958 Broadway production and recalled how true to this pattern Eric Portman had lived: "We had some blinding drunks at his Dakota apartment and horrible fights where he would say, 'You're a fucking Catholic, your fucking beady eyes are taking me all in, why aren't you queer?' I would say, 'Fuck you,' and he would say, 'Leave my house,' like the old-fashioned English dad, 'Never cross my door again.' The next day the phone would ring and he would say, 'Let's have a little lunch. Were we awful last night?' "

Barry Snider was an early replacement for an actor who had not worked out as the bartender, Mickey Maloy. Snider had recently played an Irish bartender on television's *Beacon Hill* and was cast on the basis of reading about six lines for Quintero:

> Quintero's aware that if you've done enough things that you know something about acting, and if you communicate something to him on a personal level—if he gets the vibrations that are right he'll say, "That's what I want." He won't sit around and waste time, going through all those machinations,

playing games with actors. The first day I rehearsed
with José he came up and told me this and that and
he walked off and I didn't understand a word he
said because José when he first starts to speak to
someone he doesn't quite know yet, he speaks a little
faster than he ordinarily does and his accent gets
heavier and he gets tickier and he's all over the
place.

The next day, however, Quintero brought Snider up-to-date
on his character in very concrete terms:

He would say things like "You don't believe a word
this man Cregan says, he's a liar. He's after something. He's like those people who come up to me
and say, 'You're a wonderful director.' You ask
yourself, 'What do they want?' That's what's going
on here. Milo's a charming fellow, don't be taken
in by the charm." He sailed right in in terms of relationships with the different people in the play. We
talked about the Major "whom you have no respect
for, you would dearly love to take over the whole
place from him," he said, "and you're after the girl
in the worst way. The mother is the one who sides
with you and you're buttering her up every minute." Clear specific relationships. "And the boy
upstairs," he said, "you're the one who wrote the
message to the mother." Very specific, human
things to play, a whole mass of them right away.
You don't see them in the writing, the sort of things
that you spend forever trying to dig out. Then
you're not sure that the director is going to want
to see these kinds of things imposed on the play,
but José does. The more human the better, as far
as he's concerned.

Snider had missed the opening-day discussion of the social
milieu and concluded that "José has no interest in history, anything that you would find in a book. I think he knows a great deal,
but prefers not to talk about those kinds of things. He leaves that
to the actor; it just doesn't interest him, frankly. And I think he's
right, unless, of course, the actor shows no inclination to under-

stand the social structure he's dealing with and the period, but he didn't cast actors like that. They understood something of the background."

Mitch Erickson agreed: "I've never heard José discuss external issues. His great talent is for delving into the persons and their behavior, how they confront each other. That's why he's so successful with O'Neill, his plays are full of wonderful partings, rows, and exchanges."

When asked if Quintero had attempted to place *A Touch of the Poet* in the context of the American Cycle O'Neill had been writing, Snider replied that Quintero "was more concerned with 'this is the reality that we must deal with here.' I think he feels that, when actors are doing something, if he goes into terms of these intellectual awarenesses, he tends to pull the actor out of the play rather than into the play." Erickson agreed that there had been no reference to the Cycle, that Quintero worked the play as an entity. Betty Miller played Deborah Harford, the central figure in *More Stately Mansions*, but Quintero did not refer her to that play. Miller said, "You don't really need it to play that part. She's a very strange lady in *Poet*. I don't remember her being nearly so strange in the play where she's the central character."

In working out the opening scene, Snider recalled how Quintero worked:

> José would say: "You know this man Cregan, he has a hangover because he was here last night and he wants a drink, so you offer him a drink in exchange for every piece of information you can get from him, so that we don't have *exposition* here. What we have is you searching for information to see if you can't unload this guy upstairs and then make it with Sara. That way it becomes a much more active process rather than 'Well, we're gonna get some exposition here.' " All of his direction is so far removed from the intellectual.

To bring another activity to the first-act exposition, Quintero had Geraldine Fitzgerald down on her hands and knees cleaning the floor, just as Josie Hogan had cleaned the floor in the first act of *Moon*. In *Moon*, daughter dominates father as she cleans; in *Poet*, wife is obsequious to husband. Dermot McNamara said of Fitzgerald that "she talked a lot about those Irish women who work around the house and were drudges; she knew them. She knew what it was to take up a dishcloth."

Fitzgerald already had wide experience in playing (and lecturing upon) O'Neill's work. Quintero knew that she was in control of the character and needed little coaxing. She said, "I know that self-sacrificing kind of Irish woman who makes her husband everything. She has her daughter, but Nora's husband is like another child to her and Irish men don't give up their childhood easily." Not only had Fitzgerald known such Irish women, but she is convinced that O'Neill based Nora on his own paternal grandmother and pointed out the similarities in the fourth act of *Long Day's Journey*, when James Tyrone describes his mother.

Fitzgerald recalled that "José gave me the piece of business scrubbing the floors, which was perfect, because this woman loved scrubbing the floors and tables; she wished to be useful to people, to keep them fed, warm and happy. He also gave me a wonderful action at the end of the play when he suggested I hold Con's red coat in my arms; again it was the metaphor of the wife-mother and the eternal child."

Snider recalled the difficulty of adjusting to the rehearsal techniques:

> It's a difficult part; most of the parts are difficult in that they're sort of removed from the action, they're peripheral. José tended to rehearse his major characters sort of by themselves and we got a feeling of what was going on as we would come in. Early on, he was concentrating very hard on the major scenes. The hardest part for me was that I would like to have been there when they were rehearsing the two-character scenes so I could have asked, "Now what am I doing? What does it have to do with this?" so I could be a more integral part.

When asked if he felt that these two-character rehearsals were closed, Snider answered, "Yes, to a certain degree, because he's dealing with some difficult things, intimate relationships, family relationships. No one was ever asked to come to them. As run-throughs began, I began to get a better sense of what my character's relationship was to the rest of the play."

The three Irish barflies were left very much to themselves. McNamara recalled:

> After the first day we sort of blocked ourselves in and it stayed that way forever. We were left very free by José. I couldn't get over this man who didn't block our first entrance. From day one we stood there, script in hand like three sheep, at the right-hand side of the stage. There was no set then, but they're described as going up the steps to the front door of the house. And Con says, "Get away from me, you pigs, go in the back way." The whole point is that they've begun at the front door of his house, but that's where we stayed forevermore. We always came on in the wings, but eventually there was a door and we'd say, "José, what about this front door we have to walk up to and get rejected from?" But it was never done. And Jason didn't seem to mind either. It was the craziest thing I've ever done.

The front door was not the only spatial concern. Downstage right was an area that represented arbitrarily a solid wall and then not a solid wall. In the opening scene, Cregan snuck in and stole a drink while Mickey Maloy read a newspaper (the very scene Quintero discussed with Ben Edwards in conceiving the set). For Maloy not to have seen Cregan, there had to have been a solid but invisible wall. In the third act, however, the three barflies walked right through that solid but invisible wall. Barry Snider acknowledged:

> I had trouble with that solid wall. "Is this thing solid or isn't it?" It started out as a solid wall and then changed. I don't think it ever got quite clearly defined. There are elements of logic and physical detail which José is not terribly interested in clarifying. In the end you clarify it for yourself. I think I have to criticize myself by asking, "Why didn't I clarify it sooner? Why did I wait so long to make an adjustment? Why didn't I go to José and ask, 'What is this? This is confusing.' " Because he's perfectly able to straighten it out for you. I didn't fully

understand the complications of it until we got on the set and I said, "I'm sitting right here, what do you mean I don't *see* him. He's the noisiest person I've ever seen at stealing a drink."

Snider then made a very interesting comparison between the spatial conventions of the open staging of Quintero's *Desire Under the Elms* and the proscenium staging of *A Touch of the Poet*: "I thought that the space in *Desire* was quite clear. It was clear to the actors, it was clear to me. It was somehow easier because you were dealing with only lights, you weren't dealing with a structure. Once you get into structures, like *Poet*, you have to deal with a specific demarcation. You're not doing it with your imagination."

Barbara Gelb attended some of the rehearsals and gave a detailed description of Quintero's rehearsal style:

> Quintero in action prowls the stage and the dim aisles of the empty auditorium like a lithe and restive ocelot. He is choreographer, dancer, conductor, vocalist, therapist, diplomat, spiritualist, seer and actor—most emphatically actor; the stage lost a potential star when Quintero decided to become a director. He raises an arm, index finger pointing skyward, marking a pause in dialogue. He smashes his fist onto a prop table, not so much to show the actor how to perform a bit of stage business, but because he is feeling the role. He had been silently mouthing the actor's lines in this particular scene and the emotions here dictate a violent physical comment. Quintero does not necessarily expect the actor to copy his gesture, but is merely communicating how the character feels. He hums along when the actors break into song, nods his head and stamps his feet when they perform a little jig, beams when they joke and laugh, twists his features into a grimace of despair during a speech of anguish, reaches up with both arms as a scene draws to a close, in a gesture resembling a benediction, calls softly, "curtain." He is a complete performance (Gelb, 1977:125).

In fact, Quintero never acts. Having just watched a scene through to its conclusion, Quintero will not hesitate to assume an actor's role, brandish the appropriate prop, and, with full voice and gestures, demonstrate what he wants. His demonstration, however, has none of the foundations of acting; it is all externals, it is indicating. It is meant to indicate to the actor the level of passion or commitment the character feels at that moment. Quintero is fully aware that the actor involved may not reach or justify that level of playing for an additional week or so. If Quintero were acting in these demonstrations, actors would resent being shown the chalk lines they were expected to toe.

Quintero did "act out" scenes during *Poet* rehearsals, Erickson recalled: "Lots of it. Because José has certain verbal limitations in communicating, with the language, with his accent. This is his shorthand. When he cannot find the English words, he feels that he can get up there and demonstrate. I don't think that in his wildest dreams he wants you to imitate him. He wants to show the actor the heat of the scene."

Robards says of Quintero's "acting-out" of a scene that "José knows which actors need him and which actors don't. Not that he hasn't gotten up and done it for me. *All* directors do that. I remember at the American Academy they told me 'When the director is showing you something, stand down on the apron and look at him on the stage.' There is nothing special about José. He does it no more than any other director."

Barbara Gelb (1977:126) attempted to pin down the methods by which Quintero had directed Robards for a quarter of a century:

> "Jason and I understood each other, right away," Quintero says recalling the first time he directed Robards at Circle-in-the-Square . . . "There was an open corridor between us, with no obstructions. There was never a feeling that I had to be careful, you know, not to say that. It has always been like that, also with Colleen and Gerry Page. They don't have to hear what I say, they sense what I feel. That's my kind of actor and I'm their kind of director."
>
> "I don't remember José actually telling me anything," Robards says, confirming this, at the

end of the third week of rehearsal, "he's *acting* with us."

She then contrasted the impact a director makes on a self-sufficient actor like George C. Scott and his impact on Robards who "develops a role slowly and emotionally, from within. He welcomes Quintero's suggestions and support—which is not to say that Robards is not a highly innovative actor. The collaboration between the two is far more typical of Quintero's directorial approach than is the intellectual and minimal collaboration between him and Scott" (Gelb, 1977:126).

Quintero began to see Con Melody in terms of his own father: "To understand Con Melody, I began thinking how my father felt . . . My father died in complete humiliation six years ago. To understand Con Melody, I found myself living my father's humiliation" (Gelb, 1977:120). Quintero employed a different image to get Robards started:

> All the examples I give to Jason are emotional ones. For instance, I've talked to him about how it felt to Melody to live in the past, how his life has no meaning in the present. Who is Melody without his dreams? I think he is on the verge of madness when the play begins, like Hickey in *The Iceman Cometh*. And we talk about Mr. O'Neill. What must those years have been like when he was forgotten and could no longer write? He must have said to himself, "I was given the Nobel Prize" (Gelb, 1977:127).

In putting the play on its feet, Quintero took O'Neill's stage directions selectively, according to Barbara Gelb (1977:127): "He explained that O'Neill's stage directions—elaborate and fanciful and often quite impossible—are not, in his opinion, meant to be taken literally. They are, rather, meant as guides to characterization." Nothing need be forced on Robards. Quintero explained:

> "If something doesn't become organic to Jason, we throw it out, but we're not afraid to try anything." One piece of business that became organic was the cold fury with which Robards, as Melody, crumpled a paper document whose contents he will not confront. Watching Robards in an early rehearsal,

L ro r: Dermot McNamara, Geraldine Fitzgerald, Kathryn Walker, Jason Robards. Photo by Martha Swope.

Quintero senses his wish to make the gesture—and his hesitation. Silently Quintero stepped up to Robards, ad-libbed the sense of his line and closed his fist around the piece of paper. "Once you set Jason on the right track . . . " Quintero leaves the sentence unfinished, but gestures to show that Robards will take flight. "Watch the way Jason deals with his cigar, as though it's the most deadly stiletto. His hand movements, his body movements are incredible. I will say things to him like, 'try to catch the plume-like silhouette of Lord Byron.' I never push him, because I know he is very daring. He was willing even to try taking out his bridge after his fight scene" (Gelb, 1977:127).

Rehearsals focused on the complexity of Con Melody's character, locating the touch of the poet, throwing light on an avenue of approach the audience would need to reach Melody. Dean Valentine (1978:25) pinpointed the single, overriding requirement of producing *A Touch of the Poet*:

Of all the playwright's works, *A Touch of the Poet* most resembles a buskin, dealing as it does with a hero whose immense hubris precipitates a fall. But unlike the protagonists of classical tragedy, Cornelius has few redeeming features; his ignominy is difficult to sympathize with and the audience is tempted to wish this blustery fool good riddance rather than good night. For the play to succeed then—to produce the necessary pity and terror— the lead actor must supply the character with what O'Neill did not, a self-deceit worthy of respect, as well as a nobility that can be tragically crushed by awakening from a dream of the past to the reality of a materialistic America.

For Robards, the title of the play refers not to Con, but to "the poet upstairs, that kid Simon who is never seen. That's the touch of the poet." As Robards sees him:

Con is reacting in opposition to the young generation growing up and to the society in which he's living. He's a rebel. To the Yanks like Deborah who come in, he's scum. He's angry and that's why he's still a drunk, because he never found out what it was that was eating him. It was wonderful for me to get a chance to play that kind of guy and know that underneath that he was something else. It's the mask that O'Neill puts into every play.

Robards is equivocal about Melody's military background: "Who knows what a hero of Talavara he was? I *read* all about Talavara. Christopher Plummer, who'd played Wellington, gave me a lot of stuff for research. I wanted to be familiar with the Peninsular Wars because I talk to Milo about where we were on the map so I looked up that particular battle, but maybe it's all bullshit." This is an unusual choice, or nonchoice. Whether or not Melody distinguished himself at Talavara and was decorated by Wellington would seem to be the very spine of building Melody's character. The active choice would be to make him a fighting Irish devil who showed the English how it should be done.

Dermot McNamara's memories of how Con Melody's character developed dwelt on his military and sexual prowess:

> Early in the play, Eric Portman was perfect when Con is being the British guy, a British officer immaculate on parade. He looked good. Maybe in the first act Jason who is all-American was not as happy in that cravat as he was later when he falls apart because then he was off to the races. I don't think Portman could have touched that and remained lucid. Robards has all that balls going for him all the time, no matter what he's playing. You can't dislike the man, you've got to feel what he feels. It's so powerful.

According to McNamara, Quintero built up Con's bravado until Mrs. Harford rejected his advances in the second act:

> That sets him off, in José's opinion, because he was a good-looking bloke and he had his way with the women a lot. He was a major after all, with the uniform. He says, "A kiss will not be out of place now, my dear," and she walks away from him. That killed him, that rejection, only that. He wasn't trying to get her in the sack at that moment, but

imagine a man of his vanity and ego and Irishness,
with a basic inferiority and the class distinction.

Barry Snider stressed the difficulty of locating the nature of
the poet in Con:

> That was the center of the problem of the produc-
> tion. As he was described by José, he was a soldier,
> he was the hero of Talavara, he was that as a young
> man. The problem came in with the concept of the
> "poet," in his conception of himself as a poet,
> because he tended to have a kind of elitist attitude
> which those who are rather insecure feel and
> express, and he expressed it in such a way that Jason
> would go through the lines "I have not loved the
> world" and he would say, "I feel phoney, phoney
> saying that when I get out on the stage. Preten-
> tious." The difficulty is, of course, in finding a way
> to say that the man is pretentious, because you can't
> say that he isn't. And Jason's instincts about that
> have got to be totally right. Jason is so unpreten-
> tious himself and he cuts through that sort of thing
> and he can see it a mile away. The hard part for
> an actor like Jason, who is so opposed to anything
> pretentious on stage, was to find some way to make
> this man, underneath all that, display some value.
> And he did, of course, find value in it in the tran-
> sition, after he got drunk, from there on he was
> gorgeous. Those early scenes were the difficult part.

Snider examined the manner in which he thought Robards
tried to create a poetic nature:

> If he were to ascribe a poetic nature to a character
> he would find a real poetic nature—that's not the
> sort of thing that Jason can play. He says, "that's
> bullshit." He would say that directly. The first part
> of the play—it's a problem with the play—you can
> do it as some actors do it, stand up straight and
> deliver it like that, you're a poet. Well, what does
> that mean? My impression of Jason was that he
> never felt totally satisfied with it. It's a problem

with that man going on and on about what a poet
he is. It's very difficult to solve.

In effect, rehearsals continued on the road. *A Touch of the
Poet* was scheduled to play the Toronto-Baltimore-Washington,
DC subscription circuit, but Robards had a film commitment that
ran over, delayed rehearsals, and eliminated the Toronto engagement. Mitch Erickson trembled when he recalled that "we lost
the dark week in Toronto for technicals. We went into Baltimore
on a Monday morning and had a performance on Tuesday evening. We never teched the show."

In Baltimore, according to Snider, "We ran for four hours
and got three laughs. We cut only a little in New York and of course
we were in bad shape. We didn't know what we were doing yet.
It needed a lot of tightening up just in terms of the production
but, even with that, we still had to cut." McNamara said: "No
one wanted to cut, least of all José, because it was sacrosanct, but
in Baltimore they were snoring in that theater at quarter to 12.
Finally Elliot Martin, who is a businessman, thank God, prevailed.
They got it back to 11:15. They cut 20 minutes right there in Baltimore and in New York we came down by 11:00."

In Washington, DC, Quintero absented himself from the
production, as he had done with *Anna Christie* in Toronto. He
announced, "I'm not sure what I can do with this play at this point
so I'm going down to Puerto Rico for a week. All of you do what
you have to do." Snider recalled that when Quintero returned,
he said:

> "This is good, this is good," and he straightened
> out a few things. I think it was a rather marvelous
> time because there were a lot of steps forward at
> that time because the actors were saying, in a way,
> "I'm going to have to go out there and play this.
> José is not going to be standing here holding my
> hand. We've got to go out and try to solve some
> of these problems by using our own instincts, mak-
> ing the part ours and the play ours."

Robards felt that Quintero's direction was "the clearest and
hardest work he ever did. I've never seen him stick with a play

like that. The great care that José put into the show, the preparation and the follow-up, all the way through the road to New York, paid off as the play went on." By and large the critics agreed. Marilyn Stasio's (1978:20) rave was the only review that implied that Quintero had succeeded by directing against the text:

> The character of Con is usually interpreted as O'Neill probably intended, as an irascible bull of a man very much like James O'Neill, a man whose bursts of cruelty can be forgiven because he has a speck of the artist's imagination. A touch of O'Neill if you will. Robards has the guts to defy this romantic excuse and to interpret Con's "gift" as a touch of the Devil. For all the charm and dignity he allows Con, Robards never glosses over the rough, even savage cruelty of the man.

Most of the reviews, like the production itself, sought to locate just what constitutes the implications of the title. Wherein lies the touch of the poet? They focused, inevitably, on Robards' performance as Con.

Both *Newsweek* and *Time* were lavish in their praise of Robards. Jack Kroll (1978:71) wrote that "this is the poetry of crack-up and Jason Robards is the master actor of crack-up . . . Some of his acting earlier in the play . . . is somewhat mannered and fussy." Ted Kalem (1978:68) wrote that "to the role of Con Melody, Robards brings the deep-set, brooding eyes of profound melancholy, the harsh self-lacerating laugh that masks inner pain, the actorish stance of assuming, while mocking, the grand manner, the human love that becomes inhuman cruelty under the distillation of alcohol." Kalem put his finger on, and accepted, "the actorish stance of assuming, while mocking, the grand manner." Other reviewers would not accept it.

Robards' military bearing was brought into question. John Simon (1978:57) wrote that "one does not believe in his military prowess or in his determined rise to specious respectability." Michael Finegold (1978:67) wrote that "the body, even at maximum hauteur, does not have the force needed for a major of dragoons: the voice long ago settled into a permanent rasp and is short of sounding brass."

Accents proved to be a problem. Mitch Erickson said that "José's strong suit is not dialect or speech of any kind, so he's not inclined to steer people in that direction." Milo O'Shea, Geraldine Fitzgerald, and Dermot McNamara were all Irish-born and used their own accent. Robards had a much more complicated task. As Leonard Harris (1978:40) wrote, "Robards, an American, must play an Irishman trying to sound like an upperclass Englishman. It's not quite there." Martin Gottfried (1978:41) wrote that "Robards is surely the great O'Neill actor of our time, but when he tries a high British accent, he is an actor with a hot potato in his mouth."

Beyond the technique of military bearing and English accent lay the ability to examine and project the cruel disparity between Con's military and social background in both Ireland and England and his present existence as a barkeeper. Producer Elliot Martin articulated the production's concept of Con Melody:

> The concept behind the work that Jason did on *Poet* was that this man was a bog-Irishman. That was his basic background, and he had been sent to an English academy to learn a certain amount of polish, but he never learned it. He was a tough, gutter Irishman. Rather than playing him from the other point of view, which was to cast it as an Englishman who was terribly grand and try to play the rough bog-Irishman. In our discussions, we justified it the other way around. There was a lot of baggy pants in that character, basically. When he became grand, it was phoney grand. After all, he was in a run-down, early American tavern which was very Irish-oriented and if anybody put on airs—if you go to Ireland today and put on airs, they'd throw you right out. Our point of view was that Jason was very right because he's a bog-Irishman.

Stage manager Mitch Erickson agreed: "What with Jason and his wry view of life and his sense of humor, I don't remember any attempt to make Con a great figure or person. He wasn't a great man fallen, but a man with great aspirations who was living a huge lie and gets his comeuppance."

Every critic granted Robards the grandeur of his final twenty minutes in the role, when he is beaten and humiliated, but six major critics/publications found the pivotal element of the production (as articulated by Martin and played by Robards) either misconceived or badly executed. Harold Clurman (1978:60–61), who had directed the 1958 production, wrote:

> What Robards cannot convincingly achieve is personal grandeur. I am not sure that José Quintero as director has wholly understood the play. For while Melody is something of a fool in his Byronic swagger, his aspiration to and feeling for nobility are real. He is a dreamer, not a faker; his whole being yearns for what was sound and forever worthy in the old aristocratic ideal of the English gentry, an ideal O'Neill held in high esteem . . . Melody's downfall at the hands of the wealthy New England "tradesmen" is pathetic and meaningful to the play only if we discern the idealistic truth hidden beneath his boastful postures and lordly behavior. There can be no real pathos in the crackup of a pipsqueak or a phony.

Dean Valentine (1978:25) wrote of Robards:

> He plays Melody as a foppish buffoon. Descending the stairs caparisoned in his major's uniform, he looks merely like a poseur, a man too small for his britches; certainly he has not the trace of a hero of the Battle of Talavara, the classy soldier decorated by Wellington. He crumples up his fingers, rolls his eyelids to denote a touch of the demoniac, curls his lip and sticks out his tongue. These gestures, it is true, frequently produce the desired effect; a con man whose lies and sarcasm overlay an infinite pool of disgust with the world. The desired effect, though, is not the right one, and it is difficult not to feel that Robards is hamming it up at the cost of a truly heroic Melody.

Elliot Norton (1978:30) wrote:

> It is, of course, true that Melody is in both cases mimicking manners and accents which are not quite his own. Although he was born in a shanty,

he was educated in an English school, and elevated to the rank of major in a prestigious English regiment. He would have more style and authority, even if these are faded, and a much less fraudulent manner of speech than that of Jason Robards. The major is, in a sense, a phony. But not so desperately ridiculous, so amateurishly imitative, as Jason Robards makes him.

Richard Eder, Stanley Kauffmann, and Walter Kerr all focused their reservations about Robards' Melody on the crucial seduction scene. Richard Eder (1977b:C13) wrote, "Mr. Robards acts too old. With marvelous timing and control, changing courses as suddenly as a waterbug, he spectacularly manages Melody's silky deviousness, his aristocratic airs, but his delusion is something he mostly toys with. He may get angry asserting it but it is a testy anger . . . Mr. Robards' semi-seduction is all style and buffoonery."

After commending Robards' final 20 minutes, Stanley Kauffmann (1978:24–25) went on to say:

> But in the major part of the role (pun intended), he is, frankly, appalling. I could hardly believe what I was seeing and hearing. Instead of a Byron-quoting ex-officer, a fallen emperor with a ragged retinue, we get mugging and caricature. For just one instance: when the elegant Mrs. Harford, Simon's mother, enters unannounced, Robards turns from his mirror and discovers her. Then he does a full unabashed "take" from her face to the audience, like a baggy-pants comic when a pretty girl comes in. Throughout, until the very end, he kept reminding me of Harvey Korman of "The Carol Burnett Show" playing a lord. Then I realized what was happening. Robards (and his director) took the "elevated" portion of the role as impersonation, a kind of W. C. Fields act of grandeur. Nothing could be falser or most destructive of the play. Either the grand Con is *not* "acting" or there is no tragedy. The two actors I've seen previously in the part, Eric Portman and Denholm Elliott, had their shortcomings, but both of them

understood that basic truth. Without it, without
Con's belief in himself as a gentleman, all we get
is the exposure of a self-conscious faker which is
trivial.

As soon as Elliott Martin was reminded that Kauffmann had
referred to Melody as "a fallen emperor with a ragged retinue,"
Martin burst out triumphantly, "You see! *That's* miscasting. That's
really miscasting, because this character was a low-born Irishman
whose father, somehow or other, scraped together the money and
pulled enough strings to get him into an English school where they
probably made terrible fun of him. So, for the rest of his life, he'd
send them up if he got the chance."

Walter Kerr (1978:D5) concluded:

If all this is to hold up in the theater the poetic
impulse must be constantly present and be recog-
nized for what it is. Those who cling to it may be
fools but they must be ambiguously fools: men with
a trace of actual talent, men with color on their
tongue, men of ludicrously thwarted aspiration.
And it is here that the present production collapses
completely. Until the satisfyingly vigorous final
scene, neither Mr. Quintero nor Mr. Robards sug-
gests that there is anything to be salvaged from a
fantasist's inventive brain, from a memory of hero-
ism on the battlefield under Wellington, from an
ostentatious fondness for Byron's rhythms, for, if
you will, an unquenchable thirst for blarney.

Mr. Robards looks right when he enters,
straightbacked in a black frock coat, lace at his
throat and wrists. Almost at once, however, he is
reduced to an idle poppinjay, tyrant to no purpose.
Nervously and noisily rattling a whiskey bottle
against a glass for his first sip of the morning, he
is very nearly a cartoon. The one-dimensional hum-
buggery continues as he wriggles his fingers high
in the air like a barnstorming Osric, as he turns
from self-adulation in a mirror to hike his eyebrows
at the audience in a vaudeville leer, as he adopts
stances that constantly seem to be inviting someone to slap him across the face with a glove. "Thank

God," he purrs, "I still bear the stamp of an offi-
cer and a gentleman." But he doesn't really; he
bears the stamp of a fop. When he proposes to flat-
ter the visiting Miss Miller by pawing her, the clum-
siness of the gesture may be half-right. But surely
it should have another half to it; some echo of the
suave gallantry that must have been his as a young
man.

In his review of *A Moon for the Misbegotten*, Stanley Kauffmann (1974:34) wrote of Robards' performance that "essentially
this is the fourth installment of Robards' performance of the O'Neill
character; it's virtually the same man he played in *The Iceman
Cometh, Hughie* and, of course, *Long Day's Journey Into Night*.
Robards does it superbly. It's the only character I've ever seen him
do superbly." In his review of *A Touch of the Poet*, Kauffmann
(1978:24–25) emphasizes the difference between Con Melody and
the other O'Neill characters Robards had played: "In the last 20
minutes or so of the play, Jason Robards is fine as Melody, on the
other side of the catastrophe in which Con is degraded. When the
role comes *to* Robards, when he can once again do the one character he can do well—the ironic, self-loathing drunk, the Jamie of
Long Day's Journey and *A Moon for the Misbegotten*—he fulfills
it."
　　To take Kauffmann one step further, the four O'Neill roles
Robards has played are all based heavily on James O'Neill, Jr.,
whereas Con is based on James O'Neill, Sr., and set 100 years
earlier than the Jamie characters. Robards is certainly no stranger to fatherhood or to the military. With his extended family and
his experiences in the Pacific during World War II, Robards has
all the life experience needed to play Melody. Until 1977, when
he played Melody, Robards' career, certainly his great successes,
consisted largely of sons rebelling against the imposition of the
parental will. It is a very specific acting impulse. Even if the parental figure does not appear on stage, the son is still able to lash out
at restraints. In *A Touch of the Poet*, however, as domestic drama,
it is Con the father who imposes the restraints, who behaves
arbitrarily, who sets the tone. It is a totally different acting impulse
and Robards did not seem to be at home with it.
　　Robards, understandably, rejected this theory and refused
to be pigeonholed: "This is a gift I've got and I don't know any-

thing about that gift. I'm just lucky that I've got it, that I've got *some* of it. It's rubbed off on me, from my dad or wherever it came from, my genes or my experience, but I don't question it. I don't start tearing it apart because then you end up in a Strasberg class and, Jesus, who wants to be there?"

A Touch of the Poet is not often produced, but there has been a striking consistency in trying to capture the essence of Con. In 1947, the Theatre Guild wished to cast either Spencer Tracy or Laurence Olivier. Thirty years later, producer Elliot Martin said that Con "was a tough, gutter Irishman." Until the 1977–78 *Poet*, Con had been played twice in New York City by Eric Portman and Denholm Elliott, two terribly grand (and gifted) Englishmen. Robards was the first American playing the role and he made some passive acting choices: the touch of the poet resides in an offstage character and Con may or may not have been decorated by Wellington. That's a lot to give up. It pleased some of the critics. Ted Kalem (1978:68), for instance, believed that Con is "as confirmed a dream addict as any of the tosspots in *The Iceman Cometh.*" From the six demurring critics included here, for whom the touch of the poet is *definitely* in Con himself who was *definitely* honored by Wellington, Robards was bound to take a hammering.

The production remains one of Robards' fondest achievements: "I kept learning doing that play daily, every day, until it closed nine months after we'd started. I was always learning something as an actor. I was soaring. It was like finding a new color to put on the canvas every day. It was so exciting to go to the theater to do that play."

11

Welded

Writing
　Begun late September 1922; completed February 1923.
Premieres
　Original: March 17, 1924; New York, 39th Street Theater.
　Quintero: June 10, 1981; New York, Columbia University Horace Mann Theater.

1924 Production

Cast List
Michael Cape　　　　　Jacob Ben-Ami
Eleanor　　　　　　　　Doris Keane
John　　　　　　　　　　Curtis Cooksey
A Woman　　　　　　　　Catherine Collins

O'Neill and Agnes Bolton married in 1918. By 1922, the pressures of that marriage led him to examine the relationship in dramatic form. He wrote to Kenneth Macgowan on September 23, 1922, as he began writing *Welded*, that the play "demands evolving into some new form of its own if I am to say what I want to. My conception of it as Strindberg's *Dance of Death* formula seems hard

to fit on . . . but I have no inkling yet of the 'belonging method' "
(Sheaffer, 1973:100).

Dance of Death is relevant to the thematic material, but certainly not to the style in which *Welded* is written:

> In style the play embodied what O'Neill thought
> of as a sort of suprarealism; that is, he intended
> it to be realistic in the sense of symbolic universality and truth, but not realistic in representation.
> For example, he called for a stage effect that consisted of two circles of light "like auras of egoism"
> to pick out and follow Michael and Eleanor
> throughout the action of the play. "There is no
> other lighting," writes O'Neill in his stage directions. "The other two people and the rooms are distinguishable only by the light of Eleanor and
> Michael" (Gelb, 1960:520).

The play's prose has none of the tough fiber of Strindberg's prose. Michael's proclamation that "our marriage must be a consummation demanding and combining the best in each of us! Hard, difficult, guarded from the commonplace, kept sacred as the outward form of our inner harmony" (O'Neill, 1951:262) is typical. At one point in the first act, O'Neill (1951:266) stipulates that the dialogue not be rendered realistically: "Their chairs are side by side, each facing front, so near that by a slight movement each could touch the other, but during the following scene they stare straight ahead and remain motionless. They speak, ostensibly to the other, but showing by their tone it is a thinking aloud to oneself, and neither appears to hear what the other has said." In an attempt to make the play timeless, there is not a single contemporary reference in the writing.

Welded became the first O'Neill play to be produced by the O'Neill–Robert Edmond Jones–Kenneth Macgowan triumvirate. Jones was to design the sets and lighting, Stark Young to direct, and Jacob Ben-Ami and Doris Keane to costar. The rehearsals were an unrelieved nightmare: Ben-Ami lost confidence in the play, Keane lost confidence in the play and in Ben-Ami. Both wished to withdraw, but were persuaded by Young to remain. O'Neill did not see what he called "an attempt at the last word in intensity in truth about love and marriage" (Gelb, 1960:521) appearing in rehearsals. "Not only was he critical of both leading players but halfway through rehearsals, when it was too late to change the settings, he decided that they should have been symbolic rather than realistic, that they helped to throw his script off-key" (Sheaffer, 1973:132).

Stark Young (1957:70) wrote of the O'Neills at *Welded* rehearsals: "I can see them now at some of the rehearsals sitting side by side in the third row and listening to every speech, good or bad, and taking it all as 'bona fide' and their own." Sheaffer (1973: 132) brings that published memory down to earth: "Another time, speaking privately, he put it more bluntly: 'Those God-awful speeches! Yet Gene and Agnes drank it all in as though it were poetry.' "

The actors remained, as did the realistic sets. O'Neill, uncharacteristically, agreed to a week's out-of-town engagement in Baltimore "where the playwright attended several performances and made last-minute revisions" (Sheaffer, 1973:132). When the production opened in New York, it met with uniformly disastrous notices.

In *Ritual and Pathos*, Leonard Chabrowe (1976:24–25) wrote of *Welded* that "O'Neill realized the necessity of playing this expressionistically, although rehearsals were already under way by the time he did. His idea was to hide the realistic settings in drapes and to isolate each of the characters at certain moments by spotlights that would be like halos or auras of egoism. The device didn't save the play, but it did contribute to the psychology of it." None of the contemporary reviews mentions the spotlights as focusing on the two protagonists as a motif. The only reference to the lighting was made by George Jean Nathan (1924:115):

> The staging of the manuscript by Stark Young was satisfactory save in the manner of lighting. Unless my eye deceived me on the opening night, it was high noon outside the window of the room in Act II although the time was two o'clock in the morning. Again, the dawn of the last act was of a peculiar pea-green shade, as of Maeterlinck full of chartreuse. Still again, although the room of Act I was illuminated only by a small and arty table lamp at the extreme left of the stage, the center of the stage—the battleground of the action—was whimsically bathed in a dazzling radiance by a powerful balcony spotlight.

It would appear that during rehearsals the sets became less realistic than what Jones had designed and the lighting more realistic than what O'Neill had specified. This inability to fix on a production style for the play (what O'Neill had called "the belonging method") resulted in a style of which Alexander Woollcott wrote, "the milieu of the man and wife was occasionally left to shift for itself so vaguely that there were times when the wrangling two seemed as silhouetted and alone as two back fence cats in debate" (Gelb, 1960:545).

O'Neill had gone to great lengths to redefine realism, but the critics would have none of it. Ludwig Lewisohn (1924:377) wrote:

> In the scene with the prostitute, Mr. Ben-Ami's lines are preposterous enough in form, however good in substance. Had he used a visionary simplicity of delivery one might have suspended disbelief. He preaches. The direction is rhetorical. Mr. Ben-Ami and Miss Keane act. They never do anything at any moment but act in the crass and obvious sense. The audience laughed. For on this one point the uninstructed are at one with sound critical doctrine; they want the illusion of reality. You may produce that illusion by any means you like, from stark realism to ultra-expressionism. The artistic and spiritual result must be ultimately and in effect the same—to show truth, to show life, to come a little closer to truth.

George Jean Nathan (1924:115) made the one substantive effort to examine how O'Neill was attempting to expand realism: "He has misjudged, it seems to me completely, the Strindberg method. That method is the intensification of a theme from within. O'Neill has intensified his theme from without. He has piled psychological and physical situation on situation until the structure topples over with a burlesque clatter. Strindberg magnified the psyche of his characters. O'Neill magnifies their actions."

By November 1932, O'Neill "lumped *Welded* together with *The Fountain, The First Man* and *Gold* as 'too painfully bungled to merit reviving' " (Sheaffer, 1973:108).

1981 Production

Cast List

Michael Cape	Phillip Anglim
Eleanor	Ellen Tobie
John	Court Miller
A Woman	Laura Gardner

Beginning in 1978, the Center for Theatre Studies at Columbia University had produced plays "of interest to both the professional and the educational communities" (Harris, 1981:9). The most conspicuous of these productions were *Galileo* with Laurence Luckinbill and *Suddenly Last Summer* with Dina Merrill. Andrew Harris, assistant professor and Acting Chairman for the Center for Theatre Studies, believed that "the best way to bring Columbia into competitive position as a theatre department was to have a professional theater, eventually a LORT theater. At this point, we had a letter-of-agreement with Actors' Equity, so we were working under a version of the off-Broadway mini-contract. The university seemed receptive to the idea if the participants were of the caliber of Quintero, etc."

During Quintero's 10-week residency at Columbia, Harris prevailed upon him to direct an O'Neill production:

> What José wanted to do was the early O'Neill. He had explored the older O'Neill. He wanted to see the later O'Neill in the early O'Neill's work. I said that sounds like the kind of thing you do at a university. There's a more experimental atmosphere. (That didn't turn out to be quite true.) The New York press questioned whether we were bringing a commercial product on to the market. I don't think that was the spirit in which we began. We wanted to do an O'Neill Festival, the young O'Neill, and we wanted to do more than one.

The available space was the Horace Mann Theater, which is a 140-seat house with a proscenium opening of 22 feet, 30 feet deep, and only 18 feet high, with no means of flying or storing scenery. These limitations precluded *The Hairy Ape*, which was Quintero's first choice. Harris said, "I suggested *Welded*. He reread it and liked it, more than liked it. He was very enthusiastic about doing it."

Quintero met with Harris subsequently and discussed his production concept. Harris (1981:9) wrote:

> Quintero did not consider *Welded* to be a finished script. Instead, he looked at it as if it were the script of a contemporary experimental playwright. O'Neill's acts were not acts; they were scenes. The locales were not fully realized; they were just schematic representations. What separated one place from another was a certain emblem; a bed for the prostitute, a stairway for the artist's apartment, and so on.
>
> In order to express the evolutionary process of this work, Quintero required that the actors be dressed in contemporary clothing and that they work together in a way that suggested that the playwright himself was watching them rehearse. This meant that the playwright might appear from time to time and change lines or reorder the speeches.

In interview, Harris said of the production concept:

> José wanted the various elements of the set to be moved by the actors, although he changed his mind later on. He wanted to capture that "loft" kind of feeling, that kind of bohemian feeling where people were living in a much more open fashion and to make a direct connection between the bohemianism of that era and today's. He wanted that kind of "this is in rehearsal" feeling, "this is an experimental play," "we're making no bones, it's not a finished script." He did not want to use follow spots. He wanted it non-stop. He wanted that flow in quality, a kind of fluidity, that this was kind of happening and not happening, and he felt that it was a short play and that intermissions would have killed it.

Actress Laura Gardner said of the production concept:

> I think that, in the beginning, he was going more toward a more stylistic approach. That's why we

had the poles. Initially it was just going to be chairs and a lot of miming. Very evident in the script is this sense of characters in loneliness, ego-vision, the egotism of each character. The lights were going to be very strange. To José, although the style of writing was somewhat lofty and dramatic, the way of doing it had to be simple in order for the language not to be laughable, not to be embarrassing.

On the other hand, to use that simplicity against a symbolic background, with just chairs, just having the spotlight on the stage, with just the poles as opposed to having a full set, would enable the audience to see pure emotion. José wanted to stylize the physical part of it, not the emotional part.

Harris said that Quintero wanted the set:

to look like the back of the theater, where various things start to say one thing and yet still give you that sense of being in a theater. To create the back of the theater, it was necessary for us to buy brick because we have a plastic psyche. We could not get the sense of being in the backstage of a theater, in José's mind, without having a naked brick wall. So we had to go out and put in a bigger set in some ways than we had bargained for because, not only did we have to take down all the curtains, but put up this brick wall all the way to the grid. He wanted us to remove the apron from the stage, which we did.

When asked what terms Quintero used to describe a set or the space in which he was working, Harris answered:

In speaking of the set, he uses no technical terms, but uses very emotionally charged language which is highly active. He tries to stimulate, in the same way he works with his actors. The only trouble is that there is a preconceived notion and his statement of it is not that clear. In other words, it's not quite true. He leads a designer into believing that things are probably more open than they are. There was a tremendous falling out between José and the designer, Quentin Thomas. They weren't speaking to each other and the designer wanted to withdraw because he didn't feel that José was true to the production he had originally started with. The trouble was that José's concept did change.

Welshman Quentin Thomas had designed for London's Royal Court Theater and Royal Shakespeare Company, as well as for American regional theaters. By 1981, he had already designed *Peking Man* and *Suddenly Last Summer* for Andrew Harris at Columbia, where he was an associate professor in the theater department. Harris mentioned the possibility of *Welded* to Thomas and he agreed to meet Quintero. Thomas said that "we seemed to have an overall link. He wanted to take risks, to be innovative. He didn't want to do just a standup version of the piece."

When asked how Quintero described space and staging, Thomas replied:

> He was constantly referring to "passion" and "intimacy," wanting to get as close to the audience as possible, wanting the audience to sense the physical presence of the actors as much as possible. That is why we came up with the idea of putting in that step, making the whole stage a step in the front, to break that barrier of the actual front of the stage and bring the actors to the front, to become intimate with the audience, without trying to build a thrust stage or something like that.

Thomas agreed to design *Welded* "as a simplistic piece, as a work in progress, as if the playwright were alive, and it moved pretty smoothly through the design process."

Thomas is a great believer in seeing the original concept through to completion and spoke with great conviction against the alterations made in productions such as *My One and Only* and *42nd Street*: "Theater is a hit-or-miss business. Once you're embarked, stick with it, see it through. Don't change course. If you don't see it through, if you abort it, you'll never know if it was right. One's best ideas are one's initial ideas."

By Thomas' definition, Quintero changed the concept of *Welded:*

He suddenly made a conscious decision to turn it into a finished piece, a finished theatrical production. It may have been peer pressure. He felt that people would be coming and viewing it in that way and would not give it credit if he produced it in a casual, experimental manner, that the intellectuals would feel that he had not presented a finished piece of theater, which I felt was a betrayal. The moment that one tried to present it as a finished work, one was overblowing the piece. It became more elaborate scenographically and he tried to compensate for the lack of drama in the piece by producing more drama within the location.

When we originally spoke of the actors sitting on the edge of the stage in a work light, we were then to reduce the work light to allow an atmosphere of intimacy to develop between them. I felt that it was essential to stay true to that. The lights and sets were to be designed to give the impression that one could stop and start again, to draw the audience into and then out of the production, rather than control them in the conventional theatrical sense. Instead of remaining true to the original concept, he suddenly felt compelled to turn it into a great theatrical work, an undiscovered insight into Quintero. (I mean O'Neill; that's a Freudian slip.) The design is meant to serve and augment, not meant to create theater merely for the sake of creating theater.

When asked what specific changes Quintero made, Thomas replied:

It's not as simple as a director's suddenly saying, "OK, let's bring on some walls." The set didn't change, don't get me wrong. It was the idea change. So much of it had to do with the lighting. Where there is minimal scenery, lighting is exceptionally important. At technical rehearsals he suddenly started introducing these washes of blue and

blood red. In my mind, he was telling the audience
what they were supposed to be feeling. It was supposed to be lit with a work light. We were to control the balance up and down, allowing the piece
to dictate when you take the lighting down or let
it draw in on the couple and then open it back
again. It was supposed to be overall lighting so that
people could move anywhere. José started asking,
"Why don't we have a light here, why don't we
have a light there?" I said, "You wait, the next
thing he'll want is a follow spot." That's just what
he did. That's when he went over into the outer
limits. Because you put them into a follow spot,
it's almost like watching a movie. The audience is
totally controlled, not taking part. It's the same
convention as a Broadway musical.

At this point, Quentin Thomas withdrew from the production,
although he remained the designer of record. Laura Gardner
recalled that "the scenic designer left and José started adding
pieces: the doorframe, the stairs that led nowhere, the couch."

There was also a Broadway aura around the choice of actors.
As Harris described it, "We decided to do it with the 'right actors'
and we concluded fairly quickly that that meant professionals.
I don't think José would have been interested in working with students. Students were auditioned for understudies and perhaps the
wife." For *Theatre News* Harris (1981:9–10) wrote:

Quintero wanted a young and vital cast. He read
students for the roles without much success. We had
not counted on finding students, since the Center's
program concentrates on the training of directors,
managers and playwrights. (Acting at Columbia
is still an undergraduate experience, with a major
in the School of General Studies.) Still, the process
was useful. Quintero began to focus his ideas more
concretely concerning the roles, and the acting students benefited from exhausting audition sessions
with Quintero.

Harris specified:

> Phillip Anglim was a precondition by the time we
> got around to casting. José wanted to work with
> Phillip. He had seen him in *Macbeth* and thought
> that Phillip was manhandled. Phillip needed to
> learn some basic acting lessons. He needed to make
> a connection between his voice and his body. José
> thought he could make a solid contribution to Phil-
> lip's career if he could work with him now on some-
> thing. He saw Phillip immediately in this role and
> Phillip was available.

Harris then hired a casting director, who sought out agent sub-
missions and, according to Harris, "José gave long auditions where
he gave a lot of direction."

Laura Gardner, who was eventually cast as the prostitute,
knew the casting director personally and secured an interview with
Quintero:

> José had those piercing black eyes. He asked me
> about myself and what I thought of the play and
> I told him I'd always wanted to do Josie in *Moon*
> and that I thought the character was a lot like Josie.
> A few days later I went to Columbia for an audi-
> tion. I started reading the scene and he kept stop-
> ping me and starting me and giving me direction.
> He was very strong on "Don't act, just listen and
> be there and just allow it to happen." The audi-
> tion was really about an hour. I was reading with
> a reader. José was giving me different ideas and
> the dialogue for the characters is so stilted. I wasn't
> sure about an accent, whether it was Irish or Brook-
> lyn or Jewish. He said not to worry about it, just
> talk.
>   A lot of his way of directing, even then, was
> just grunts. He would say, "You know," then a low
> whisper, "you *know*." For some reason, the rela-
> tionship that he and I developed right from there
> was that he would not really have to express some-

thing in a very clear way because there was an incredible understanding. It was a real psychic communication. I would say, "OK, gotcha, gotcha, gotcha." I would do it and he would say, "Yes, yes, yes." We were in a little room at Columbia. A lot of the audition he spent sitting and then he would get up and come closer and then pull away. It was a lot like film because he would get that close. In rehearsal, too, he would get that close. I thought that was real exciting.

Quintero himself found much of *Moon* in *Welded.* In a *New York Times* (Dunning, 1981:II, 28) interview he said that "the prostitute and Michael's coming for revenge and ultimately finding forgiveness reminds me of A *Moon for the Misbegotten.*" Their common feeling for the character Josie and their ability to "read" each other made for an excellent relationship between Laura Gardner and Quintero.

Ellen Tobie, who was cast as Eleanor, said of Quintero's casting methods:

> He saw every actress in New York who was remotely right for the role. He was very caught up in the auditions, almost obsessed with what the Agnes Bolton character would be like. He got it into his head that I looked very much like Agnes; in fact, I do. Also he knows a good actress when he sees one. He was certainly wild about the auditions. I read with him, he played the other role. It was very instinctual, perhaps the most instinctual casting situation I've ever been through. It was certainly not just casting on looks. It was a long audition with several callbacks, pretty exacting.

Andrew Harris said of the first day's rehearsal:

> José spoke very much about his relationship with Carlotta and the way Carlotta had mistaken him for Eugene and what he sensed from that about Carlotta's relationship with Gene. And he made the leap that the character that Eleanor was modeled on was not really Agnes Bolton but Carlotta. Agnes Bolton ceased to exist as anyone

he was ever interested in. This was a fallacy because, in a sense, he was reading the old O'Neill into the young O'Neill. That was an historical fallacy. He made the leap and that was that.

He saw this as a war for the soul, for possession, that only one would survive, that if there was such a thing as a marriage it was a marriage where the two people made up one, like Plato's *Symposium*. And that's what José had in mind, that kind of love-hate thing. That's also what Strindberg had in mind, but I don't think he talked about Strindberg. I think he just talked about O'Neill. He has made O'Neill into a mountain of a figure who is mythic and the same with Carlotta, so he doesn't feel the need to explore anything else. He talks pretty much in those terms.

Laura Gardner said that "José talked a lot about Carlotta because it was real to him; he hadn't met Agnes. But the character in the play, Eleanor, was always Agnes for José."

Laura Gardner said of the first day's rehearsal that "José talked a lot about O'Neill and Carlotta and his experience with them and the fact that he was taking on a piece that he knew was problematic but that he had total faith in it. He had a vision that this could work and that he wasn't quite sure exactly where it was going to go, but he *believed* in the piece, that it was valuable. It was more feeling than an intellectual experience."

Rehearsals lasted four weeks, most of them held at the Horace Mann Theater. Laura Gardner said, "José sat on a chair at the front of the stage. He did a lot of acting it out, or he would get up and do this grunting thing. He would not say the words but he would move around." As usual, Quintero did not rehearse the full eight hours. According to Laura Gardner, "We never went eight hours, maybe five or six with big breaks." Andrew Harris said that "José seemed to want to have a sense of relaxation among the members of the cast and then sneak up on it and work very intensively." The rehearsals were *not* relaxed.

As Laura Gardner had indicated, she and Quintero understood each other immediately:

I get along with my directors. I'm malleable. He never made me do anything. He never said "you must." When I was having a problem he would say, "Go back to where you pitched the ball, how you pitched the ball, and you'll find out where the problem is, instead of where you are now which is after the ball has been tossed." That image was so clear to me that it helped me enormously. He would say, "Don't stop, don't edit. Go as far as you can. Don't worry, I'm here. Don't worry that you will lose control. It's all right." So I always knew that I was going to be caught. He helped me emotionally with my work because I had always been somewhat stopped up and he knew that. So maybe I was a challenge to him too because I would always just stop short of the tears and it would always get caught in my throat and become inaudible. What began in rehearsals and periodically in performance was that it just went.

Gardner's ability to work well with Quintero did not, however, make the scene successful. She elaborated:

José and I knew what we wanted, but what Phillip was doing was really not what José was talking about. I was trying to play simplicity and realism and Phillip was—well, when you have a gay actor playing a straight man you immediately have a problem in a scene which is primarily physical, with a man trying to make it with a woman and can't make it. I felt more than anything else that I was being thrown around and I wasn't being spoken to. To a certain degree that's what the scene is about, a man blurting these things out to a woman who doesn't understand, but there was never a sense of the two of us talking. I didn't feel in rehearsal that I was being looked at or dealt with. Maybe that's inherent in the piece or appropriate, but there was more there. There was Phillip's inability to just talk, to be there, and José's frustration at dealing with him. José would say, "I don't believe it, I don't believe it," and Phillip would say, "I don't understand what you're saying," and José trying again and Phillip saying,

"OK" and then doing it and not changing an inch. Phillip can't just talk. He gets on stage and starts reading his script and it's very actorish.

Many of the reviews of Anglim's Macbeth at Lincoln Center made all-but-blatant references to his homosexuality. If Quintero and Anglim ever discussed the difficulty a homosexual actor has playing heterosexuality, it was never discussed in Laura Gardner's presence.

Relations were much worse between Ellen Tobie and Phillip Anglim. Laura Gardner recalled:

> Phillip and Ellen had major disagreements and problems. There was such enormous conflict going on among those three people that there were days when Ellen would tear out and José would start screaming and he'd disappear. I wasn't sitting in on those rehearsals because they didn't want us there. I would have loved to be in on everything, but there was such tension among those three. Ellen blamed it on José, everyone was throwing it at each other.

Andrew Harris said of relations between Quintero and Ellen Tobie:

> José needs a type of actress whom José likes. The kind of actress he enjoys working with has a certain kind of training, a certain theatrical knowledge: Colleen Dewhurst, Geraldine Page. He gave long auditions where he gave a lot of direction. He has a love-hate thing with women and it's very strong. He needs a woman who's strong enough, in terms of her own feelings of confidence about her sexuality, that she can stand his onslaught because he loves them and he hates them. He wants to be able to tear them apart—to pull the gold out, as he would put it. And there aren't too many young women who can take someone as potentially terrifying as José Quintero when he's on the "let's tear them apart" routine. And this woman got fairly hysterical. She developed but, as much as she wanted to succeed, she just couldn't handle José.

Welded, 1981. L to r: Ellen Tobie, Court Miller, Phillip Anglim. Photo by James D. Radiches.

She felt that José and Phillip were conspiring against her and she got paranoid and she got hysterical. And in her hysteria she started doing a little work offstage that was not under José's supervision and broke one of the bones in her hand. Emoting, she hit Court Miller in the collar bone. That was a mess because she had to go on stage with a soft cast. There were scenes where Phillip was supposed to fling her literally across the stage, very physical, and now he couldn't do that. We were afraid that the audience would think that Phillip had broken her hand. If there had been tension between José and Ellen before that incident, after that incident he really had no use for her.

Laura Gardner recalled that "at one of our previews, Ellen said something horrible to José, just hateful. José followed her to our dressing room and said, 'You are a very bad person, and I don't like you.' It wasn't just name calling. It was as though José was saying to Ellen, 'You are dead to me.' We opened and José disappeared."

Ellen Tobie said of her relationship with Quintero:

I was enamored of José. He wasn't grounded in reality, but he certainly had a great sense of human behavior, what one did in a love relationship which was manipulative, etc. The character would do this here and not that there. What I did not like was the fact that there was no freedom, absolutely none. He wouldn't give you room to create anything. I was so hemmed in, so claustrophobic; yet at the same time I was aware, he told me early on, that he thought that I was brilliant. It's just that José is like a painter. He wants to get his painting up on the stage.

When asked if she meant that there is a preconception, if Quintero already has a specific painting in his mind, Tobie responded:

Exactly. In particular, the movement he gave us was very interesting. I hate to say this but it was very '50s, but he did create that kind of theater, that kind of blocking. Also he would get his images from photographs or pictures, like the image of me at the end of the staircase. He took that from a famous photograph of Isadora Duncan. There's no question about the artist in the man. What made it most difficult is that he stuck us in a completely ridiculous spatial situation, ridiculous because of his concept. All I remember was its being so abstract that there was nothing to ground you. It was like we were out there floating in space, which he probably liked, conceptually.

Tobie said of Quintero's rehearsal techniques:

He was inside the space. We were not Colleen Dewhurst or Jason Robards. We would have been infinitely better off if he had stood back and at least given us the room to let it happen. I probably walked into that audition and that situation with as many credits as young Colleen Dewhurst did when she worked for him for the first time, but I'm not like Colleen Dewhurst or Geraldine Page. As actresses they are much more earth-mothery, harder. (I don't mean hard, good God they're legends. I mean in terms of temperament as actresses, very different.) I didn't like not having freedom. I didn't like not being trusted.

On the Sunday before previews began, the *New York Times* Arts and Leisure section carried a long article by Jennifer Dunning entitled "Quintero Takes on an Early O'Neill." There were no fewer than three photographs: one of Quintero, one of Phillip Anglim and Ellen Tobie, and one of O'Neill and Agnes Bolton. Very few Broadway productions with stars achieve this level of coverage. The article covered Quintero's manner of staging the play:

Mr. Quintero says he has sought to capture that sense of ritual in movement that is a little stylized, in almost the way of dance. "The conventions of the theatre in 1923—the ways of communicating— were entirely different than they are now," he says. "Mr. O'Neill has the characters sitting down. I just make them move around when they fight, keeping the light on their faces as much as possible. I make the two engage in battle, instead of just letting the words battle themselves in the air" (Dunning, 1981:II, 28).

Quintero appeared to be delighted with his working conditions: "It reminds me of my early days off-Broadway at Circle-in-the-Square. That little miracle still happens . . . It's wonderful to have a chance now to do this, free of all the fears and pressures of a commercial production. I can talk, for instance, with such honesty about the play! I can try to communicate the simple joy of the work, and of finding out that at my age I still have that joy" (Dunning, 1981:II, 28). Harris said of the interview, "I think the expectations were set up by Jennifer Dunning's article. José knew he could get that article because the Gelbs were very sympathetic to him. He was fairly happy with that article."

During the three-and-a-half week run of the play, major critics were invited and those who came savaged the production. Mel Gussow (1981:C22) called the production an "unwarranted exhumation . . . Mr. Quintero's production does nothing to salvage the evening. Under Mr. Quintero's heavy-handed direction, the actors deliver their lines in dead earnest, while occasionally provoking unintentional laughter." John Simon (1981:39) spoke of "Mr. Quintero who elicited all that mechanistic huffing and puffing and almost random stage movement," and of "trekking up to the remarkably unappetizing Horace Mann Theater to see this play being given a production that manages the almost impossible task of making it look worse than it is."

Both Gussow and Simon made the salient point that the production smacked of a classroom exercise, not a public performance, professionally mounted. Gussow (1981:C22) wrote that "the staging is threadbare, with several wooden chairs serving as scenery and curved overhead bars looking like open pipe racks in a clothing discount store. Plays such as this should not be revived or, at most, they should be performed as classroom exercises." Simon (1981:39) wrote:

Having arrived a moment or two late, and unable to consult the program, I labored under the delusion that this was—except for the staging by José

Quintero and starring by Phillip Anglim—a student production and an unusually poor one at that.
To my amazement, I later learned that the terrible performances, including Mr. Anglim's, were all
by experienced professionals, the set and costume
design by an apparently much-working British
designer and the lighting (both candleworths of it)
by the Center's technical director, who is also an
instructor at Columbia University . . . Should
drama-school productions, even if bolstered by
professional talent, or in this case, lack of talent,—
invite critics to review them as if they were professional offerings? Actually, everyone here is a professional, but it may be that the school atmosphere
somehow undermines the acumen. Schools, I think,
should remain schools and not compete in a commercial market.

Of all Quintero's productions of O'Neill, *Welded* most resembled its original. The 1924 production began with a realistic set
and moved toward a stylization; Quintero's production began with
a stylized set and moved toward more realistic set pieces. Both
companies had bitter personality conflicts. Neither production was
able to develop or discover what O'Neill had called "the belonging method." The 1924 production, at least, was a fully professional, commercial production and when it failed, it failed on its
own terms.

From its inception, Quintero's production straddled the academic and the professional. The budget and physical circumstances
almost precluded a professional production. Quintero appears to
have cast the production with people who needed to learn more
of their craft. For the first time in his O'Neill career, Quintero
cast away from the play's heterosexuality—not that the production was effeminate, but in a play about the need to possess women
who are too individual to be possessed, there was no significant
desire to possess. If Quintero had confined his work here to the
studio, much of the rancor that blighted the rehearsal period might
not have occurred. Most young actors can afford to be trusting
and open in a studio, but when John Simon and the *New York
Times* loom on the horizon, their worst insecurities are kindled.

Quentin Thomas stoutly maintained that the production's greatest advantage was that it was academic in conception, which was the reason for his withdrawing when Quintero altered the conception:

> It was no longer an academic learning experience: it was suddenly show biz, the critics are coming. Why isn't the theater painted? It made the step from being academic to sending the wrong message. If he'd stuck to its being an academic exercise, Frank Rich and Clive Barnes or anyone can come and give valid criticism; they're not unintelligent people. But if you present it as a piece of commercial theater, if they think it stinks, they will vent all their wrath in large letters in a widely read publication. Even the epic pieces of O'Neill are not staged commercially, so if the earlier or lesser pieces are to be seen, explored, the academic halls of Columbia University or wherever are the perfect location.

Part Five

FULL CIRCLE

"Only robbers and gypsies say that one must never return where one has once been"—Soren Kierkegaard.

By 1985, Quintero was finally willing, if the circumstances were favorable, to reexamine his successes of a generation before. In conversation with David Richards (1985:K10), he effortlessly combined his investment in both *Iceman* and *Long Day's Journey:* "I understand the characters in *Iceman* with their tomorrows that will never come. Because part of me is all mañana. But there's part of me that carries about the weight of the past. I have my mother and father in me—they are so tangible—and sometimes they flare up." The favorable circumstances arrived in the form of commissions from the Kennedy Center for *Iceman* and the Yale Repertory Theatre for *Long Day's Journey*.

Just before preparation for *Long Day's Journey* began, Quintero learned that he had cancer of the throat and that his vocal cords would have to be removed. He was afraid that he would no longer be able to work: "And my first thought was of O'Neill, in the last ten years of his life, when he could no longer work because of the tremor in his hand . . . And I thought, my God, I understand now exactly what he felt during those last ten years, unable to communicate" (Rothstein, 1988:C21). Quintero was fitted with a speaking device and continued to work.

12

The Iceman Cometh, 1985

Premiere: September 29, 1985; New York, Lunt-Fontanne Theater.

Cast List

Rocky Pioggi	John Pankow
Larry Slade	Donald Moffat
Hugo Kalmar	Leonardo Cimino
Willie Oban	John Christopher Jones
Harry Hope	Barnard Hughes
Joe Mott	Roger Robinson
Don Parritt	Paul McCrane
Cecil Lewis	Bill Moor
Piet Wetjoen	Frederick Neumann
James Cameron (Jimmy Tomorrow)	James Green
Pat McGloin	Pat McNamara
Ed Mosher	Allen Swift
Margie	Natalia Nogulich
Pearl	Kristine Nielsen
Cora	Caroline Aaron
Chuck Morello	Harris Laskawy
Theodore Hickman (Hickey)	Jason Robards
Moran	Paul Austin
Lieb	Walter Flanagan

There had existed for some years the possibility that Quintero and Robards would revive their production of *Iceman*. Stage manager Mitch Erickson stated that "for a period of about five years, *Iceman* was announced on the Kennedy Center subscription list, but it never happened. It had been high on Roger Stevens' list for some time."

On October 19, 1981, the Theater Committee for Eugene O'Neill met at the uptown Circle-in-the-Square to celebrate O'Neill's birthday. As part of the festivities, Jason Robards performed Hickey's fourth-act monologue from *Iceman* to cheers from the audience. Circle codirector Paul Libin recalled that "later that night the key participants said, 'Let's do it together' " (Mitgang, 1983:C11). Robards later traced the *Iceman* revival to that party: "Barney Hughes was there that night. José and I thought, Wouldn't Barney be a great Harry Hope! I thought maybe we should go with it. But I decided I was not going to say anything, unless that would jinx it" (Tallmer, 1985:28).

Quintero and Robards had been estranged from Ted Mann for 20 years, but negotiations did inch forward. By October 6, 1982, Circle-in-the-Square had teamed up with Roger Stevens at the Kennedy Center and scheduled a coproduction costing a quarter of a million dollars. The schedule provided for a four-week run at the Kennedy Center and a limited run of three months in New York, to be extended if successful. Most specifically, "the play would not be presented at Circle-in-the-Square's theater, but at a theater with a proscenium—a condition of Mr. Robards and Mr. Quintero that the Circle-in-the-Square producers were willing to accept" (Mitgang, 1983:C11). This stipulation, a combination of aesthetics and personalities, precluded taking advantage of the Circle's nonprofit status and effectively returned the project to the commercial marketplace for which *Iceman* has never been suited. It meant Broadway salaries for 25 actors on a return of six performances a week, rather than the customary eight. Agents, producers, and executors negotiated until the first week in December when Robards signed on for another project and *Iceman* was shelved.

By 1985, Peter Sellars had been appointed artistic director of the Kennedy Center by Roger Stevens. When Sellars had to postpone his production of Mae West's comedy *Come On Over*, Stevens arranged for Quintero and Robards to revive *Iceman* under the auspices of the American National Theater. The Kennedy Center, however, was interested in the production only as a part of its series and Quintero and Robards were not interested in such arduous work for only a short run in Washington, DC. Producer Lewis Allen brought the problem to Ben Edwards, who "told Lew 'yes,' and then called José and Jason to say that we would guarantee a New York production and they agreed. Kennedy Center was to pay for the production down there: scenery, costumes, the works. We needed $250,000 to get it to New York. Of course, it wound up costing $325,000."

With the production finally set, Quintero's biggest problem was the past. Mitch Erickson said that "they had a very hard time persuading José to revive *Iceman*. He was very frightened of competing with himself, that people would remember the 1956 production as better no matter *what* he did. It was a no-win situation." With Robards playing Hickey again, Quintero had one foot irretrievably in the past, but started the rest of the production from scratch.

Ben Edwards described the proscenium set he designed for Quintero:

> As the play is written, you see the bar and, when the set moves, you see the backroom. In the 1946 production, which I saw at the Martin Beck Theater, they had enough wing space to have a railroad-like device that the bar was on so that it could slide back and forth, parallel to the footlights, and show you the backroom. We weren't going to have that kind of wing space, so I devised a thing that would not be a complete turntable, but would work like an arc and move off to stage right leaving most of the bar and then off to stage left leaving most of the room.

Stage manager Mitch Erickson described Edwards' set:

> The set of *Iceman* was designed as a turntable. There was a wedge, about 60 degrees of a circle to be swiveled from side to side to display the back room or the bar itself and front entrance. While the back room was in view, the bar and front door would recede into the wings, unlit, but without

being blocked from sight. There was to be a divider, or partial arch, between the two areas. The set was mounted on a raked deck of real floor boards, not painted ones. Outside the bar, stage left, the actors were three and a half feet up in the air. There were nine tables on the set. It was very stripped down, it lacked a detailed realism and gave the whole play a size and shape it would not have had if it had been done in a set appropriate for *Time of Your Life*.

Robards said, "José mentioned to me that he had thought of a set that moved in and out. I don't know why the set had to move. When José works on a proscenium he always looks for a forestage or a way to do it semiround or semithrust. He's always looking for the round, circular sort of thing. It's almost never straight on."

Quintero's casting habits could not possibly have changed more since 1956. Robards was a given, Barney Hughes was pre-cast as Harry Hope, and Jimmy Greene repeated his 1956 Jimmy Tomorrow. Everyone else auditioned and *auditioned*. Mitch Erickson recalled that "we read endlessly for certain roles, Parritt and the girls. We read endlessly for the girls. Even Donald Moffat had to read for Larry Slade." Moffat said, "I had waited for years to work with José Quintero and Jason Robards. When I heard about this, I went after the role of Larry" (Shepard, 1985:C9).

Paul McCrane, who was finally cast as Parritt, had three auditions: "We talked a lot. José asked me what actors I liked; he wanted to get a sense of who I was. The final time we dug into Parritt and José told me a very personal story to illustrate Parritt's guilt. He's a driven man, Parritt. He's killed his mother, or feels that he has, and has a need to repent, to be punished. Finally, killing himself is the only release. He can't live with what he's done."

Actress Kristine Nielsen is blessed with a memory for detail and recalled her four auditions for one of the whores:

The first one was just a meeting. I talked to him about my father's illness. I think this made me vulnerable to him. The second was very specific. He stopped my comic speech immediately. He wanted

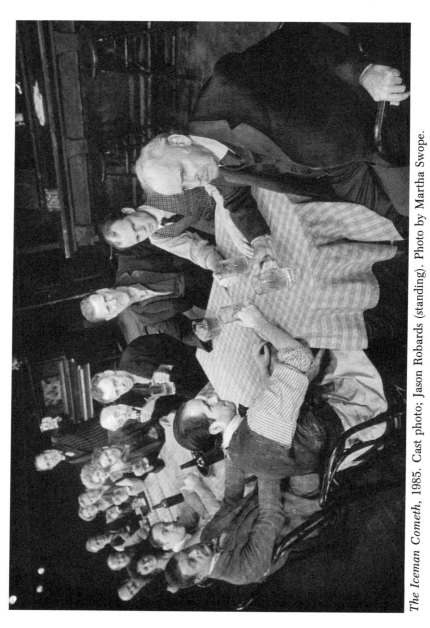

The Iceman Cometh, 1985. Cast photo; Jason Robards (standing). Photo by Martha Swope.

no stereotypic dumb blondes. He wanted her very tough, someone that nobody would ever think of as vulnerable, a woman who's very good at what she does. The third audition was very much like an acting class. I did Pearl and José played my pimp. He kept pushing me to a higher emotional level, he wanted it on the edge of tears. It was very heightened. He kept asking the questions an acting coach asks you, prompting you, going for what Bobby Lewis calls "your middle column." He makes the demands, you can't pull out of the scene. On the fourth audition, I did it once with no interruptions and he asked me to play Pearl and understudy Cora.

Because of the length of the play, Actors' Equity permitted a fifth week of rehearsals. The production was rehearsed at 890 Broadway, known unofficially to all New York actors as the Michael Bennett Building, named for the late choreographer/director who then owned it. It is a very attractive rehearsal space, large rooms flooded with natural light.

Peter Sellars made the opening welcome speech. In terms of actual producing, Mitch Erickson commented that "it was strictly Roger Stevens. Peter Sellars was a gracious host, but had virtually nothing to do with it. He was wildly busy."

Kristine Nielsen remembered the first day of rehearsal as a reunion, "what with José, Jason, Jimmy Greene, Ben Edwards, and Jane Greenwood. We were scared at how important this production was, historical even; how could we equal it? There were stories of the 1956 production. It was something to be gotten rid of."

Erickson recalled that Quintero mentioned "a production of *Iceman* in England where the entrance to the bar was way up center and José hated that. Here he took the proscenium for granted. He hadn't worked in the round for over 20 years, I don't think he ever referred to the round. In fact, I should have thought that it was a great weight off his shoulders not to have to block for the people on the other side. He did, however, fuss a lot about the position of the tables so that everyone would have as clear a view as possible."

Erickson had no fewer than three production books in front of him: "We had the 1956 production book, the cuts that Sidney Lumet made for his Play of the Week telecast, and a fresh one that José had gone over scrupulously. But José doesn't really cut, he nibbles a bit." Kristine Nielsen specified that "whatever material was cut, the women never got anything back in."

Quintero was subdued on the first day and stuck to his usual five-hour rehearsal day. Erickson stated that "we were never seriously behind. José would wear out after his five hours. On occasion he was hot and we would work longer, but that was not often. On the first day we just read the play."

There was a major discovery, however, on that first day. The set had been taped out on the rehearsal floor. Erickson said that "the plan had been for José to move from side to side to focus on the playing space, but he was upset by this great gaping hole on one side of the stage or the other. It was a great offstage expanse not being blocked off; it was just open. Jason, for instance, would have to enter from way offstage and walk through a dead space to enter the party." Paul McCrane recalled that Quintero said, "Things don't move at the bottom of the sea; it cannot be fluid."

Ben Edwards acquiesced. "At Circle-in-the-Square, of course, nothing had moved except what they moved themselves, the tables and chairs. So we changed it to a one-set show, completely stripped down, just lights and the bar, tables and chairs. José and I agreed. Jason asked, 'Isn't there going to be anything on the wall?' and José said 'No.' " Mitch Erickson said of the set that "the pie wedge was compressed. The piano went from the back wall to the side wall. We centered the wedge and brought in both sides to the proscenium arch. We compressed the set from right to left."

Although Hickey is the great showpiece of *The Iceman Cometh*, he does not enter until more than an hour of the first act has passed. It is the atmosphere into which he enters that makes for the play's tension. Quintero informed his company that he had overdirected the first act in 1956. Paul McCrane recalled that "in the first act, José wanted stillness. There was to be no card playing or eating sandwiches: that was announced to the company. It was to be a graveyard." Mitch Erickson stated that "we would keep a wary eye out for people pulling focus, but, you see, the nature of the piece was such that unless they arbitrarily scratched or yawned, that wasn't likely to happen." Quintero said of the characters that "their activity is to be and to dream."

Quintero reversed himself totally from his usual practice by discussing the musical nature of the play's structure. Nielsen remembered "very much discussion of symphonic repetition. There was even a rehearsal with the lights out and José spoke of 'the tune coming to life, as slow as it takes.' " McCrane said that "José did speak of the play as composed symphonically, with thematic repeats, themes and undercurrents. It was to be a slow building, relentless, with huge tension. It was to be like the earth moving; slow, of course, because it's so massive."

The musical terminology spilled over into the interviews. Donald Moffat told Richard F. Shepard (1985:C9), "I wanted the role because it is a great piece of theater music, one of the leitmotifs that keep recurring . . . How did I get Larry's voice? Hard work, drilling and drilling, like finger exercises." Jason Robards told David Remnick (1985:D2):

> It's an aria Hickey sings. There are other voices, but it's mostly his . . . You don't want to strain your voice, not with a part that has big arias, one in the second act and the really big one in the fourth. The play is scored that way. Themes repeat. The full orchestra plays, then the second violin, then me, then bass. It's got a great tone to it, this play. It's beautifully written, but you don't realize it for a while. Finally it occurs to you—the rhythm, the tones.

There was agreement in the way Quintero achieved his musical effects. Nielsen said that "the conducting was done in the moment: to get the music, he got the emotional moment. I paused on one entrance and José said 'Don't pause at the beginning, the play is long enough.' He was very aware of unnecessary pauses. It was rehearsed as an act and he always kept the act going. He never rehearsed one man at a time and only Don Parritt and Larry Slade got much time as a unit." McCrane recalled that "José did not conduct. Notes were given individually for the energy in a specific section. There wasn't much stop and start. We would work an act until something struck him that he needed to communicate to us, like filling out the skeleton with marrow. It came in sudden bursts."

Quintero confided to Nielsen that it had been some time since he had directed women of her generation, but he quickly assimi-

lated: "José said that only the women went in and out of the bar.
Only the women made money. He insisted that the women were
to be real, there was to be no playing for comedy. They were to
be hard and angry because they're *scared*." When Quintero
explained to the company, from his own experience, how important a drink was to these characters, Nielsen exclaimed, "I'd never
worked with *that* vulnerable a director."

McCrane recalled that "at one point an actor was making
an entrance and José asked him, 'Why are you coming into the
room?' The actor jokingly answered 'Because it says that I do' and
José blew up. He couldn't take the joke and said, 'This is life and
death.' Then he went up to the actor and said, 'I'm not angry at
you.' He has an enormous heart, great openness." McCrane, however, felt intimidated by Quintero's reputation, that Quintero must
know the play too well for his judgments to be questioned. He
concluded that "I ought to have given in more to my natural inclination to ask questions."

It was inevitable that Robards' Hickey would change, but
not because of any conspicuous direction from Quintero. After all,
he was 29 years older, heavier, and he was acting on a wide
proscenium stage rather than the original, intimate setting. Rhoda
Koenig (1985:38) wrote of his 1985 Hickey, "His performance is
sweeter than the first time, he says—more restrained. 'I let the
hate creep in much later now. Then I was a *mean* son of a bitch.' "

There can be a large misconception about Robards' work—
that his own troubled personal life so mirrors the lives of the O'Neill
and F. Scott Fitzgerald figures he has played that his gift must
be for emotional identification: "Jason's been there. He knows that
character. That's how he does it." The 1985 revival of *Iceman* gave
Robards the incentive to insist that that is *not* how he does it: "People ask if I see Hickey in myself. That's not for me to say. My thing
is to learn the lines, learn where I'm supposed to stand and listen
when other people are talking. That's it. We go moment by
moment. You are there to serve the play and the playwright, who
is serving us. And we serve the audience. And they serve us" (Remnick, 1985:D2). Robards is Rabelaisian in his contempt for any
acting approach that is not based on bedrock technique:

> You *must* have technique. That's why we have peo-
> ple who can't hold on to a performance. They go
> up and prepare for an hour and nothing comes out.

L to r: Bernard Hughes, Jason Robards, James Greene, John Pankow, Donald Moffat.
Photo by Martha Swope.

> You've got to make the points and stay within a
> form that we've set up. And if you do it often
> enough, you might, once in a while, get a moment
> that unites you with the play and God, and real
> time may break and it may be a beautiful thing,
> but that's rare. You can't 'not feel it,' you've got
> to have a technique to do it every night.

The production opened at the Kennedy Center's 1,100-seat
Eisenhower Theater on August 10, 1985. The actors worked on
a three-tiered favored-nations contract, the same salary to each
actor on that level. "All the woman were on the bottom rung,"
commented Nielsen. The daily reviews were good as were several
periodicals. Producers Lewis Allen and Ben Edwards were then
joined by the theater-owning Nederlanders to find a house for the
New York run. The choice of theaters was a major question. (The
word "choice" is misleading; a Broadway production accepts or
rejects the theater offered by the Schuberts, Nederlanders, or Jujan-
cyn organization.) Ben Edwards preferred the Martin Beck where
Iceman had had its world premiere, but Robards did not want
that theater and the only other theater offered was the Lunt-
Fontanne. No Broadway house could have recaptured the
atmosphere of the original Circle theater, but the Lunt-Fontanne
was perhaps the worst possible substitute. It is a long bowling alley
of a musical house. It has had its share of musical successes but,
unlike such swing houses as the Imperial, Martin Beck, or 46th
Street that can also do justice to a drama, hardly a man is now
alive who can remember a dramatic success in the Lunt-Fontanne
Theater. Nielsen conceded that "the Lunt-Fontanne was not the
first choice. The sound absorption made it quite difficult. You had
to shout."

Only four 1985 critics claimed to have seen the 1956 production. Of these four, only John Simon (1985:70) played devil's advo-
cate, comparing the two productions in detail. For Simon, the
proscenium production was in every way—Quintero's staging, pacing, and casting—inferior to the Circle production. Jason Robards
"seems to have lost just about everything losable; energy, elegance,
speed of reaction, vocal flexibility, that fevered elasticity of being
and springiness of soul shared by salesmen and actor that made
Robards' 1956 Hickey archetypal; now the kick has gone out of
Hickey, even as it has at one point out of Harry Hope's booze."

The other three repeat critics concentrated primarily on Robards. Brendan Gill (1985:110) found that, "In this production, Robards is so subdued as almost to equal in sullen impassiveness his new-found adversaries."

Edwin Wilson and Mel Gussow both picked up on the subdued elements of Robards' performance, but interpreted it differently. Wilson (1985:19) wrote that "along with the effervescence of the salesman, Mr. Robards also conveys the underlying sense of the toll that life takes and of impending death—the iceman of the title who is on his way. This dimension Mr. Robards invests with tremendous insight and conviction, a result, no doubt, of his own experience and maturity." Gussow (1985:3) wrote in the same vein:

> In 1956, Robards charged the play with energy and intimacy. His Hickey was a drummer on a roll and one could immediately feel the almost fatal attraction he had for his less colorful companions. In contrast, the Hickey that comes on stage in 1985 is world weary, a salesman who has been too long on the road and has begun to question the validity of the product (himself) he has sold so well. During his last absence from the saloon he has suffered a breakdown; though seemingly born again, he is actually on the verge of becoming a burnt-out case. But, with one final crack of his whiplash he arouses his listeners and gives them his eye-opening message on panaceas. One cannot say that Mr. Robards' performance has deepened; in 1956 he had already plumbed to the heart and viscera of this saintly sinner. The return performance is different, more subdued, but no less effective and no less an evocation. Mr. Robards remains more persuasive than the actors who have followed him in the role.

Larry Robinson, who had appeared in the 1956 *Iceman*, said of Robards that "because of the accident Jason suffered to his mouth, teeth, and vocal cords, he became a different actor, in terms of dynamics. His first Hickey was like a coiled spring; he was subjective, the man in the ring. His voice was tireless. He was a fire-breathing evangelist who'd come back to help clean up the act of his friends. His Hickey in 1985 had lived life more; he was more contemplative, more objective, more controlled. He was more careful of his voice. I missed that caged animal. The Hickey of 1956 never clearly understood what he had done. In 1985, he understood much more of what he had done."

Both Clive Barnes and Howard Kissel, neither of whom had seen the 1956 production, maintained that the play is better suited to the round. Barnes wrote that "the hugger-mugger proximity of such a staging adds to that sense of experience the play needs to convey. The only aspect of the play to emerge better with proscenium arch is the odd 'Last supper' effect of Harry's birthday party" (1985:59).

For Kissel (1985:12), the proscenium arch diminished the play's claim to reality:

> *Iceman* may have been one of the few plays that benefited from Circle's arena style which minimized the distance between the audience and the denizens of Harry Hope's bar. In a conventional proscenium approach, like the current revival at the Lunt-Fontanne, the bar is likely to seem all too stately a tableau. As each of the characters wakes up to tell his life story, the utter mechanicalness of the play is all too apparent . . . At any given moment, one looks at the stage and sees heads on the table, presumably in drunken stupors. One by one the heads pop up, tell their tales and flop down again—it seems like a medieval clock on the quarter hour, figures go through their appointed routines and then return to immobility.

Ben Edwards' stripped down set, per se, was not well received. John Simon (1985:70) wrote that "Ben Edwards, a designer specializing in seediness, has outdone himself here by making the squalor of the set not even theatrically interesting." Howard Kissel (1985:12) complained that "Ben Edwards's set seems needlessly dismal—even flophouses have some odd pieces of decoration to give them character."

When Edwards' set was seen in the context of Thomas Skelton's lighting, however, the results sounded much more creative. Gussow (1985:8) wrote that "the dimly lit barroom, frozen in tableau at dawn, brightens with the entrance of Hickey and momentarily achieves the conviviality of a George Bellows painting. Then, as Hickey sews disillusionment, the setting takes on the starkness of Edward Hopper, the characters are placed in pockets of isolation. After Hickey's confession, the 'survivors' are scrutinized under a piercing white light that makes each man stand in bold relief." Frank Rich (1985:C11) commented that "Harry Hope's saloon of 1912 looks as ghostly as bottom of the sea glimpses of the Titanic."

Donald Moffat received superb notices as Larry Slade. The notices gave the impression that the philosophical dialogue between Hickey and Larry Slade had never been so realized.

In spite of two rave reviews in the *New York Times,* the production ran only from late September to Thanksgiving week. "We closed several weeks earlier than expected," commented Mitch Erickson. "It ought to have been announced as a limited engagement and then extended, if necessary. We had a good advance, but it was spread thin over a long period of time." The production was moved successfully for four weeks in the 1,100-seat Doolittle (formerly Huntington Hartford) Theater in Los Angeles.

O'Neill had known that the timing of *Iceman* was crucial. Mel Gussow (1985:3) wrote that "in its Broadway premiere the play had apparently been victimized by a flawed performance and by postwar euphoria. The bleakness of O'Neill's message—that illusions, pipe dreams, were essential to man's survival—met with resistance. Ten years later there was enough disillusion in the air to give the play a biting relevance." The 1985 *Iceman* was produced within a year of Ronald Reagan's 1984 landslide. *Iceman* is not a play to flourish alongside the Reagan Revolution and Yuppiedom. If it had been produced after Black Monday and the Iran-Contra hearings, it might have found a more receptive audience. Or, perhaps, as Howard Kissel (1985:12) commented, "We are less easily shocked than O'Neill's contemporaries and we go to a Broadway theater with less innocence than people trekked to the Village thirty years ago. One has no sense of discovery, only of doing one's cultural duty." No sense of discovery? Can a mystery be solved only once? If so, Quintero and Robards had already done that in 1956.

13

Long Day's Journey Into Night, 1988

Premiere: June 14, 1988; New York, Neil Simon (formerly Alvin) Theater.

Cast List

James Tyrone	Jason Robards
Mary Tyrone	Colleen Dewhurst
James Tyrone Jr.	Jamey Sheridan
Edmund Tyrone	Campbell Scott
Cathleen	Jane Macfie

In 1987, Quintero agreed to direct *Long Day's Journey Into Night* and *Ah, Wilderness!* in repertory at the Yale Repertory Theater for O'Neill's 1988 Centennial. The discovery and treatment of Quintero's illness precluded his doing both; he chose to direct only *Long Day's Journey.* Arvin Brown, artistic director of New Haven's Long Wharf Theater, agreed to direct *Ah, Wilderness!*

It was generally agreed upon that the production would be designed by professionals rather than by students. Michael H. Yeargan is the resident designer at the Yale Repertory Theater (a proscenium house seating approximately 550), but, understandably, Quintero needed to work with people whom he knew intimately. Ben Edwards was hired to design the *Long Day's Journey* set for Quintero and Yeargan designed the *Ah, Wilderness!* set for Arvin Brown. Because the plays were being produced in repertory, it had to be a unit set. Ben Edwards said that "the sets for both plays are the same architecturally, but the atmosphere cannot be the same. Michael Yeargan and I simply adapted to one another."

In O'Neill's stage directions for *Long Day's Journey*, there are double doors on the back wall. There is a porch door on the stage right wall, which is the front door of the house and a series of windows on the stage left wall, which is the back of the house. O'Neill intended the changes of light to come from both sides of the stage. As he had done in the 1956 production, Quintero placed all the windows on the back wall and designated one exit downstage left and the other upstage right into a hall. Quintero wants *Long Day's Journey* lit from the back wall. Ben Edwards, however, no longer does lighting as well as sets because "it's gotten very complicated. Years ago, the designers did the scenery, costumes, and the lighting. But, years ago, from the heart of Times Square, you could walk to the electrical shop, the costume shop, and the scenery shop in five minutes. Now they build the scenery way up the Hudson River, paint it in Brooklyn, the lighting company is way up in the Bronx, only the costume shop is still nearby; the logistics, it's just impossible."

Jennifer Tipton teaches lighting at the Yale School of Drama and, despite a very full schedule, agreed to light both productions. Tipton normally discusses the set with the designer as it develops: "Perhaps with this project, the set was more developed before I spoke to Ben." Tipton described the unit set she was to light: "Working in repertory *did* complicate the work, but the two set designs were close enough to . . . it was much easier to change the lights, shall I say, than to change the set. In *Ah, Wilderness!*, the sitting room and dining room doubled, so we only had to pull the basic set back 10 feet for the barroom scene and the beach scene. *Long Day's Journey* was very stark while *Ah, Wilderness!* was a lived-in home with lots of dressing. The walls were removable panels, stained wood for *Long Day's Journey* and wallpaper for *Ah, Wilderness!* In general, I changed the color of the light; a cool white for *Long Day's Journey* and lavender for *Ah, Wilderness!* "

Tipton did not speak to Quintero until the first day of rehearsal:

> José doesn't say very much. Maybe he would have
> said more if he had been more comfortable with

his voice. He spoke of the lighting's being stripped down: a blast of light in the beginning and then a slow progression to midnight, to the fourth act and a lack of light. It was always in very simple terms that he expressed himself. It was assumed on my part that it was to be simple and stark. [In the theater, during technical rehearsals,] José indicated that when the family sat down at the table that the lights should come down around them a bit and when Edmund got up they had to open up a bit again. He did indicate certain things like that. He preferred that the lights really isolate the characters than be totally naturalistic. The lights were to show the passage of time, but also to isolate.

Tipton was perfectly at ease with the deviations from O'Neill's description of the set:

To me, that description is a circumstance rather than specific indications from the text. I don't think there are any playwrights of whom I would say that you have to do it exactly the way they wrote it. Of course there is light in it, but as to exactly where that light comes from is usually left to the designer.

Placing the porch upstage made possible the following two lighting effects: You saw the fog at the back of the stage in this production rather than at the side. Many people were surprised that real fog was not used. We lit scrim *behind* the scrim so that you could see through it. We lit the face of the scrim and that opaqued it. With a gray scrim you can make fog, which is what we did. And Ben felt strongly that there should be something painted on the drop so that it would disappear and that the porch railing would fly out, so that you had been looking during the first part at objects; the railing and a land mass (Long Island Sound, if you must, but it didn't have to be that), and then after the intermission the fog had closed in and they were no longer visible. The fog was so thick that you couldn't even see the porch rail.

Long Day's Journey Into Night, 1988. L to r: Colleen Dewhurst, Campbell Scott, Jamey Sheridan, Jason Robards. Photo by Peter Cunningham.

The initial package, the selling point, included Jason Robards and Colleen Dewhurst playing both sets of parents, although neither was a natural choice for the roles. Robards had played James Tyrone in 1976, but circumstances compelled him to direct the production as well as play Tyrone. When discussing the role of Mary Tyrone, Dewhurst told Amy Hersh (1988:9), "I never thought of her as one of O'Neill's women that I would be right for." Actor Campbell Scott, the son of Dewhurst and George C. Scott, jokingly told Quintero before rehearsals that "Colleen isn't exactly Mary Tyrone," and Quintero responded, "It's going to be difficult, but I know she has that in her."

Campbell Scott knew Quintero as a family friend, but because Quintero has lived on the West Coast since the early '80s, he had never seen Scott's work. Scott had been submitted for Don Parritt in *Iceman* and when he auditioned, "All sense of family acquaintance was thrust aside immediately. I was totally intimidated and scared to death. He acted it out a little; he was very passionate about it. I did a sort of meandering audition and he didn't hire me. At the time, though, he mentioned that some time maybe I could do Edmund." By 1987, Scott was in Los Angeles and got a call from casting directors Simon and Kumin in New York City saying that Quintero wanted him to audition for Edmund:

> I knew that Colleen was going to do it and I said "no" because I didn't want to be in a play with my mother. I thought I owed it to José to see him in person and say no, which was my big mistake. We immediately began to talk about the play, which I didn't know all that well. He insisted that I read the play overnight and, indeed, it's a great play and a great part. I called to tell him that I wanted to audition, he told me he didn't want me to audition, "I just want you to do the part, I have a feeling." Now we had already discussed the part and agreed on some things and I'm certain that he had some very subconscious ideas that the mother/son thing might work (not that he ever played with it), but I kept saying, "You've got to audition me or you'll make me totally paranoid. This is *too* strange." Then he told me that, in the old days,

with Geraldine and Colleen, he never auditioned them. He assured me that this was not a new practice for him.

Jane Macfie, who was a third-year student at Yale School of Drama, said that "José had been open to the possibility of using a Yale student as Cathleen, so we had auditions—almost every woman in our class who was of Irish descent or could be. The audition was crazy, all the producers were there. I walked into a room expecting to see one person there and there were 10 people, but José was so warm to me and relaxed me. I started to read the scene with Mary and he stopped me and gave me a lot of direction. He was apparently happy with the way I took direction. I think that's one of the reasons why I got the role. José was such a force, even in the audition."

Quintero had assembled a cast whose elder generation were his most trusted associates and whose younger generation worked with him for the first time. This relationship was very much in keeping with his conception of the new production:

> I was about 30 when I first did *Long Day's Journey* in its American premiere. I understood the problems of the young members of the family, and I imagined, I think, the problems of the father and the mother. Now, of course, I look at the play and my feelings are more with the parents. So I have viewed the play from both sides. And that means vast areas of the play are illuminated for me. The tragedy of the father, for instance. You know, when you get to an age when you look upon your entire life and what you've done with it, you're far more aware of the waste, the unfulfilled promise. And there lies the tragedy of James Tyrone, which I only vaguely perceived the first time I did the play, and now I am so moved by it (Rothstein, 1988:C21).

The two productions were rehearsed in New Haven, in a rehearsal room at the Film Studies Building several blocks from the Yale Repertory Theater. Each production was rehearsed for six weeks in repertory, with *Long Day's Journey* beginning a week earlier than *Ah, Wilderness!* Quintero began in the morning, worked his five hours, and then Arvin Brown took over. The rehearsal schedule made enormous demands on Robards and Dewhurst.

The opening speech was given by Lloyd Richards, artistic director of the Yale Repertory Theater. Jane Macfie recalled that "José spoke briefly about how eager he was to do the play. He spoke of the 1956 production only in respect to Jason's moving from one role to another and that he was not attempting to re-create that production. He warned those of us who had not worked with him before that it might take some time to get used to work-ing with him, because he works in a very definite way." Macfie said that it took about a week to adjust to Quintero's speaking device. During that first week, "We read the play a lot and he blocked everything, the entire production. He was very 'Move here, do it this way.' He explained to us that he was going to do that and then back off, which is what he did. Which is the reverse of the way most people work. I think a lot of that was due to time considerations."

Campbell Scott said that "on the first day, José stressed the need for communication. He was concerned about that for obvi-ous reasons, but he was comfortable with Colleen and Jason there. I'm the kind of actor who hangs out for a while anyway. I don't want to know things up front. I want to learn by osmosis if I can."

Scott's willingness to hang back coincided with the approach Quintero felt imposed upon him by circumstances. John Heard, who had been cast as Jamie, could not accommodate himself to that style. Scott observed:

> Unfortunately, John's way of working and José's didn't jibe. John wanted to work it out up front, and José had trouble because he likes to get it up on his feet so he can start. It's like a painter and you're his colors and once you *trust* that, then you can go with it. In the wrong hands, that can be horrendous for an actor. José is dominating, but not tyrannical in the least. He's dominating because he knows the text so well. He has his thoughts visually. John has been screwed around by direc-tors who aren't as good as José and he didn't know how to trust José's approach.

The decision was eventually taken to replace Heard. Arvin Brown and producer Manny Azenburg recommended Jamey

Sheridan to Quintero. Sheridan had appeared in Brown's *All My Sons* and in Azenburg's *Biloxi Blues.* Sheridan, however, had just moved to Los Angeles. He was contacted on a Friday afternoon and boarded a red-eye flight several hours later. He went from New York City to New Haven with no sleep and auditioned on Saturday morning:

> José had me read with Mitch Erickson. I was pretty blitzed, as you can imagine. All José said was, "Relax. I know you've had no time to look at it or prepare it, but trust me to know the person I'm looking for." He offered me the role and I had to stay, even though I had only a couple of T-shirts. We began to rehearse immediately. I think they had been together for two or two-and-a-half weeks. I had 14 days of rehearsal before the first performance.

Scott said that "Jamey looked at José and said, 'Let's go.' Suddenly there was hope." Sheridan and Quintero got right down to work:

> When we first started out, he had to find out if I trusted him or not and I think there was a little residual effect of the trouble that had gone on before me. So, basically, he gave me all my blocking and told me where to go and when, which is a difficult way to begin. But I knew that I was behind the eight ball and that everybody needed me to get going, so I just did what I was told. I did everything that way for two or three days until I did something wrong, something other than what I had been told to do, and immediately apologized to him. He said, "No, that's it, now you're on your way." So I realized that he was just giving me a skeleton to work from. It *was* difficult because I felt that I had to rehearse and give the result at the same time. I was just trying to be a good soldier. So—it did not have a lot of slow building and cool consideration of the piece. It was more a reared-back attack on the passion inside of Jamie. And the antecedents, the history of the character, I took

what I could from the play, from *Moon for the Mis-begotten*, and my imagination filled in what had gone on before, on my own.

Jane Macfie described the way Quintero broke down the scenes: "It was essentially beats in the sense of two people on stage confronting each other, a scene. He would work the opening of Tyrone and Mary for an hour or two, then he'd work the boys coming in and then work the whole pig story. He usually broke it down into one-on-one confrontations because there are so many in this play. And we did run it a lot." Jamey Sheridan said, "We would work scenes at a time, half-hour units; the fourth act scene between Edmund and Jamie would be an independent unit, the first scene between my father and myself. Maybe an act."

If Quintero "acted out" scenes a great deal when he still had his voice, it grew exponentially with his limited vocal resources. Macfie said that "he 'acted out' all the time. Like most actors I do not like being given line readings, but he never made it sound like line readings." Sheridan said, "I felt that he directed me by pure passion. He would come into the space and begin performing my role, saying the words of my role, but in such a way as to show me a graph of the heart. He would show you the pain which is buried somewhere, how big or small it was. You have a front when you're rehearsing, where the audience would be; he would come into the space and very quickly I would turn around and become the audience to watch him, to see what it was he was trying to give me." Campbell Scott had the final word on Quintero's "acting out" of a role:

> He does act it out for you. If you don't know him you feel invaded. What you have to trust and real-ize about him is that he doesn't want you to do it the way he does it. That's the only way he can com-municate it to you, perhaps because the text is so personal to him. He'd do the women, he'd do the men. He'd do the women more gracefully than the women, and the men just as macho if not more so than they, which is a testament to his range. And yet he's not an actor. The danger with actors-turned-directors is that they act it out and want to see it immediately, they change it right away

if you don't do what they do, so there's no room
for trust. With José, there's a great deal of patience
involved. He's showing you what he wants and you
get there any way you want. Then, when you get
it, snap, it's nothing like what he did.

Macfie and Sheridan remembered isolated instances of Quintero's mentioning musical structure. Scott put the question of musical structure into the context of Quintero's direction:

He did discuss musical structure with us, but not
extensively. He's very passionate, but all his passions are based on very simple things. If we ever
had a discussion that would elevate to a certain
point, if actors asked large questions, he would
always say, "Look, she's angry because he just said
this." All right, back to the text. It's a very simple
language he reverts to. It seems more complex
because of the passion. If we tried to intellectual-
ize the piece, he would bring us back down with
literal things you can hold onto. If we couldn't find
a reason for the way things were going, he'd say
"It's like music; we have this here, so we must have
that there." Sometimes that's all actors need. You
can't always do what he does, sometimes you *need*
the sense that you're in something larger. Then he
would throw in something large, but not often.

Quintero said in an interview with Mervyn Rothstein
(1988:C24) that, since he'd first directed the play in 1956, he had
honed his craft: "I think I am far more economical in my staging
than I was in my early years. You are prone to loud statements
when you are younger. I think I have grown toward greater simplicity. In terms of props, for instance, this time I used one bottle
of whiskey, three glasses and one book. That's all. In the other
production I had Edmund reading, I had him writing, there were
pencils and papers, a great many props. I no longer feel they are
needed." Campbell Scott said, "José has a wonderful way of cutting your indulgences without your knowing it. He says, 'I don't
understand . . .' and if you couldn't explain it, you'd cut it. With
this production, he wanted nothing extraneous, we were to respond
only to each other. We would suggest pieces of business and he

would answer, 'Try it without, try to get across that sense of anxiety just with the words.' "

In terms of working individually with the actors, Jane Macfie said that "José didn't talk to me about accent or characterization." Macfie carried a cassette tape recorder into a screening of John Huston's *The Dead* to get the accent and deportment of the servants in the film. She concluded:

> If you're not hearing anything from José, you don't have to worry. If he has a problem with something you're doing, he'll let you know. You don't have to second-guess him. He didn't give me a lot of direction, but what he gave me sometimes changed everything I was doing, if that's what he wanted. Tiny hints could explain a good deal to me. In the scene with Mary, he told me that I was inebriated to the point that things were slipping out rather than being planned and that transformed the way I looked at the scene. I was being way too literal with it. He'd give you little things that you could work with rather than 50 suggestions that really didn't do anything.

Campbell Scott said that "You can go through a whole act and he'll say only one thing. In the fourth act, all he said to me was that 'you've got to come on angrier. You've got to bring the past act on with you.' And, of course, he was right, as opposed to just beginning the act and then trying to make it a bulldozer."

Jamey Sheridan remembered that:

> We didn't talk much about what he wanted. I was convinced that José was going to die right there, that he would kill himself to get this material. Then we started to come together and as I made him feel my trust he would hang on me more and more; his frailty was so moving, his courage was so moving that I felt that I had to go as far as he would go. In two weeks, you can't, but I tried. I probably went over the top with a lot of those things and got some of them right, I was doing it for him for a long time. It was like he threw down a gauntlet

to me, "Are you willing to sacrifice? Are you willing to believe this much?" I said, "OK."

It was bad enough for Sheridan that he began two weeks behind the other actors, but he was named Jamey, playing Jamie, opposite the actor who took out the patent on Jamie Tyrone: "Jason welcomed me very warmly and was very flattering after a week of what I was doing. He did not let me know what he had done with the role with one exception: a staging problem which was pure mechanics." Just before the opening at Yale, however, "I asked Jason to go over some things with me. We talked through the fourth act scene, that was great. He had a lot to say, not all of which fit me, but there was that kind of father and son thing that we could share over the role."

Sheridan had actually gone to the West Coast to get his own life settled and *Long Day's Journey* was a difficult adjustment for him to make:

> I was ripped out of there and back on the East Coast with this role. I got kind of desperate. I began to wonder why O'Neill wrote this play. Did he just want to hammer a big, fat, black nail in everybody's head? There is no hope, only a black hole. Why live? Why don't we all die and get it over with? That's how it began to look to me, and Jason caught me in that mood and said, "Remember, it's about love. That's what it's about." And to hear that, knowing how harshly he'd played the role (I'd seen the movie and remembered some of the nastiness), well . . . And some of the choices we've made with Jamie in this production, especially early on, have been choices of love. When I was nasty with Jamie early on, José would say, "The sun had to rise for Jamie, there had to be hope." He had to be out there to save Mom, everything hangs on him. He had to have every chance to survive until he realizes that she's back on dope again and that's when the slide begins. He even hopes against hope later. In the morning, though, he's got the sun in his eyes.

Quintero felt secure working with Robards and Dewhurst, but for the first time, he was directing both of them against type. Unlike many a director, Quintero never set in concrete the 19th-century romantic actor Robards had to portray nor the fragile, convent-reared girl expected of Dewhurst. He proceeded by suggestion rather than mandate. He held back and let them make their explorations. Sheridan said, "I watched Jason change a lot, to build that guy, adopting various rhythms and stances. There were times when I would notice him arch up a little bit, not only physically, but mentally and in his language." Scott said that "Jason would, on occasion, do the Broadway sport. Sometimes he would find the 19th-century actor and afterwards José would say, 'That's it, hold onto that.' " According to Macfie, "José spoke about where Mary was emotionally at any given moment, about regression to childhood, the way she regresses into this little girl." Scott concluded, "José let her find the fragility without ever setting it as an objective. He spoke only when he'd seen a glimpse of it."

The production opened in early April at the University Theater. During the run in New Haven, according to Jennifer Tipton, "José felt that it was too much of a star turn for Colleen, that the lights went down too much on her. We had to brighten the other three considerably and make it not so isolated on her at the very end."

Both productions were brought into New York City as part of the city's first International Festival of the Arts, with Ken Marsolais, Alexander H. Cohen, and the Kennedy Center as producers. Because of the proliferation of theatrical events in the arts festival, *Long Day's Journey* received less critical attention than would have normally been the case.

Only Howard Kissel (1988:42) experienced the play as contemporary, rather than as a given American classic:

> When O'Neill's *Long Day's Journey Into Night* was first done, in 1956, the Tyrone family, which consists of three alcoholics and a morphine addict, seemed odd. Now they're a quintessential American family. The two sons, after all, are dropouts, disappointments to their father's dreams of upward mobility. He was a penniless Irish immigrant who became a matinee idol, then abandoned his own

ideals, settling for commercial success. It's like a parable of America, bewildered by its legacy of wealth and idealism, narcotizing itself against the goadings of remembrance and responsibility. At heart it is about people who lie to themselves and turn to alcohol and drugs when they can no longer believe their lies. Perhaps because he is anatomizing a family rather than trying to modernize myth, it is the one play in which O'Neill's language fulfills his ambitions.

The production, per se, was well received. Linda Winer (1988:II, 9) called it "the closest our time will come to a classic edition of one of the few genuine classics of the American stage." Clive Barnes (1988:31) called it "splendidly authoritative and richly evocative . . . Here is American classic theater at its greatest." John Beaufort (1988:21) called it "probably the definitive production of this overwhelming autobiographical masterpiece."

Frank Rich called attention to the staging evolutions in Quintero's work: "It's unlikely that Mr. Quintero has the same view of the text now that he did over thirty seasons ago. The current version has the bare-bones simplicity and sepulchral darkness of the director's 1985 *Iceman Cometh*—as befits the abstract, dream-like, classically unified quality of the nominally realistic late O'Neill masterworks" (1988:C2).

In reviewing the New Haven opening, Hilary De Vries (1988:21) wrote of Quintero's barebones simplicity:

> It is a wholly conventional staging that labors mightily but elicits no new insights, does little to reaffirm the director's singular artistry and leaves its gifted actors, with one exception, floundering. This production lacks point of view. It also lacks a certain directorial energy. Quintero has all but rooted three of the play's four principals at the Tyrone family table. With the exception of Miss Dewhurst's Mary, O'Neill's fierce, pitiable matriarch, the others hug the spotlit table like drowning men clinging to a capsized ship.

Variety (Humm, 1988:70) and *Time* (Henry, 1988:57) made the same point: "Coming hard on the heels of Jonathan Miller's startling and often fascinating, swiftly paced production, this is a return to the classic American O'Neill style of psychological clarity and overt emotionalism"; "Director José Quintero's lugubrious staging, well nigh perfect in its conventional way, lacks the revelatory quality of Jonathan Miller's fast-paced and fiercely funny version on Broadway in 1986." Quintero's staging was conventional. Who but Peter Sellars would *not* be conventional if judged by the standard of Jonathan Miller's production?

In judging the performances, Frank Rich spoke for the majority when he wrote that "like other renditions of this work, Mr. Quintero's staging illuminates one parent-child axis—Mary and Edmund—more brilliantly than the other" (1988:C2).

Douglas Watt (1988:51) said of Robards that "He has outdone himself with the most rending and majestic account of the much-played part we are ever likely to see." Julius Novick wrote that:

> Jason Robards is not the handsome, golden-voiced charmer that James Tyrone is supposed to be nor is it possible to believe that his James Tyrone could once have been a fine Shakesperean actor of the old school. Mr. Robards is very much a modern, realistic actor, in-turned, understated, anti-rhetorical (and not very good in Shakespeare). He gives us not a noble ruin, just a sad old man. But he does finely by much of the pathos in the part. You can see the moment when James realizes that his wife had begun taking morphine again and you can feel his devastation (1988:11).

Colleen Dewhurst had done appreciably less O'Neill than Robards in New York City, and those appearances had been evenly spaced. This was very much to her advantage in *Long Day's Journey*. When Dewhurst appeared "in her Gibson Girl 'do' and empire-waisted gowns" (DeVries, 1988:22) she was an unfamiliar presence, a discovery. Frank Rich (1988:C2) wrote that "Miss Dewhurst has a rending tragic dimension, to be sure . . . Yet this Mary, for all her ethereal beauty and maternal silver hair, is no Dewhurst earth mother—she's a killer, forever twisting the knife in old familial wounds." Julius Novick (1988:11) captured how Dewhurst had adapted her persona to Mary Tyrone:

The most impressive figure among them, in this production, is Mary Tyrone in the person of Colleen Dewhurst; not the usual delicate wraithlike, virginal Mary but a tall, erect, stately, powerful woman. (With the upswept gray hair, her jewelled earrings and her long gray gown she looks like old Queen Mary of England.) Like all truly tragic performances, perhaps, this one is built on the tension between strength and suffering. Mary's withdrawal, under the morphine's influence, is all the more strange because her presence is so emphatic.

Both productions closed on July 23, 1988, having run for six weeks.

SUMMATION

José Quintero's directing career falls neatly into two periods: the years at Circle-in-the-Square and the years after Circle. The Greenwich Village of the '50s and early '60s was the golden age for Quintero. He was able to rent a space and, with a company living as a commune, experiment with a wide variety of plays. Costs were low and failure was acceptable. There was a minimum of interference from the unions, and actors could work for love, if supported by a day job.

When Quintero left the Circle in 1963, he gave up his power base. He was no longer in a position to choose material or make policy. Off-Broadway was behind him and he chose not to work in regional theaters. He wished to direct on Broadway. Even in 1963, however, the amount of dramas being staged on Broadway was finite. Unlike Elia Kazan, Josh Logan, or Mike Nichols, Quintero was not a bicoastal power broker, whose successful movies could make Broadway projects happen. And Quintero was a director of revivals, not new plays. The offers that came (or at least the offers he accepted) were for revivals of O'Neill, provided they starred one of his Circle loyalists—Robards, Dewhurst, or Page— or a bankable star like Bergman or Ullmann.

In the first dozen years of his career, Quintero directed only two productions of Eugene O'Neill. For the next quarter of a century he directed 11 O'Neill productions in New York City alone (plus one *Ah, Wilderness!*, three *Moons*, and a number of *Hughies* elsewhere). This was not an active choice, the equivalent of Leon Edel's devoting a scholarly lifetime to Henry James or Richard Ellmann's doing the same for James Joyce. This was an accommodation to earning a living in the theater. O'Neill's plays became the vise for Quintero that *The Count of Monte Cristo* had been for James O'Neill, Sr.

Quintero's O'Neill career also falls into two periods: his productions of seven plays from O'Neill's mature period, 1920–1939, and his productions of the four plays from O'Neill's final period, 1939–1943. (Quintero has directed none of the pre-1920 plays.)

In the seven mature plays—*Anna Christie, Desire Under the Elms, Welded, Strange Interlude, Marco Millions, A Touch of the Poet*, and *More Stately Mansions*—Quintero's production focused on solving an O'Neill experiment: asides, quick set changes, or simultaneity of interior and exterior. The performances in these productions were largely conditioned by the staging. Even when the performances were exceptional, they were subordinate to the staging. Quintero's solutions to O'Neill's experiments were appropriate to each production without being definitive.

Quintero's greatest successes have come with O'Neill's final plays—*The Iceman Cometh, Long Day's Journey Into Night, Hughie,* and *A Moon for the Misbegotten*—postexperimental plays written for a single set, without masking devices for the actors. Where O'Neill is most biographical, when his family rises nakedly to the surface, Quintero has provided the icons. The O'Neill family in 1912 *looks* like Fredric March, Florence Eldridge, Jason Robards, and Bradford Dillman, clinging to that living-room table. Whenever the wasted life of James O'Neill, Jr., appears, whole in *Long Day's Journey* and *Moon,* or partial in *Iceman* and *Hughie,* Jason Robards has defined it. And O'Neill's redemptive whore/mother is best embodied in Colleen Dewhurst. These archetypal figures have been played by such gifted successors as Laurence Olivier, Ralph Richardson, Robert Ryan, Geraldine Fitzgerald, Zoe Caldwell, Katherine Hepburn, Stacy Keach, Ben Gazzara, Lee Marvin, and Kate Nelligan, without supplanting the images Quintero first captured. He is the Matthew Brady of the O'Neill family.

REFERENCES

Anthony, George. "Woman of the Seventies." The Toronto *Sun*, December 26, 1976.

Atkinson, Brooks. "*Strange Interlude* Plays Five Hours." *New York Times*, January 31, 1928.

_____. "O'Neill Tragedy Revived." *New York Times*, May 9, 1956.

Barnes, Clive. "O'Neill's *More Stately Mansions* Opens." *New York Times*, November 1, 1967.

_____. "Landmark *Moon for the Misbegotten*." *New York Times*, December 31, 1973.

_____. "Liv Ullmann's *Anna Christie*." *New York Times*, April 15, 1977.

_____. "The *Iceman* Arriveth to Adorn a Season." New York *Post*, September 30, 1985.

_____. "Hellish Family Portrait." New York *Post*, June 15, 1988.

Beaufort, John. "Robards' Long Journey with O'Neill." *Christian Science Monitor*, June 16, 1988.

Bentley, Eric. "Trying to Like O'Neill." In Eric Bentley, *In Search of Theatre* (New York: Alfred A. Knopf, 1952).

Bergman, Ingrid. "A Meeting with O'Neill." In Virginia Floyd, *Eugene O'Neill: A World View* (New York: Frederick Ungar, 1979).

Bogard, Travis. *Contour in Time: The Plays of Eugene O'Neill.* New York: Oxford University Press, 1972.

Bolton, Whitney. "*Hughie* Is Fascinating O'Neill: Touching and Compassionate." New York *Morning Telegraph*, December 24, 1964.

_____. "Controversial *More Stately Mansions*." New York *Morning Telegraph*, November 2, 1967.

Bowen, Croswell. *The Curse of the Misbegotten.* New York: McGraw-Hill, 1959.

Brackett, Charles. "Not at Their Best." *New Yorker*, February 11, 1928.

Brown, John Mason. "New York Goes Native." *Theatre Arts*, March 1928.

Bryson, John. "Jason Robards' Long Journey Home." *New York Magazine*, December 24, 1973.

Bunce, Alan N. "*Stately Mansions* Stars Ingrid Bergman." *Christian Science Monitor*, November 6, 1967.

Burke, Tom. "Mary McCarty—The Quintessential Character Actress?" *New York Times*, May 15, 1977.

Chabrowe, Leonard. *Ritual and Pathos: The Theater of Eugene O'Neill*. Lewisburg, Pa.: Bucknell University Press, 1976.

Chapin, Louis. "*Marco Millions.*" *Christian Science Monitor*, February 25, 1964.

Chapman, John. "Lincoln Center's Production of *Marco Millions* Stylized Bore." New York *Daily News*, February 21, 1964(a).

_____. "Lincoln Center Is Not Rep Yet." New York *Sunday News*, March 22, 1964(b).

_____. "Robards in O'Neill Bit." New York *Daily News*, December 23, 1964(c).

_____. "Have We Had Last O'Neill Play?" New York *Sunday News*, November 17, 1967.

Chase, Chris. "Colleen Has Broadway 'Moon-Struck.' " *New York Times*, February 17, 1974.

Clark, Barrett H. "Eugene O'Neill and the Guild." *The Drama*, March 1928.

_____. *Eugene O'Neill: The Man and His Plays*. New York: Dover, 1947.

Clurman, Harold. *The Fervent Years*. New York: Hill and Wang, 1957.

_____. *Nation*, February 2, 1963(a).

_____. *Nation*, March 30, 1963(b).

_____. *Nation*, April 30, 1977.

_____. *Nation*, January 21, 1978.

Crawford, Cheryl. *One Naked Individual*. New York: Bobbs-Merrill, 1977.

Dash, Thomas R. *Woman's Wear Daily*, May 9, 1956.

De Vries, Hilary. "*Long Day's Journey* Gets Conventional Staging from Quintero." *Christian Science Monitor*, April 5, 1988.

Dunning, Jennifer. "Quintero Takes on an Early O'Neill." *New York Times*, June 7, 1981.

Eder, Richard. "Liv Ullmann: Actress, Mother and Now Author." *New York Times*, January 26, 1977(a).

_____. "*A Touch of the Poet* Staged by Quintero on Broadway." *New York Times*, December 29, 1977(b).

Edwards, Ben. "Setting *A Touch of the Poet*." *Theatre Crafts*, July/August 1967.

Eldridge, Florence. "Reflections on *Long Day's Journey Into Night:* First Curtain Call for Mary Tyrone." In Virginia Floyd, *Eugene O'Neill: A World View* (New York: Frederick Ungar, 1979).

Finegold, Michael. "O'Neill's Way." *The Village Voice.* January 19, 1978.

Fitzgerald, John E. "Looking and Listening." *Our Sunday Visitor*, July 5, 1959.

Floyd, Virginia. *Eugene O'Neill: A World View.* New York: Frederick Ungar, 1979.

_____. *Eugene O'Neill at Work.* New York: Frederick Ungar, 1981.

Freedley, George. "*Iceman Cometh* Proves O'Neill Is America's Greatest Dramatist." New York *Morning Telegraph*, October 11, 1946.

Funke, Lewis. "Mann, O'Neill Producer, Gaining Fame as Director." *New York Times*, July 5, 1968.

Funke, Phyllis. "José Quintero and the Devil of Success." *Wall Street Journal*, May 15, 1974.

Gardner, Paul. "Columbia Tapes a Full O'Neill Play." *New York Times*, April 8, 1963.

Garfield, David. *A Player's Place.* New York: Macmillan, 1980.

Garvey, Sheila Hickey. "Not for Profit: A History of the Circle-in-the-Square." Unpublished doctoral dissertation, New York University, 1984.

Gaver, Jack. "O'Neill's Play Has Moldered." New York *Sunday News*, January 13, 1963.

Gelb, Arthur. "O'Neill's *Hughie* to Make US Bow." *New York Times*, January 25, 1960.

Gelb, Arthur and Barbara. *O'Neill.* New York: Harper and Row, 1960.

_____. "As O'Neill Saw the Theater." *New York Times Magazine*, November 12, 1961.

Gelb, Barbara. "Quintero in the Square." *New York Times*, February 16, 1964.

_____. "The Child O'Neill Tore Up." *New York Times*, October 29, 1967.

_____. "Jason Jamie Robards Tyrone." *New York Times Magazine*, January 20, 1974.

_____. "A Touch of the Tragic." *New York Times Magazine*, December 11, 1977.

Gent, George. "Flanders, 39, Ages to Cheers in O'Neill Play." *New York Times*, January 4, 1974.

Gibbs, Walcott. "Good Old Hickey." *New Yorker*, May 26, 1956.

Gilder, Rosamond. *"The Iceman Cometh."* In *Theatre Arts Anthology* (New York: Theatre Arts Books, 1950).

Gill, Brendan. *New Yorker*, October 7, 1985.

Gottfried, Martin. *"More Stately Mansions."* *Woman's Wear Daily*, November 1, 1967.

_____. "What's a Nice Girl Like Liv Doing in a Play Like This?" New York *Post*, April 15, 1977.

_____. "Cult of the Second-Rate." *Saturday Review*, March 4, 1978.

Gussow, Mel. "O'Neill's *Welded*." *New York Times*, June 18, 1981.

_____. "O'Neill's *Iceman* Retains Its Riveting Power." *New York Times*, October 6, 1985.

Hammond, Percy. "Eugene O'Neill's Romantic and Sarcastic *Marco Millions* Presented as Admirably as Possible by the Theatre Guild." New York *Herald-Tribune*, January 10, 1928.

Harris, Andrew B., Jr. "A Tangible Confrontation: *Welded*." *Theatre News*, Fall 1981.

Harris, Leonard. "Quintero Given Blessing by Mrs. O'Neill." New York *World Telegram and Sun*, February 19, 1964.

_____. "An American Chronicle." *SoHo Weekly News*, January 12, 1978.

Hatch, Robert. *Nation*, May 26, 1956.

Helburn, Teresa. *A Wayward Quest*. Boston: Little, Brown, 1960.

Henry, William A., III. "A Coney Island of the Mind." *Time*, June 27, 1988.

Hersh, Amy. "Colleen Dewhurst: At Home with the O'Neills." *Theater Week*, June 20, 1988.

Hewes, Henry. "Less Stately Farmhouse." *Saturday Review*, January 26, 1963(a).

_____. "Actors' Studio's First Long Pants." *Saturday Review*, March 30, 1963(b).

_____. "Life of a Salesman." *Saturday Review*. March 7, 1964.

_____. *Saturday Review*, January 16, 1965.

_____. "Unreal Estate." *Saturday Review*, November 18, 1967.

Hipp, Edward Sothern. "*Marco* Saved by Direction." Newark *Evening News*, February 21, 1964(a).

_____. "Three Square Deals." Newark *Evening News*, March 22, 1964(b).

Hobe. *Variety*, March 13, 1963.

Hopkins, Arthur. *To a Lonely Boy*. New York: Doubleday, Doran, 1937.

_____. *Reference Point*. New York: Samuel French, 1948.

Humm. *Variety*, June 23, 1988.

Issac, Dan. "*A Moon for the Misbegotten*: Radiance Beneath the Grime." *The Village Voice*, July 19, 1973.

_____. "Quintero—Keeper of the Eugene O'Neill Flame—Returns to Broadway." *New York Magazine*, April 18, 1977.

Kalem, Ted E. "Liv in Limbo." *Time*, April 25, 1977.

_____. "Dream Addict." *Time*, January 9, 1978.

Kauffmann, Stanley. *New Republic*, January 26, 1974.

_____. *New Republic*, January 28, 1978.

Kerr, Walter F. "*Iceman Cometh* Revived at Circle-in-the-Square." New York *Herald Tribune*, May 9, 1956(a).

_____. "Little Hope of Hope Denoted." New York *Herald Tribune*, May 20, 1956(b).

Kerr, Walter. New York *Herald Tribune*, January 10, 1963(a).

_____. New York *Herald Tribune*, March 13, 1963(b).

_____. "*Marco Millions*: Kerr and O'Neill Revival." New York *Herald Tribune*, February 21, 1964(a).

_____. "Walter Kerr Reviews Eugene O'Neill's *Hughie*." New York *Herald Tribune*, December 23, 1964(b).

_____. "No One Will Ever Live in It." *New York Times*, November 12, 1967.

_____. "It's a Rich Play, Richly Performed." *New York Times*, January 13, 1974.

_____. "There's More to *Anna Christie* Than This Production Knows." *New York Times*, April 24, 1977.

_____. "Vintage O'Neill—But with the Critical Ambiguity Missing." *New York Times*, January 8, 1978.

Kissel, Howard. "*Anna Christie*." *Woman's Wear Daily*. April 15, 1977.

_____. "*The Iceman Cometh*." *Woman's Wear Daily*. September 30, 1985.

_____. "A Worthwhile *Journey*." New York *Daily News*, June 15, 1988.

Koenig, Rhoda. "Robards and *Iceman* Cometh Again." *New York Magazine,* September 16, 1985.

Kroll, Jack. "Liv's *Anna." Newsweek,* April 25, 1977.

_____. "Symphony of Despair." *Newsweek,* January 9, 1978.

Krutch, Joseph Wood. "*Marco Millions." Nation,* January 25, 1928.

Langner, Lawrence. *The Magic Curtain.* New York: Dutton, 1951.

Lawson, Steve. "José, Jason and 'Gene." *Horizon,* January 1978.

Lewis, Emory. "Journey Uptown with O'Neill." *Cue,* November 3, 1956.

Lewisohn, Ludwig. "Pseudo-Marriage. *Nation,* April 2, 1924.

Little, Stuart. "First American Production for O'Neill's *Hughie.*" New York *Herald Tribune,* December 1, 1964.

McCarthy, Mary. "Eugene O'Neill—Dry Ice." In *Sights and Spectacles, 1937–1956* (New York: Farrar, Straus and Cudahy, 1956).

Millstein, Gilbert. "José Quintero." *Theatre Arts,* May 1960.

Mitgang, Herbert. "Why *Iceman Cometh* Did Not Arrive This Year." *New York Times,* March 7, 1983.

Moeller, Phillip. "Silences Out Loud." *New York Times,* February 26, 1928.

Morehouse, Ward. Long Island *Star Journal.* March 21, 1960.

Morton, Frederick. "Quintero the Fortuitous." *New York Times,* May 6, 1956.

Murray, Michael. "Inside His Script He Wrote: 'Jason, Trust Yourself.' " *New York Times,* December 30, 1973.

Nadel, Norman. "O'Neill Bares Ax in *Marco Millions.*" New York *World Telegram and Sun,* February 21, 1964.

Nathan, George Jean. *American Mercury,* May 1924.

Nichols, Dudley. "The New Play." New York *World.* January 31, 1928.

Norton, Eliot. "Liv Is Unforgettable in O'Neill Melodrama." Boston *Herald-American,* May 18, 1977.

_____. "Robards Falters in *Touch of the Poet.*" Boston *Herald-American,* January 2, 1978.

Novick, Julius. *New York Observer,* June 27, 1988.

Oliver, Edith. "O'Neill on Bleecker Street." *New Yorker,* January 19, 1963.

_____. "Trick but No Treat." *New Yorker,* November 11, 1967.

O'Neill, Eugene. "The Mail Bag." *New York Times*, December 18, 1921.

_____. *Six Short Plays of Eugene O'Neill*. New York: Vintage, 1951.

_____. *Three Plays*. New York: Vintage, 1952.

_____. *More Stately Mansions*. New Haven, Ct.: Yale University Press, 1964.

"O'Neill Magic." *Newsweek*, March 2, 1964.

Oppenheimer, George. "Long Night's Journey." *Newsday*, May 25, 1956.

_____. "The Great O'Neill." *Newsday*, January 16, 1963(a).

_____. "The Electrical Display of God." *Newsday*, March 20, 1963(b).

"Overwhelming." *Newsweek*, March 25, 1963.

Pryce-Jones, Alan. *Theatre Arts*, February 1963.

Quintero, José. "Postscript to a Journey." *Theatre Arts*, April 1957(a).

_____. "The Dance: What It Means to Me." *Dance Magazine*, June 1957(b).

_____. *If You Don't Dance They Beat You*. Boston: Little, Brown, 1974.

_____. "José to Fred March." *Playbill Magazine*, August 1975.

Remnick, David. "Robards, Renewing the Role." Washington *Post*, August 10, 1985.

Rhodes, Russell. "Robert Edmond Jones Says It Was O'Neill Who Really Did Designing for *The Iceman*." New York *Herald Tribune*, December 29, 1946.

Rich, Alan. "A Coal Barge Named Desire." *New York Magazine*, May 2, 1977.

Rich, Frank. "Jason Robards in *The Iceman Cometh*." *New York Times*, September 30, 1985.

_____. "The Stars Align for *Long Day's Journey*." *New York Times*, June 15, 1988.

Richards, David. "An O'Neill Classic Undercut by New Values." Washington *Star*, March 16, 1977.

_____. "The Iceman Returns." Washington *Post*, July 28, 1985.

Rothstein, Mervyn. "Quintero and O'Neill Resonate." *New York Times*, June 16, 1988.

Seldes, Gilbert. *Dial*, April 1928.

Shaeffer, Louis. *O'Neill: Son and Playwright*. Boston: Little, Brown, 1968.

_____. *O'Neill: Son and Artist*. Boston: Little, Brown, 1973.

Shepard, Richard F. "Donald Moffat, Listening in *Iceman*." *New York Times*, October 1, 1985.

Simon, John. "A Great Compassion." *New York Magazine*, January 21, 1974.

_____ "A Touch Is Better Than None." *New York Magazine*, January 16, 1978.

_____. *New York Magazine*, June 29, 1981.

_____. "The Sandman Cometh." *New York Magazine*, October 14, 1985.

Smith, Cecil. "Building a Mansion for Ingrid." Los Angeles *Times*, September 10, 1967(a).

_____. "*Mansions* Debuts in a Series of Theater Firsts for L.A." Los Angeles *Times*, September 14, 1967(b).

Smith, Michael. "*Desire Under the Elms*." *The Village Voice*, January 17, 1963(a).

_____. *The Village Voice*, March 14, 1963(b).

_____. "*Marco Millions*." *The Village Voice*, February 27, 1964.

Stasio, Marilyn. *Cue*, February 20, 1978.

Stern, Harold. New York *Standard*. January 10, 1963(a).

_____. "*Interlude* Revival." New York *Standard*. March 13, 1963(b).

"Strange Interlude." *Commonweal*, February 22, 1928.

"Suffocated Souls." *Time*, January 18, 1963.

Sullivan, Dan. "Liv Enlivens *Anna Christie*." Los Angeles *Times*, ?, 1977.

Tallmer, Jerry. "José Quintero: On Keeping the Faith." New York *Post*, January 19, 1974.

_____. "29 Great Years Between Drinks." New York *Post*, September 26, 1985.

Taubman, Howard. "New *Desire*." *New York Times*, January 11, 1963.

_____. "O'Neill's *Hughie* Opens." *New York Times*, December 23, 1964.

Valentine, Dean. "Blarney and Bluster." *New Leader*, January 30, 1978.

Ver Meulin, Michael. "A Grand Reunion for Jason." Chicago *Sun-Times*, July 11, 1976.

Watt, Douglas. "To See Liv Is to Love Her." New York *Daily News*, April 15, 1977.

_____. "*Journey* of a Lifetime." New York *Daily News*, June 24, 1988.

Watts, Richard, Jr. New York *Post*, January 10, 1963(a).

_____. "O'Neill's *Strange Interlude* Retains Its Dramatic Power." New York *Post*, March 13, 1963(b).

_____. "A Superb Play, Superbly Done." New York *Post*, December 31, 1973.

Weales, Gerald. "Less *Stately Mansions*." *The Reporter*, November 30, 1967.

Welch, Mary. "Softer Tones for Mr. O'Neill's Portrait." *Theatre Arts*, May 1957.

West, Anthony. "*Desire Under the Elms*." *Show Magazine*, March 1963(a).

_____. "The Big Guns." *Show Magazine*, June 1963(b).

Wilson, Edwin. "Great Performance." *Wall Street Journal*, October 4, 1985.

Winer, Linda. "A *Long Day's Journey* Revisited." New York *Newsday*, June 15, 1988.

Woollcott, Alexander. "Giving O'Neill Until It Hurts." *Vanity Fair*, February 1928.

Wyatt, Euphemia Van Rensselaer. *Catholic World*. July 1956.

Young, Stark. "O'Neill and Rostand." *New Republic*, October 21, 1946.

_____. "Eugene O'Neill: Notes from a Critic's Diary." *Harpers*, June 1957.

INDEX